HOW TO RUN A
SMALL BUSINESS

HOW TO RUN A SMALL BUSINESS

Fifth Edition, Revised and Enlarged

by **J. K. LASSER TAX INSTITUTE**
Editor: **Bernard Greisman**
Directors: **Bernard Greisman and Bobbi Lasser Gray**

McGRAW-HILL BOOK COMPANY

New York St. Louis San Francisco Auckland Bogotá
Hamburg Johannesburg London Madrid Mexico
Montreal New Delhi Panama Paris São Paulo
Singapore Sydney Tokyo Toronto

Library of Congress Cataloging in Publication Data
Main entry under title:

How to run a small business.

Includes index.
1. Small business—Management.   2. Business.
I. Greisman, Bernard.   II. J. K. Lasser Tax Institute.
HD62.H68   1982   658'.022   81-15584
                                        AACR2

1 2 3 4 5 6 7 8 9 0   BPBP   8 9 8 7 6 5 4 3 2

ISBN 0-07-036566-0

The editors for this book were William R. Newton
and William B. O'Neal, the designer was Elliot
Epstein, and the production supervisor was Sally
Fliess. It was set in Melior by J. M. Post Graphics
Corp.

Printed and bound by The Book Press.

CONTENTS

PREFACE

For over 30 years, *How to Run a Small Business* has been a popularly accepted guide to business operations. The fifth edition of this book reflects changes in contemporary economic conditions, current business practices, and the law which affect small business.

Whether you are planning a new business or operating an existing one, *How to Run a Small Business* will assist you in making decisions and organizing your thoughts, as well as aid you in solving your business problems by suggesting possible solutions you may have overlooked in the course of a busy workday. Accepting the challenge of running a small business can be rewarding, but you must meet the challenge with knowledge and understanding. We believe that this new edition of *How to Run a Small Business* will contribute to the success of your enterprise.

We acknowledge with appreciation the contributions of Alan Lasser and Barbara E. Weltman with the assistance of Joyce Clarke, Henrietta Danson, Linda Seymour, and Kay Torak.

Bernard Greisman
Director, J. K. Lasser Tax Institute

HOW TO RUN A
SMALL BUSINESS

1
ENTERING THE
BUSINESS WORLD

We constantly make economic and financial decisions which affect our lives, and we must live with the consequences of these decisions. However, too often we make our decisions on whim or after a superficial appraisal. We can usually survive such decisions when they involve the purchase of, say, a car. We can buy and drive it without knowing what makes it run; it will operate without our knowledge of its inner workings. We cannot afford, however, to adopt a casual attitude about buying or starting up a business. We dare not be ignorant in this matter. We must have the patience to learn all there is to know about a particular business before we invest our time, energy, and financial resources in it.

As an introduction to the complexity of making business decisions, consider the experience of Mr. and Mrs. Smith, who are considering buying a business. They illustrate how those who move slowly and carefully have the best chance to survive.

John and Marie Smith have some free time on their hands now that their children are in college. Marie is from a restaurant family and has dreamed of recapturing the childhood joy she knew from being involved in the operation of a restaurant. John, a full-time executive, can use his business contacts to help fulfill his wife's ambitions. Marie will handle the operational details, such as hiring talented people to staff the operation. Knowing Marie's background and her decision-making ability, and realizing that restaurants can be very profitable, John believes this type of gastronomical venture will be right for them.

The Smiths choose to investigate restaurants in a coastal resort area about an hour from the city. A large, year-round tourist population guarantees a sizable group of people who regularly dine out. John and Marie proceed carefully, arranging for both a lawyer and accountant to help them. They are undecided whether to build the restaurant and develop the clientele from scratch, to buy an established restaurant and run it their own way, or to buy into a nationally franchised restaurant chain whose meals must be prepared in a manner dictated by the franchise.

The attorney first discovers that the local zoning board is hostile to the construction of a new restaurant because of the already existing urban sprawl. However, the zoning board is receptive to the construction of the nationally known franchise, deciding that the addition to the existing overdevelopment would be outweighed by the attention the franchise would bring to the town. An attempt to fight the zoning board's peculiar prejudice would be costly and time-consuming, and would only serve to hurt the restaurant's business when it finally opened. These considerations convince the couple to drop the idea of building their own restaurant and to concentrate on the other two possibilities, buying an existing restaurant or buying into a franchise.

A check of local real estate brokers reveals that there are two restaurants on the market. One is on the shore, available at a bargain price, and the other is farther inland, with a good reputation and a high asking price. Upon request, the franchisor mails John and Marie a disclosure statement, an earnings claims document, and a copy of the franchise contract. These papers are forwarded to the attorney for evaluation. Because each state has different laws pertaining to franchises, the attorney must study what effect the contract will have on the operation.

Meanwhile, the Smiths concentrate on evaluating the potential of the two restaurants that are for sale. The proprietors of both restaurants grant interviews and access to the documents John and Marie want to see.

The reason that the owners of the successful inland restaurant are selling becomes obvious at the interview. They are beyond retirement age. They are tired of the hectic life of food preparation, but their pride in what they have accomplished is visible as they point out the various facets of their operation. In a convincing manner, they discuss recipes, cooking tips, and the preparation of the house specialties. They provide photocopies of 3 back years of income tax returns, which John and Marie forward to their accountant for analysis.

When John and Marie visit the shore restaurant, they observe that too much of the restaurant's floor space seems devoted to the bar. During the brief time they are there, one of the few diners complains to the waitress that the chowder is too salty to be eaten. The owners, a couple in their forties, seem anxious to get out of the restaurant business. The owners also provide copies of their tax returns.

At home, John and Marie discuss the two restaurants. Both operations buy their raw food from the same markets. The kitchen equipment of each is in good condition, although the facilities of the inland restaurant are a little older. County health officials state that there has never been a problem with either restaurant. The employees of the inland restaurant seem to be about a generation older than the staff of the shore restaurant. The shoreline restaurant has a smaller parking lot than the inland restaurant, but more of its customers walk to dinner. There is an empty lot next to the shoreline restaurant that the owners have offered to include in the sale. The lot could be cleared and paved to provide additional parking, but it is not clear if the local zoning board would allow the improvement.

The next day John and Marie meet with their accountant to go over the figures presented by the two restaurants. The inland restaurant shows good, consistent profits. The income and expenses are in a ratio that is normal for restaurants, indicating an efficient operation. The tax deduction for repairs is small, so presumably the machinery is in good working order. The payroll records show little turnover. The inland restaurant seems to keep everyone happy—customers, employees, and owners.

Marie notes that the menu prices at the inland restaurant were moderate for an eatery with a good reputation. The accountant confirms that the restaurant would be even more profitable if the menu prices were raised to keep up with inflation. The accountant and the Smiths postulate that the restaurant's reputation would survive modest price increases without losing many customers. Since the asking price of the business seems to be composed of the value of the assets and 2 years' profits, raising prices might make a significant dent in the length of time needed to recover their investment.

Casual conversation with local residents failed to reveal anyone who would admit to eating at the shoreline restaurant. The figures for the shoreline restaurant seem to confirm the emphasis on tourists, with little effort to attract repeat customers. The accountant points out that an unusually high percentage of the restaurant's income is from the sale of liquor, a ratio more akin to a bar and grill. The couple and the accountant agree that they must consider, in addition to the purchase price, the cost of renovations necessary to deemphasize the cocktail lounge. This is still a relatively inexpensive purchase since the asking price for the shoreline restaurant is a figure representing the value of all the assets and less than 1 year's profit, a profit that was low to begin with.

After meeting with the accountant, John and Marie go to their attorney to complete the investigation of the two restaurants and compare these opportunities with the franchise offer. The attorney says the owners of both restaurants have clear title, free of legal attachments and mortgages. Also, the attorney sees no obstacle to obtaining a building permit to remodel the shoreline restaurant. However, because the zoning board can be unpredictable, the attorney recommends that an escrow clause be written into the purchase contract so that John and Marie do not buy the lot unless paving is approved. The part of the restaurant purchase price to be paid to the seller for the empty lot would be placed in escrow, in trust of a local bank until the zoning board reaches a decision. If the zoning board were to approve paving, the bank would turn over the escrow fund to the seller to complete the transaction. If the zoning board were to forbid paving, the bank would return the escrow fund, the purchase of the adjacent lot would be canceled, and the lot would still belong to the restaurant's former owners. A contract escrow clause protects the buyer from paying for something unusable, while the rest of the sale goes through.

According to the attorney, the franchise offers the usual entanglements, although it is no fly-by-night scheme. King Craw, the Louisiana-based seafood chain, is rated highly by business credit bureaus even though it has been in business only a few years. The attorney attributes King Craw's success to the direction it gives to franchise operators, as evidenced by the guidelines and restrictions contained in the contract. Other King Craw owners contacted by the attorney (from the list provided in the disclosure statement) confirm that controls are tight. However, the attorney points out that there is no way to tell whether the failures of some outlets were really due to the tight controls or to the public's mixed reactions to seafood restaurants. To judge the possible effects of the company guidelines, the contract has to be studied very carefully.

In return for the franchise fee, King Craw provides the basic supplies and a completed building ready for operation. The franchise purchaser has no say in the location other than to select the town to do business in. The company then sends professionals to choose the exact site and to see that the building is constructed according to company specifications. According to the contract, the company arranges for all licenses and permits, provides publicity for the grand opening, and handles all advertising, national and local.

The franchise purchaser must pay all other costs of day-to-day operation, including freight charges for the shipment of genuine Louisiana crawfish. Most of the specialized foodstuffs must be bought directly from the company at the company's price. Certain seafood can be bought locally if it meets company specifications; lobsters, for example, must weigh between 2 and 2¼ pounds. The menu itself is limited to the dishes sold at all the other franchise locations. The contract allows the company to set menu prices, restaurant hours, and even the design of the employees' uniforms. The attorney thinks these guidelines are reasonable to protect the integrity of the King Craw image.

In addition to a one-time franchise fee, the operators must also pay King Craw a percentage of the receipts. The attorney points out that there is no minimum sales provision; the contract cannot be canceled if a monthly sales quota is not met.

Of greater concern is that the company does not protect the location; it has the right to put up new outlets wherever it pleases. If the sales volume from John and Marie's outlet is heavy, the company could open another King Craw nearby. The figures on the earnings claim document state that a typical King Craw makes a 10 percent profit on sales that average $500,000 a year, a decent return on the $250,000 franchise fee. However, if the company can limit John and Marie's profit by licensing competitors, the incentive is reduced.

The attorney agrees that, given the measure of Marie's faith in her skills, the franchise would be too limiting to her. The restaurant opportunities seem to offer more in the way of self-determination. In trying to summarize the reasons for the choice of one of the restaurants, John, Marie, and the attorney arrive at some conclusions. The shoreline restaurant appears to be a bargain purchase, even including the cost of redesigning the interior. The inland restaurant offers the chance to buy in on a successful tradition, with the challenge of upholding it. The shoreline restaurant has the greater profit potential in the long run because of its favorable location. However, first, its earnings picture must be turned around.

Because Marie has the skills to make either restaurant pay off, the Smiths eventually decide, with the help of their counselors, to accept the greater challenge. They decide to buy the shoreline restaurant. Another couple, with different skills, could easily have reached a different conclusion. For example, a less well financed investor might have chosen the inland restaurant because it would be an income producer right away. On the other hand, John and Marie's careful consideration of price, location, profitability, and various complicating factors enables them to predict what true effect each of the three choices would have upon their lives. In the end, they made their selection not on the basis of appearance, but on perceived realities.

Business decisions are not easy—especially the far-reaching decision to enter business in the first place. In making your decision, do not let your judgment be clouded by dreams of success or by fears of failure. Listen to suggestions from your banker, your lawyer, and your accountant, and then consider the future coolly and calmly. Whatever the results of that decision are, you and your family will feel better about it if you have left no stone unturned in your preparation. In an endeavor as serious as entering the business world, you must take the steps necessary to give yourself the best possible chance of success.

2
FINANCING THE SMALL BUSINESS

Your ability to finance a business depends on your business reputation and prospects, the amount of money you need to start and operate the business, and your personal resources.

If you are well known in your field or have a product or service which others believe will be profitable, you may be able to finance your venture with a substantial amount of outside capital. But if you are starting without these advantages, you will have to depend on your own resources. Many businesses have successfully started on an owner's personal savings, the mortgage raised on a house, or cash borrowed against insurance policies. However, few businesses can operate long on personal financing. Inevitably, more money is needed for additional assets and for operating funds to pay for wages, supplies, and merchandise and to extend credit to customers. Also, it may not be advisable to place all of your personal resources into a business venture because of the risk of losing all of your capital.

Searching for funding can provide a sobering glimpse of reality. Potential backers may be candid about your idea and prospects. Also bracing can be the task of drawing up financial projections and financial statements. Loan applications will provide insight as you detail all business charges and expenses. Full attention to the financial demands of the business can prevent your dream of enterprise from becoming a nightmare.

EVALUATE YOUR CAPITAL REQUIREMENTS

Insufficient capital is a major problem for the new entrepreneur. Before you take a decisive step, work up a detailed set of figures indicating how much capital you will need to launch your business.

You must itemize expenses you will incur in setting up your organization, including a regular salary for yourself. The actual funds you have to invest from all sources must be sufficient to meet these costs—if they are not, you obviously cannot start your venture.

You must be able to meet three kinds of expenses: *capital* expenses, *fixed* expenses, and *variable* expenses.

Capital expenses are one-time-only costs necessary to bring your business to the point of operation. For example, the purchase of a large machine is a capital cost. A machine that is leased instead of purchased is an example of a fixed expense. A fixed expense is one which must be paid regularly, perhaps every month or every week. Variable expenses are those which fluctuate or those which are unforeseen. The energy costs of operating the machine would be a variable expense, depending upon how much the machine is used. Cash reserves may be necessary to meet unexpected variable expenses.

The following checklists will help you to make a projection of expenses you must meet.

CHECKLIST OF CAPITAL EXPENSES

Capital expenses are costs of:

- Buildings, machinery, equipment, and land used for your business
- Professional fees incurred in the purchase of business facilities, such as real estate commissions, legal fees, and architects' design fees
- Obtaining building permits and zoning changes
- Outside business improvements, parking lots, landscaping, paving, sewer connections, payments for rights-of-way or access routes
- Remodeling or redecorating the inside of the business structure to suit your needs, including rewiring, special pipes, outside windows, and ventilation
- Installation of heating systems and water lines
- Typewriters, fire extinguishers, dollies, vacuum cleaners, and portable tools
- Patents or copyrights necessary to the business
- Promotion or advertising costs for your grand opening
- Neon sign and other displays or exhibitions to be outside the building; for example, a swimming pool company may have a pool constructed on the grounds outside
- Inside and outside lighting fixtures necessary for your store and parking lot
- Shelves, files, cabinetry, and display counters

- Safes, strong boxes, cash registers, and employee lockers
- Burglar alarms, window gratings, antitheft devices, and sprinkler systems
- Water cooler, soda machine, and time clock and punch cards
- Reference books
- Inventory necessary to start retail operations or raw materials necessary to start production
- Vehicles needed by the business

CHECKLIST OF FIXED EXPENSES

- Rent for premises and for leased machinery and equipment.
- Lease of rights for patents, copyrights, rights-of-way, or other rights you must secure to do business.
- Insurance: comprehensive, fire, crime, theft, disaster, liability, malpractice, casualty, business interruption, worker's compensation, marine insurance, business overhead expense insurance, extended coverage for vandalism and malicious mischief, etc.
- Yearly registration fees and certain taxes that are fixed annually, such as the federal highway use tax, federal aircraft use tax, federal alcohol stamps, state automobile license and registration, city property tax, state certification, professional accreditation, registry fees, etc.
- Garbage collection, snow removal, landscaping, ambulance services, building maintenance, exterminators, and furnace cleaners can be paid for monthly, as needed, or on a yearly contractual basis.
- Collection agencies, accountants, lawyers, credit services, and other professionals regularly dealt with can be put on yearly retainers.
- Rotary Club membership, Lion membership, business cards, participation in town fairs or trade show, tickets to the firemen's and policemen's ball.
- Membership in business associations.
- Cleaning of premises.
- Security protection.
- Subscriptions to trade and professional magazines and journals.
- Salary costs not related to sales or production (these wages vary with volume of business and overtime): secretaries, typists, bookkeepers, personnel department, research and development staff, and management positions.
- Supply costs not related to production: paper, typewriter materials, ledgers, pencils, stamps, paper towels, toilet paper, staples, paper clips, paper cups, etc.

CHECKLIST OF VARIABLE EXPENSES

These are costs of:

- Production-related salaries, including overtime pay
- Commissions paid to sales personnel
- Contributions to employee health and medical plans and to company profit-sharing plans
- Rental of extra machinery to match peak-production demands
- Social Security contributions made on behalf of employees
- Federal and state unemployment taxes
- State and federal fuel taxes, excise taxes, customer and tariff duties, sales taxes, and value-added taxes
- Advertising
- Delivery
- Telephone
- Repairs
- Heat, utilities, and air conditioning
- Uniforms, work clothes, safety shoes, and equipment provided by employer
- Disposal of industrial wastes, incineration, purification, and other special handling
- Compliance with federal, state, and municipal regulatory agencies, such as the Environmental Protection Agency
- Travel and entertainment to solicit new business
- Customer services such as warranties, repairs, and complaints
- Raw materials and supplies necessary for production

PROJECTING INCOME

You may have the money to invest and the energy to work hard, but if you do not have customers, your business will fail. The fact that many businesses open and then close is evidence that their owners were able to estimate and raise an initial investment to start the business, but that they were not capable of developing and keeping sufficient sales volume to meet expenses and return a profit. Although it is difficult to project an income return for a new business, you must make a realistic estimate based on your experience and the experience of others. If you are unsure of your income prospects, you are really not going into business, you are gambling—betting against the odds.

Even when you are experienced and optimistic, you should make an in-depth appraisal of your prospects and have someone else check your projection of business prospects. You can hire a market research agency to undertake a study to determine your potential sales area or customer base. In some cases, you can make your own survey. A simple example: An individual planning to start a service station for foreign cars should visit other foreign-car-service businesses in town. If an appointment must be made 3 weeks in advance to do a simple tune-up, this is good evidence that there is room for another foreign-car-service business in the area.

Determine how long it will take you to develop sufficient volume to make a profit. If you are starting a business which may have to rely largely upon word of mouth to advertise it, you may experience a long period of little or no cash flow while waiting for customers to come around. The longer it takes for you and your product to be recognized, the greater the chance your business will fail. Eventually, the cost to keep the business running may overwhelm your ability to finance it. For quicker recognition, you may have to consider a large initial outlay for advertising even before you open. Some kind of grand opening and attention-getting promotion may help your business get off to a quicker, more successful start.

If you are buying a going concern, income projections will, of course, be based on the past experience of the business. But, even here, check the accuracy of the figures, whether there were unusual circumstances during the period they were compiled, and whether a change of proprietors may adversely affect customer relationships.

FACING TEMPORARY LOSSES

When projecting the extent of possible losses, you may not be out of pocket by as much as you estimate. Do not overlook the fact that the federal government shares in your risk. Should your business have losses, especially in the early start-up years, you may write them off against your other income. If it were not for the tax write-offs, you would have to shoulder the entire loss. By permitting the write-offs, the government shares your loss by forgoing part of the tax otherwise due on your other income. In states which impose income taxes your risk is further reduced to the extent of state tax reductions.

If you have large losses and insufficient income from other sources to absorb them, the excess loss will not go unused. Excess losses may be used to obtain a tax refund from prior years or to reduce taxes in certain future years. These excess losses, called *net operating losses*, help to minimize your risk.

The ability to reduce your risk by writing off losses is not without limits. Your business must be organized in such a way that income and losses are taxed directly to you. If the business itself becomes a taxpayer, losses will remain in the business and will be unavailable to offset your other nonbusiness income. When organizing your business, you have several choices of business form: proprietorship, partnership, Subchapter S corporation, or corporation. Your choice will affect your entire tax picture. Bear in mind that the ability to write off losses is just one factor that will influence your ultimate decision. The consequences of your choice are explained in detail in Chapter 5.

SOURCES OF EQUITY CAPITAL

Equity financing means sharing the profits and, to some extent, the control of your business with other investors. In times of "tight money," however, when the cost of bank loans is prohibitive if available at all, equity capital may be your primary means of raising the funds to begin operations.

Relatives, friends, employees, or people you have contacted through advertisements or brokers may want to invest in your business. Your accountant or lawyer, seeing that you have a potentially profitable venture, may also contact possible investors.

The key to obtaining outside capital is convincing potential investors that you have the ability to run a successful business and that your projected venture has a good chance to succeed. Likely investors may not necessarily want a current return of income, but they want to be assured that, within a period of time, their capital will have appreciated.

If you do have offers of capital from outsiders, consider their personalities and business reputations. They may prove to be incompatible business associates. Some may demand a voice in the business and its management, others may fight for greater control, and some may be dishonest. If you have to take in associates, make sure you keep a majority equity interest in your business.

Short-term venture capital may be available from companies whose sole business is taking a gamble on a new business with the expectation of a sizable profit. Venture capital is advanced for a short term, say, 5 years, at which time refinancing is necessary to retire the venture capital company's interest. Sources of venture capital (other than small business investment companies) are usually known to bankers, lawyers, and accountants. The U.S. Small Business Administration issues a pamphlet, *A Venture Capital Primer for Small Business*, which may be of assistance to you in securing venture capital.

SEEKING FINANCIAL
ADVICE AND FUNDS
THROUGH THE SMALL BUSINESS
ADMINISTRATION

The Small Business Administration (SBA), an independent federal government agency with field offices across the country, helps small business owners by giving financial advice and guaranteeing business loans. Although you may not want or be eligible for SBA support, you can take advantage of their financial counseling services by writing or visiting a field office. The SBA tries to give special assistance to minority businesses, and its offices will have information on aid programs which are current at the time of application. The SBA does not charge for advice. You may also write for information from the Small Business Administration, 1441 L Street, N.W., Washington, D.C. 20416.

There are businesses that are ineligible for SBA aid, such as a newspaper, a radio or TV station, or a liquor store. You cannot obtain SBA funds to pay off inadequately secured creditors; to provide payments or distributions to owners, partners, or shareholders; or to replenish working-capital funds which you have already used to make such payments.

The largest proportion of SBA aid is in the form of guaranteed loans, and before you can qualify for such assistance, you must show that you cannot obtain other financing. If your request is approved, you can borrow up to $350,000 from a bank and the SBA may guarantee up to 90 percent of the loan. Guaranteed loan applications are processed faster if your bank has been certified by the SBA. Some other financial institutions, including certain stockbrokers, have been given permission to make SBA-guaranteed loans.

Even if you qualify for an SBA loan, be aware that funds may be delayed—or strangled—in red tape. For this reason, you may decide not to ask for SBA help. However, the SBA is likely to be the source of assistance should your business suffer damage in a disaster, such as a flood or a hurricane.

FINANCIAL AID FROM
SMALL BUSINESS INVESTMENT
COMPANIES

Under the Small Business Investment Act, small business investment companies (SBICs) are licensed by the SBA to supply equity capital to companies unable to raise funds from other sources. The SBICs are chartered under state law; they are privately owned and operate for profit. Under SBA guidelines defined by federal law, SBICs are usually willing to take greater risks than banks. Negotiations between an entrepreneur and an SBIC are private business arrangements and are not supervised by the SBA.

Types of SBIC Investment If you are a sole proprietor or in partnership, with no intention of incorporating, SBIC financing is available in the form of long-term loans (over 5 years), secured by real estate or other collateral. If you are incorporated, you may seek long-term loans or equity financing. Equity financing may come through purchase of stock in your company, loans with stock-purchase warrants attached, or convertible debentures. The SBIC supplying equity capital may demand board representation and a voice in your business. Some small businesses refrain from seeking SBIC financing because their equity would be diluted. But, given a mutually satisfactory arrangement, the SBIC can be a source of valuable business counsel.

SBA Offices List SBICs Your choice of SBIC will be determined by the type of financing you are seeking. If you want equity financing, you must contact an SBIC that deals in equity financing and be prepared to show your company's history, current status, and projections for the future. Your financial statements should be comprehensive. Be ready to describe how the equity financing (or term loan) would relate to your financial projections. SBICs are profit-motivated, and you have to convince the SBIC representatives of your company's growth and profit potential. You may have to apply to several SBICs before you find one prepared to take a risk with you.

Finally, some SBICs are bank-related. Inquire if your bank has such a connection. You may more readily obtain backing from a company that can check on your financial status and prospects through data at the bank.

BORROWING FROM A BANK

A bank makes money by lending money and will generally lend you funds if your business reputation is good and your business venture is profitable or has profitable prospects. When applying for your loan, you will have to provide business and personal credit data for yourself and any partners or other associates or stockholders. The application form may require information about life insurance, business insurance, personal bank accounts, business and civic organizations in which you are involved, the organization of your business (corporation, partnership, or single proprietorship), indebtedness to other banks or lending institutions, outstanding contingent debts, and, most important, the purpose of the loan and how you plan to repay it. For example, is the loan needed to finance the purchase of merchandise which can be sold before the loan is due? How did you arrive at the amount of the loan requested? Is it the minimum amount necessary for the intended purpose?

The loan officer will discuss your *prospects.* You should be ready to:

● Give a brief account of the future of your business. Discuss such questions as the probable demand for your product or services, and the presence, absence, or likelihood of competition.
● Show your ability to obtain raw materials or supplies of merchandise in the future and show what the costs will be.
● Show what you think future price levels will mean to the valuation of your present inventories.
● Provide a *balance sheet,* listing your business assets and liabilities, and a summarized statement of prior sales, costs of doing business, and net profit before income taxes. At least 1 previous year must be shown for established businesses. Several years' data are even more desirable. Your figures should include the amount you and your partners are drawing from the business, or how much has been paid out in dividends in recent years.

If you are starting a *new business,* you will not be able to furnish much of the foregoing information. What, then, should you present?

● Have some ideas about how you will use the financing to operate your business with success.
● Prove that you have a reputation for paying your obligations when due.
● Show that you have had adequate business experience in this or a similar area.
● Show that you have sufficient financing of your own to warrant a lender's taking a reasonable risk by advancing part of your financial needs.
● Show, if possible, that you have unfilled orders on hand or business prospects which are likely to produce sufficient income to repay the loan.

Banks are conservative lenders as far as new enterprises are concerned. However, in certain circumstances, your project might merit a bank's consideration. The bank will spell out the conditions of lending. Although a bank loan may not currently be available, the loan officer may be favorably impressed with you and your project and may suggest other sources of capital, or be willing to extend aid at a later stage in your business's development.

From the start, set up a good working relationship with your bank. Personal contact with the manager, officers, and staff will be helpful. You want to earn the bank's confidence in your business so that you can establish and increase a line of credit. Look ahead to the time when you will be expanding your business. Your banker should be kept abreast of your plans and financial developments.

Bankers generally prefer to limit their loans (especially in hard economic times) to businesses that are not pressed for funds to meet current obligations. They prefer to make loans to a problem-free business which needs funds to expand operations to a new city or to develop a new product. The bank will readily consider such a loan because, if the new venture fails, the company continues to operate its regular line and has the resources to pay off the loan.

A bank loan will not be forthcoming if the bank suspects that the money is needed to pay off your debts to other creditors. The bank does not want to pay off other creditors and be left as the only remaining risk taker. A bank wants to see its funds put to a constructive use, not used as a bailout.

TYPES OF BUSINESS LOANS

Character Loans This term is used for short-term, unsecured loans, made without collateral. Only a company or an entrepreneur with the highest credit standing, business integrity, and ability to manage a company is likely to be eligible.

Line of Credit A banker extending a line of credit makes an advance commitment to lend money up to a certain maximum and on specific conditions. A credit investigation will precede the arrangement; then, when loans are called for, they are usually granted on a revolving basis, so that not more than one may be outstanding at any time. Approved customers usually find the arrangement highly adaptable to their financial needs, especially when those needs are seasonal in nature. When short-term bank notes are due, the customer may protect the line of credit by borrowing elsewhere to meet the obligation. If an annual clearance of debt is part of the arrangement, the business will ensure a buildup of funds by refraining from other outlays until that line of credit is cleared up.

Term Loans Short-term loans cover periods of less than a year, perhaps only 30 to 60 days; *intermediate* loans extend over 1 year but less than 5 years; and *long-term* loans run over 5 years, sometimes for as long as 10 or 15 years. Collateral as well as a high standard of credit may be necessary to secure a term loan. A bank will review the current financial position of a business, and it may require an equal ratio of equity capital to debt. It may require payments each month, each quarter, every 6 months, or annually. A series of notes due at specified times may be the method of payment.

Collateral Loans Inventory may be accepted as collateral for short-term loans. Longer-term loans may be secured by chattel or real estate mortgages, by stocks and bonds, or by life insurance. Since forced sale of collateral may not repay the lender in case of default, the demand for a good credit background and for sound prospects in the business will also be required.

Cosigner Loans If a cosigner or comaker joins with the borrower on a loan, that person is equally obligated to see that the loan is repaid. A cosigner with good credit standing at a bank carries some weight when a loan is authorized.

Warehouse and Field Warehouse Loans A bank or commercial finance company may lend funds to a small business on the basis of a warehouse receipt delivered directly by the lender. The staple or standard merchandise of a readily salable type is placed either in a public warehouse or in the proprietor's own warehouse where a warehousing company takes over responsibility and places a bonded employee in control. There are variations in field warehousing, some of which involve interbusiness financing. The basis of this type of loan is that the bank or other lender has security and legal possession of the merchandise while the loan is in effect. Use this method of financing when you want to take advantage of favorable buying conditions or when you anticipate a seasonal drop in business. It enables you to obtain more working capital if cash is short at a time when production and operating costs are high.

Equipment Loans   Equipment may serve as collateral for a loan. Or the cost of new equipment may be financed through installment purchases.

Accounts Receivable Financing   Commercial credit or finance companies accept accounts receivable as security for loans; so do some banks. With this type of financing, you remain responsible for the repayment of the loan when the proceeds of the accounts receivable do not cover the advance. In factoring, the factor *purchases* accounts receivable at a discount for cash. Unless other arrangements are made, the factor assumes all collection responsibilities.

There are two plans used by finance companies, banks, factors, and other lenders that deal in accounts receivable financing. Under the *notification* plan, customers are asked to pay the lender directly. But many businesses prefer not to reveal to their customers that they are financing through accounts receivable. Unless state law requires that the notification plan be used, they therefore use the *nonnotification* plan, accepting payments as usual and channeling them to the lender.

TRADE CREDIT

A business short of working capital may find it financially expedient to delay payments to suppliers—in effect, taking short-term loans through trade credit. However, to encourage you to pay within 10 days, suppliers will usually give you a small cash discount which you may deduct from your bill if you pay within 10 days. It may be advisable to take advantage of the discounts rather than delay payment. For example, if you order merchandise and the invoice reads "2/10, n/30," a 2 percent discount may be deducted from the bill if you pay in 10 days. If you delay payment until the end of the 30-day period, you are incurring an "interest" charge by not taking the discount. This interest charge is 36 percent, calculated as follows: Each credit period is 20 days. During the year, there are eighteen 20-day periods during which a 2 percent discount is not taken. Two percent multiplied by 18 equals 36 percent a year.

Some newcomers to small business eagerly seize on trade credit to acquire fixed assets, a mistaken course which may compound financial troubles. If the credit is used, it should be to generate more business, to satisfy customers, and to build up a cash flow so that you can pay bills within the discount period.

3
BUYING AN
EXISTING BUSINESS

Buying an existing business seems an easy and advantageous way to enter the business world. You may avoid some of the headaches involved with starting up a new business, if you proceed cautiously. Before you buy, plan to spend weeks—if not months—investigating the business. How much time you need depends on the size and scope of the enterprise.

Find out why the present owner is selling. In some cases, it may be because of age or failing health. It is also possible that the business is failing and the owner is eager to unload it. You do not want to pay for his or her mistakes. However, if you believe that the fault lies with the owner, you may have an opportunity to buy the business at a bargain price. Investigate the reputation of the business in the community. If the owner's poor choice of equipment, unwise inventory purchases, or unattractive floor layout seems to be the cause of failure, the situation may be correctable. However, since the former owner's practices have driven off many customers, it may take time before people become acquainted with your operation. Extra publicity steps can help make people aware that the business has changed hands or changed methods.

EVALUATING THE BUSINESS

Determine exactly what you are buying. Purchasing a business is much more complicated than buying a single piece of investment property, such as a building. Many different assets are involved—equipment, trucks, machinery, a building—and their physical condition will have to be examined. The size and salability of inventory will have to be assessed. Agreements with employees and customers must be reviewed, and the existence of liens and other liabilities must be researched. You need the assistance of an attorney and an accountant.

A lawyer will check the following: (1) the chain of legal title, leases on machinery, patent arrangements; (2) registration of patents, trademarks, formulas, copyrights, franchises, and their transferability; (3) the existence of any encumbrances on the property, such as mortgages, liens, or chattel mortgages against machinery and fixtures; (4) restrictions, either in zoning or on ownership, and any rental or building regulations; and (5) unfulfilled contract commitments.

An accountant will ascertain receivables and liabilities and will check whether the company endorsed or guaranteed any obligations of others, including negotiable instruments sold or discounted; whether there are any disputed assessments or possible tax liabilities; and whether there are cumulative dividends in arrears. The accountant will review records going back at least 3 years, preferably 10. If the company is a relatively new one, the accountant will familiarize you with its entire record.

Your accountant will determine the gross profit margin of the company and will calculate whether it is high enough to give you a comfortable profit. You want to know the growth rate of the company over the past 5 years and whether there are any factors which indicate that such a growth rate will not continue.

A valuable source of information will be the firm's federal income tax return, which the owner should show you. You can be fairly sure that the receipts are not overstated, although expenses may have been exaggerated and the inventory may have been adjusted for tax purposes. Sales tax records can be used to double-check the receipts. Property taxes can be checked with the county treasurer. Insurance expenses can be verified with the company's insurance agent. Production costs can be reviewed by examining freight costs, vendors' invoices, records of merchandise payments, bills of lading, and inventory records. Payroll and Social Security records can be used to determine salary costs. At the same time, consult union officials to find out when the labor contracts expire; there may be future wage increases on the horizon with the possibility of prolonged wrangling over other pay benefits. Salespersons' reports will give a good indication of the size of the clientele and the volume from the geographic sales area. Sometimes the company's suppliers or bankers will help you estimate the amount of the company's business.

Find out how the inventory is appraised. Is it valued at the price of the oldest item bought awaiting sale or is the inventory valued at the price of the most recent item purchased? Both methods are acceptable, and each gives a different value depending on price fluctuations. Examine the inventory; there may be items in the storeroom that cannot be sold or that have no value to you. Also have these points checked out to avoid unexpected future costs and liabilities:

- Are invoices discounted? Old customers will expect you to continue this policy, which may affect your cash flow.
- Are there unfulfilled contracts? Check what projects are ongoing against what receipts are due for them. Are there penalties for late completion?
- Has the company guaranteed the obligations of others (like being the cosigner on a loan) which may produce unexpected debts later?
- Will key personnel leave if the owner leaves?
- Consider labor relations and employee morale. Find out what benefits will continue after you buy the business, such as holidays, paid vacations, sick days, and health insurance.
- Are there any pending damage claims, lawsuits, disputed assessments, or possible tax liabilities?
- Are there pending matters before government agencies, such as a suit for equal opportunity claims or over minority hiring practices?
- Are there any problems with government regulations concerning the design of the product?
- Are there any new environmental standards that will affect the way the company does business?
- Are there any changes needed to comply with building, health, or sanitation codes?

SETTING YOUR PRICE

The seller will offer you the business for a price and give you an opportunity to examine records and check up on promises. The seller is, of course, trying to get the most from the business. The price will be based on the fair market value of the assets of the business plus an amount set for the value of a going concern, that is, its capacity to provide profits. The excess value is usually viewed as goodwill. You must accurately determine the value of the assets and the expected yearly profit. Once you have determined the asset values and profit projections, you can determine a fair price to offer for the business. After your review, you may very well agree with the seller and still try to pay less through negotiations. On the other hand, you may disagree with the values set and his or her claim of sales, production costs, profit margin, and goodwill.

Set your price for the business from your financial perspective, by considering your earning power as compared with that offered by the business: (1) Start with the investment required to buy the business. (2) Figure how much this amount would earn if invested elsewhere. (3) Add to the income figured in (2) the amount of your current salary that you would be giving up to run the business. (4) Compare the projected business profit claimed by the seller with your total earning power. (5) The excess is the earning power of the business. (6) Multiply the excess earning power by 5 for a well-established business or by 3, if you have any concern about the stability of the business, and add the result to the value of the assets of the business. For example, a business with assets of $200,000 earns $60,000 a year. If you invest $200,000 in bonds at 11 percent, you would get a return of $22,000. You are now earning a salary of $30,000. Your total earning power is $52,000. Therefore, the excess annual earning power of the business is $8000 ($60,000 − $52,000). Five times that figure is $40,000. According to the formula, a fair price for the business might be $240,000 ($200,000 + $40,000). If you used 3 years as your measuring rod, the price would be $224,000 ($200,000 + $24,000).

Another method bases price on the capitalized value of future earnings. The rate used coincides with rate of return realized on investments involving a similar amount of risk. To find the capitalized value, divide annual profit by the expected rate of return. Assume, for example, that the estimated profits over the next 5 years will average $30,000 per annum, as they would in the foregoing example ($60,000 minus salary of $30,000). If the business is considered as safe as an investment in corporate securities earning 10 percent, an offering price would be $300,000 ($30,000 divided by 0.10). However, the risk factor in a small business is considerably higher than the risk in a stock market investment, so that a rate of 20 to 25 percent might be applied. A rate of 20 percent gives a purchase price of $150,000. Of course, a low offer might not be realistic. Yet, if the proprietor is eager enough to sell, he or she may agree to it and you would be able to recover your investment in about 5 years. In any event, this figure provides you with a starting point in your bargaining. Another formula uses the value of inventory at cost plus profits of 1 year.

Whatever formula you use to set a price, there is bound to be a gap between the asking price and your bid price at the onset of negotiations. The amount you offer for the business is one thing; the actual sales price of the business is determined after negotiations between the seller and you, or the agents who represent you. How badly does the owner want to sell? How badly do you want to buy? What is the price of other businesses for sale? Are there other prospective buyers? What are the possibilities of expanding the existing operation?

Once you and your seller agree on price, you will bring in your lawyer to draw up a contract. A favorable contract from your viewpoint will give you clear title, good payment terms, warranty protection against false statements by the seller, a covenant preventing the seller from competing with you, and a provision giving you protection from the time the contract is signed until the actual settlement takes place. This action prevents a dishonest seller from depleting assets or inventory with a "going out of business" sale or destroying goodwill that you had agreed to pay for. You should have full access to the premises and records. You may even require the seller to put up a good faith deposit in escrow for 6 months or longer to back up the warranty.

GETTING YOUR BEST TAX ADVANTAGE

Tax planning should begin before any purchase is completed to determine how the purchase agreement will affect future tax liabilities. Even though you buy the business as a whole, for tax purposes the purchase of an unincorporated business is viewed as a purchase of individual assets. The total purchase price must be allocated over the various assets. You generally get your greatest tax advantage by negotiating with the seller to allocate the purchase price to those assets that give you the greatest tax deductions during operations, and largest capital gain on disposal. Be aware that this allocation process is not as straightforward as it may appear. This is because the seller may prefer a different allocation. Prepare to negotiate the allocation vigorously with the help of your attorney or accountant.

Value the following at a *high* price:

- *Merchandise inventory.* A high cost reduces taxable profit.
- *Supplies and similar items not used in the manufacture of your product.* These supplies are fully deductible as expenses.
- *Accounts receivable.* If some go bad, the loss is fully deductible.
- *Patents, copyrights, franchises, and amortizable intangibles,* if the remaining life is short.

- *Machinery, equipment, and buildings.* The cost of these assets is recovered under the accelerated cost recovery system over periods and at rates fixed by law.
- *Covenant of the seller not to compete* (discussed more fully below).

The following should be valued at a *low* price:

- *Land.* You get no depreciation deduction to recover cost. Gain on sale would be a capital gain.
- *Stocks, bonds, and securities.* You get no annual depreciation. Gain would be taxed at capital gain rates.
- *Goodwill.* You get no annual deduction for depreciation. The cost would be recovered only through eventual sale of the business. Any profits on a sale would be capital gains.

BUYING A COMPANY WITH ITS OWN FUNDS OR EARNINGS

Sometimes, the purchase of the business may be transacted by using in part the company's own funds or future earnings. This may be possible where the corporation holds substantial cash which will be used to redeem part of the seller's stock from the company. You buy from the seller only a portion of stock. The corporation redeems the balance of the stock from the seller with the cash it has. As you have the remaining stock, the only outstanding stock, you are in full control of the purchased corporation. In planning such a transaction, both you and the seller must arrange the steps of the transaction so that both of you are not subject to an IRS challenge that dividend income has been earned.

COVENANTS NOT TO COMPETE

A business purchase usually includes agreements not to compete for a specified time or in a specified area or both, but the buyer will seek to characterize the "noncompete" agreement in one way, and the seller in another, because of the different tax consequences attached to each characterization.

As the buyer, you should seek deductions for your payments to restrain the seller from competing. The seller will usually resist your demands because, under the tax law, if you deduct the payments, he or she must report the payments as ordinary income. The seller will try to avoid this. To get the deduction, you may have to do some hard bargaining and possibly allow for an adjustment of the price.

To get a deduction for the covenant, the sales contract must include the covenant and allocate a specific amount to it. Further, the contract should state that the agreement not to compete is not part of the transfer of goodwill. Retain other evidence to corroborate the agreement. Show that it has an independent value and that its chief function is not to assure the beneficial use of goodwill.

PURCHASING A CORPORATION

When you are interested in acquiring an incorporated business, you have two choices. You can buy the stock of the corporation and thereby acquire control of its assets, or you can buy the assets themselves, either directly from the corporation or from the shareholders, if the corporation is liquidated and its assets distributed in the liquidation process. As a buyer, you would generally prefer to acquire the assets of the corporation, rather than its stock. By buying stock, you may inadvertently acquire hidden or contingent corporate liabilities, such as unpaid withholding taxes. While you can protect yourself from such liabilities by guarantees or by placing part of the purchase price in escrow to cover potential problems, these protections may be costly to you in excess legal fees and may be unacceptable to the seller. Also, you may not want or need all the assets and might prefer a selective purchase. Your desires, however, may run counter to those of the seller. The seller typically prefers a stock sale; it is a clean one-step transaction for which capital gains may be realized. Thus, your choices may be more apparent than real. Consider the tax consequences to you of these alternatives.

Purchase of Assets   When you buy the assets, the price you pay becomes the basis for those assets. If you assume liabilities when you buy the assets or if the assets are subject to liabilities, the liabilities also become part of your basis. This basis is the figure upon which depreciation will be figured and against which gain or loss on a future sale will be measured. When you acquire assets, your attorney will, of course, check for any preexisting liens or mortgages on the property. You may be entitled to a 6 or 10 percent investment tax credit on the purchase of certain equipment and machinery.

When you have acquired the assets, you may then choose to incorporate or not. The corporation from which you acquired the assets is completely independent of your business.

Purchase of Corporate Stock   When you buy the stock of a corporation, the corporation remains intact and you step into the shoes of the former owners. Your stock basis is the amount you paid for it. This amount reflects the present value of the corporation's assets. The corporation's basis for its assets does not change as a result of your acquisition. Several assets may have appreciated, but depreciation deductions are still figured on the old basis. As a buyer, you are forsaking important deductions unless you liquidate the corporation as discussed below. Also, you face the possibility of contingent or undisclosed liabilities.

Stepping up the basis of assets following a stock purchase.   If the basis of corporate assets differs from market value, you may step up the basis of the assets by acquiring the stock and liquidating the corporation at no tax cost to you. This will provide you larger tax deductions for depreciation, an operating cost. Normally, when a corporation is liquidated, the stockholders pay tax on any gain (the difference between the value of the property received on the liquidation and their stock basis). But when you buy stock and immediately liquidate the corporation, little or no gain results; your stock basis approximates the value of the assets.

The liquidation may entail tax consequences to the corporation. The Internal Revenue Service has ruled that investment credit must be recaptured on a complete liquidation by the corporation even though the sole shareholder continues to use the property in the same business in which the corporation was engaged.

CHECKLIST FOR CLOSING TITLE

Your attorney and accountant should cover and acquaint you with these facts:

- The total contract price and assets you are receiving on closing date.
- Steps you must take to comply with state or city bulk-sales acts on the purchase of merchandise, stock-in-trade, and fixtures.
- How you or the seller is to satisfy any chattel mortgages, liens, and conditional bills of sale.

- Adjustments for all payments of real estate taxes or water taxes; payments to mortgagee; payments for utility services, such as electricity, gas, and telephone; and insurance payments.
- How the sale affects employees' pension or profit-sharing plans.
- How accounts receivable are being transferred. You may wish to acquire these accounts to continue doing business with the customers.
- Adjustments for uncompleted contracts with unions, sales or service agencies which must be notified (for example, Internal Revenue Service, Social Security Administration, state unemployment insurance agencies).

Your attorney must see that all legal documents (titles, leases, mortgages, etc.) show the change of ownership. You should see that insurance policies are converted to provide for proper coverage under your new ownership. Finally, you must notify customers, suppliers, and employees of the change in ownership.

4
DECIDING THE LOCATION OF YOUR BUSINESS

The importance of location depends on the nature of your business. For example, if you are running a mail-order business, location is not vital. You may operate from your home, store, garage, or loft. On the other hand, if you are planning to open a retail store, you will want to locate where you will be in contact with the largest number of potential customers for your product. If you are locating a plant, you must look for an area which provides adequate facilities at a reasonable rent, which is accessible to your market and suppliers, and which is within the commuting distance of employees. If you are a wholesaler, you want facilities with access to major highways.

USING POPULATION DATA TO DETERMINE MARKET LOCATION

Sales are made to people, and the number of people in a particular area can be counted; of this number only a percentage are potential customers. Before you decide on a location, you must estimate the number of people in the area who may be your potential customers.

You may obtain population data from various sources: a local chamber of commerce, a town office, the Small Business Administration, the Department of Commerce, and, of course, the Bureau of the Census. For example, assume you plan to start a florist shop. You have the following information:

1. Population of the community: 120,000
2. The number of stores in it similar to the type you want to open: 11 plus your store makes 12

3. The average number of people in the town per store: 10,000
4. Based on government statistics, the national average number of inhabitants needed to support the store: 9000

A comparison of the averages under points 3 and 4 tells you the margin for another florist shop is narrow. In addition, you estimate that for 5 months of the year private gardens are in bloom and business declines. You might decide to supplement the new store with a seed and garden department which would produce business in the spring and summer, or decide to consider another community where you would have about 15,000 inhabitants per store.

Determine the growth trend in the market. Assume a town has grown from 100,000 to 120,000 people in the last 2 years. New plants are going to open in the next year, bringing in workers and new residents. You might consider opening your store if you believe your abilities are impressive enough to claim the patronage of an expanding market. Also consider population shifts. For example, those entrepreneurs with the foresight to see the population boom in the sun belt and in California were able to capitalize on unusual expansion in these areas. Do you foresee a similar population shift that will aid your business prospects?

Other statistics can be found in the *Statistical Abstract of the United States*, published by the Bureau of the Census. This book contains a wealth of data, including the average hourly wage for each state, which a manufacturer may use to locate a plant in an area with low payroll costs. Statistics for the educational level of a state's residents may also give clues to a pool of skilled labor or a market for consumer computer products.

LOCATING THE RETAIL
OR SERVICE SHOP

Visibility is a most important factor in the choice of location. Just as advertising increases your public awareness, presenting people with the opportunity to look at your goods in your store will increase the traffic coming into your store. Corner locations are preferable as they are passed by pedestrians coming from two different streets. An important intersection may also increase trade, especially if it is regarded as a landmark or a point of reference for people to meet each other. Another favorable location may be close to a store that runs large advertising campaigns, such as a supermarket. Customers attracted to such a store will also pass your location.

When considering a site, make firsthand observations at regular intervals to determine the flow and destination of pedestrian traffic. Note the proportion of men to women and their relative ages. Chart whether they fit the profile of the clientele you seek for your store: young adults for a record store, professionals for a men's shop, affluent women for a jewelry store. If pedestrians seem to be hurrying to bus stops or train stations, the chances are that that location will not attract passersby to a store which requires more leisurely shopping. On the other hand, a stationery store or newspaper stand might do well there. Perhaps your area contains other businesses which may draw trade at lunch hour. Consider the entire work and leisure cycle of a neighborhood before you accept or reject it as a likely spot for your firm.

Some stores will succeed wherever they are located because their uniqueness serves to draw the customers to them; for example, a piano dealership or a furrier. Other stores actually benefit from being near the competition. Apparel stores frequently locate in the same district, offering shoppers a choice and comparisons. Together, they attract more buyers and can offer more items. The customer can usually find what is desired, so there is more overall spending. However, two nearby specialty shops, such as pet stores, will end up dividing trade to the detriment of each.

If you have to rely on customers who will come to a location by car, you must consider parking facilities. Drivers will not travel to shop in an area where they cannot find parking space or where parking may be subject to strict overtime fines. Sometimes, to make an area attractive to shoppers, retailers can persuade authorities to reset the time periods on nearby parking meters to better coincide with the time customers must be inside the establishment. For example, where a fast-food shop might be content with 15-minute meter parking, a beauty parlor may press for longer periods so that its customers do not have to worry about being ticketed for a stay of less than an hour. A local merchant's association can often help to take steps to improve parking conditions for retail customers.

If you plan to provide parking facilities, you must have at least 200 square feet of parking lot per car. This takes into account the dimensions of the car, room to open doors, and sufficient turnaround space. A lot for 10 cars would need 2000 square feet. However, in estimating the amount of space, you must also consider the length of time customers spend in your store and the availability of other parking space in the area. Also, consider the eventual need to expand parking facilities as business improves. Sometimes adjacent stores can share the investment for customer parking.

LOCATING IN
A SHOPPING CENTER

Malls and shopping centers have radically changed shopping habits since the end of World War II, draining business from the old, established districts in the center of towns and cities. In fact, at least 40 percent of the nation's retail transactions take place in shopping centers.

Before you sign a lease, investigate the center carefully. What competition would you face from similar businesses within the center? Has the center fulfilled the promoters' stated expectations? Check for yourself on its potential in relation to competition, traffic patterns, and the big-name stores scheduled to open on the site.

Can you afford occupancy in a shopping mall? Developers extract the highest rents they can get, and the small shop is usually the victim. Although a full-line department store may be able to drive a bargain because it is the main tenant, small stores have less leeway in negotiating rents.

Suburban homeowners, the country's biggest spenders, do gravitate to the shopping centers. Attractions have been added at many centers to gain shoppers' interest. Some feature art shows, modern bazaars, fashion shows, or sports car rallies. Consider what value such gimmicks might have for your type of business. Record shops, ice-cream franchises, and moderately priced fashion boutiques often thrive in lively surroundings. But if you are running a conservative gift shop or a women's half-size dress store, a carnival atmosphere is not likely to enhance your business. Also, if your business is highly prone to pilferage, losses are likely to be greater in a shopping center.

Shopping centers can be classified under three headings: *neighborhood, community,* and *regional.* The neighborhood center, perhaps a few minutes' drive from a specific residential area, will feature a chain supermarket and shops selling drugs and sundries. Ideally, it will also offer such personal services as laundry, dry cleaning, and shoe repair. Ample parking space is available on the premises. If space is available and consumer interest high, you might find the neighborhood center a good location for your small hardware or meat store or delicatessen.

A community center is likely to be dominated by a branch department or discount store. It may serve a population of 40,000 to 150,000 people. In the regional center, one or more full-line department stores exert the major drawing power. The trading area may extend outward as far as 10 to 15 miles in all directions. The most ambitious of these centers are climate-controlled, enclosed malls with fountains, gardens, and supervised play areas to lure customers. Several department stores usually exert a cumulative attraction and powerful traffic pull. Many malls include theaters, restaurants, bowling alleys, game rooms, and all the facilities possible to encourage a family not to leave the shopping area.

LEASING IN A
PROPOSED SHOPPING MALL

Use caution in signing a lease for space in a shopping mall that has not yet been constructed. Such agreements usually work to the advantage of the contractor, not the store owner. If the contractor should decide that the shopping mall venture is not attractive after all, he or she can usually default on the agreement without penalty. The courts seldom compel the contractor to proceed.

If you do lease before the premises are constructed, be sure the agreement states the dimension of your area, its exact location in the mall, its position in relation to other firms, and all its specifications.

Be aware of the various interpretations that can be given your "finished" facilities. Try to avoid the *shell* specification which requires the developer to supply you only with four walls, a roof, and a dirt floor. You will have to furnish all the internal construction on this bare cavern—a considerable contracting job. A *half-shell* will provide you with certain other items: front and rear doors, gypsum wallboard, concrete floors, and perhaps a toilet and heat. Ideally, you should arrange for *key* specifications. With this plan, the developer supplies the tenant with complete facilities ready for the addition of fixtures and decor.

What other types of retail stores will be included in the center? The designation "retail" can include insurance offices, service stores, theaters, and bowling alleys. Be sure you know exactly which establishments plan to locate in your center and what effect they might have upon your business.

LOCATING IN TOWN

If rent costs are prohibitive in the shopping centers, you may find as large a clientele in the proper downtown location. With the government offering programs of financing assistance and tax abatements, real estate developers have been revitalizing downtown areas, building high-rise structures for offices, parking garages, and shopping facilities. These downtown areas seem to attract many older couples. With the increase in lower-income housing and renovations, many young families and an increasingly large group of single people are moving back into the cities as well.

The variety of merchandise your store carries will help you decide the type of shopping area in which to locate. For example, clothing, jewelry, and department stores are more likely to be successful in the main or outlying central shopping district. On the other hand, grocery stores, drugstores, gasoline stations, and bakeries succeed on principal thoroughfares and neighborhood streets outside the main shopping districts.

Deciding on a location in a small town is sometimes secondary to the determination of the economic health of the community itself. What is the shopping pattern of the inhabitants? Are they inclined to travel to the city for major purchases, or do they rely on shopping centers situated on their route to work?

Beware of some of the inducements promised by local governments. Mayors and council members change with each election. Even the obvious has a way of not occurring. For example, the West Side Highway, a major automobile artery in Manhattan, collapsed in 1973. Downtown merchants were led to believe it would be rebuilt. Since all commerce would suffer without it, rebuilding seemed inevitable. Nine years later the West Side Highway has still not been completed.

Highways are not the only transportation services that fall into disrepair. Regional airlines are chronic money losers and do occasionally go bankrupt. If your business is going to rely upon air supplies or deliveries, investigate the financial condition of the local carrier before commencing operations. Railroads may also cut back services or drift into bankruptcy. Either arrange for alternate shipping methods at the first sign of trouble or, at extra cost, insure your business against service interruption.

Other municipal problems that may cripple your business include police, fire service, or sanitation strikes; municipal water shortages; and civil disorders. Any one of these disturbances occurring during the crucial Christmas season can spell failure for a retailer. Again, there is no inexpensive protection from these problems, but you should make every effort to gauge well the local mood before commencing business in a community.

LOCATING THE WHOLESALE BUSINESS

In this day and age of energy efficiency, the location of the wholesale business should be determined with an eye toward minimizing transportation costs. Centrally locate your warehouse to cut delivery costs to the most frequent customers. Easy access to major transportation arteries is an important consideration. If snow or other local weather conditions can make it difficult for you to receive and ship goods by truck, you might consider locating the warehouse near a railway line. A wholesaler of frozen foods, desiring a constant supply of electricity for freezing, should not locate in an area where power interruptions are frequent (unless the warehouse has a generator of its own).

For many urban wholesalers, delivery costs are raised by perpetual double-parking problems. Your location should have ramps or bays to ease your receiving problems. Your location may enable you to reduce shipping costs as well, if you can organize goods well enough to use smaller vehicles for better maneuverability in the streets.

LOCATING A SMALL PLANT

When choosing a location for a small plant, consider the proximity to your market, availability of labor, local wage scales, and access to raw materials. Before deciding between a metropolitan, suburban, or rural location, analyze your particular needs. If you require few skilled workers, especially at the outset, and if your process relies mostly on purchased parts, you may thrive in a small town. Wages are often lower outside the metropolitan area. An operator who prefers locating in a small town will have to consider the availability of repair service for machinery and the expense of bringing in raw materials and supplies from a distance. The plant that needs to be near big labor pools, with skilled workers, specialists, and consultants, will be more likely to prosper in the large city. This is also true of any factory that needs to be near customers and suppliers, such as those concerns which also maintain a retail factory store outlet.

Many areas of the country have an abundance of manufacturing space available. Especially tempting for beginning businesses are low rentals offered on space found outmoded by a former tenant. Furthermore, an owner of such a factory building (particularly abundant in the northeast) may be willing to make improvements to suit your needs in order to gain an occupant. If a municipality owns the building, the offer may be even more generous.

Industrial parks may offer attractive plant sites. Designed to be near transportation lines, water access, and sewage facilities, they may have solved many of the problems you have in choosing a site. Again, as industrial parks are usually organized under a municipal development plan, there may be tax breaks and other incentives for locating there.

If your plant creates noise, odors, or other pollution problems, the community may be hostile to your presence. Even if zoning regulations allow a plant to make certain environmental incursions in an industrial area, near a residential area, or in a retail zone, you will never feel secure or comfortable when popular opinion opposes you. Sound out potential opposition before you move in. Local newspapers and town meetings provide forums for local approval. If your desire to see your company expand coincides with the community's growth plans, there should be few problems.

THE LOCATION OF
AN EXISTING BUSINESS

Location is just as important when you are buying a business as when you are starting one from scratch. Just because the business being bought is a going concern does not mean the location problem has been solved. Location may be the very reason the business is being sold, in which case even the best business expertise may be unable to turn an unprofitable situation around. Consider the following when buying an existing business.

Has the composition of the immediate neighborhood population changed so as to be adverse to the business? A farm nursery may be unable to function in an area where local farms are being converted to suburban developments. Northern cities may be losing population to the south, so that there are no longer enough people in the immediate area to buy your goods. A change in the average income of your neighborhood can spell doom for a yacht basin. As families move out and singles move in, a store that sells maternity clothes can fail. If the crime statistics for your area increase, the cost of insurance and security can make it hard for you to do business.

Have the suppliers of materials important to your business moved farther away? Many clothing factories were once located near New

England textile producers. Once the textile concerns moved nearer southern cotton fields, the clothing makers could no longer make a profit. A snack shop will fail if the factory that provided lunchtime customers goes out of business.

Have transportation arteries passed the business by? A new interstate highway means that a formerly viable roadside cafe is now on a secondary road. New mass transit facilities encourage customers to make an easy trip to the city instead of finding their bargains locally.

LOCATION AND DESIGN OF YOUR FACILITIES

Locations influence design. Whether an architect is planning your building from scratch or you are renovating an existing structure, the aesthetic or functional appeal of the design will be influenced by the location. For example, a location in a mall, redevelopment plan, or industrial park limits your design to something conforming to the tone set by the development.

Another example of design limited by location is a building conversion, for example, a barn converted into a restaurant or an abandoned factory turned into a roller-skating rink. If your intention upon securing a location is to radically alter the interior, consider the cost of these alterations in planning for what you must spend to start or purchase a business.

Ideally your design will project the personality of the business in such a way as to attract customers. For example, a drug manufacturer might wish to create a clean-cut, antiseptic look, whereas the owner of an exclusive women's dress shop might add glamour with some rococo flourishes on the store exterior. Your basic design can be traditional, contemporary, neoclassical, or very modern. Just be certain that your architectural style matches the nature of your product.

You will be able to choose from many building materials: stone, brick, wood, glass, cast concrete, ceramic tile, plastic, aluminum, and steel. Which is most practical and attractive for the terrain or street on which your property is located?

If you can afford it, hire a consultant to direct studies for your interior design. An industrial engineer can plan layout, a general contractor will direct the building operation, and an interior decorator can advise you on interior finishing. Some store architects specialize in doing an entire job from site selection to decor. Be sure to find one whose tastes and objectives are compatible with yours.

SOLAR ENERGY

Many business facilities are now designed to minimize energy costs—for good reason. If you have the opportunity to design your own building or make sweeping renovations, consider the installation of solar devices to heat the air or water or to provide electricity. Systems utilizing roof or window units are practical for many businesses, not just greenhouses. The best of the current solar energy systems, photovoltaic, may soon cost about $15,000 to provide about 60 percent of the electricity for a 3000-square-foot building. Other systems are less expensive, but do require unusual construction. However, your business may be eligible for tax credits, special loans, or other government subsidies if you construct a solar system. Consult your architect for further details before you choose a location. Such a system may require a southern exposure.

5
CHOOSING A FORM
FOR YOUR BUSINESS

You can operate your business as a sole proprietor, in partnerhip with others, or through a corporation. Your choice of business form will affect your personal liability, how you will draw profits, the amount of your taxes, the amount of capital you can raise, and the way you manage your business.

The nature of your business may dictate the legal form of your business. If you want to limit your personal liability because of investment or liability risks, you may incorporate. A corporation will generally protect you from being personally liable for debts and liabilities of a corporate business.

Where legal or financial considerations do not require you to incorporate, your decision may be motivated by the tax advantages of one business form over another.

Remember, you are not bound by your initial choice. You may make a new choice as circumstances change. You may start out in business as a sole proprietor. As business expands, you may choose to incorporate so as to take full advantage of fringe benefits, capital gains opportunities, and perhaps to raise additional capital by taking in associates.

SOLE PROPRIETORSHIP

A sole proprietorship is a business owned and operated by one person. To operate as a sole proprietor, you do not have to get special permission or pay an attorney to prepare a charter or special papers. However, you may have to get certain local licenses, and if you are doing business under a business name other than your personal name, you may be required to file a notice of your name at your local county office. You may also have to place a notice in a newspaper, noting your business name. Your county clerk will give you the requirements.

As a sole proprietor, you are personally liable for your business debts; your business creditors may force payment from your personal assets. To protect your personal assets from claims of business creditors, you may decide to incorporate, thus limiting your personal liability.

The business operations of a sole proprietorship are considered an integral part of your personal activities. Business income and expenses for the year are reported in Schedule C on your personal income tax return. The net result of entries on Schedule C, profit or loss, is combined with your other income. If you incur business losses, the losses will reduce the amount of your nonbusiness income subject to tax.

In addition to paying regular income tax on business income, you must also pay self-employment tax for Social Security coverage.

PARTNERSHIP

A partnership exists when two or more persons agree to operate a business as coowners. A partnership is a more complex form of doing business than a sole proprietorship. Partnerships are easily disrupted, and friction may lead to dissolution of the business. You must have an attorney prepare a written partnership agreement to define the rights and obligations of each partner. While you and your partners will be on amicable terms during the formation of the partnership and all may agree to have one attorney act as partnership attorney in preparing the partnership agreement, have your own personal attorney review the agreement to ensure that your interests have been protected, especially in the event of the death, bankruptcy, or retirement of any partner. The agreement should also anticipate how certain tax problems are to be treated when they arise.

Partner's Share of Special Income or Loss Items Generally, a partner's share of parnership income (or loss), deduction, or credit is fixed by the partnership agreement. Partners can agree to any division of income, deduction, or credit items unless the formula is motivated by a tax-avoidance or -evasion scheme.

Gain or Loss on the Sale of Contributed Property A partner may contribute property to the partnership instead of investing cash. If there is a difference between the partner's cost (basis) for the property and its present market value, fellow partners may be burdened with tax costs they never bargained for. A partnership agreement can overcome the inequity by providing for methods for adjusting the calculation of profit.

Interest and Salary Payments to Partners   Partners' salaries and interest payments on capital can be treated (1) as distributions of profits or (2) as guaranteed payments. The partnership agreement can determine which method is to be used.

Buy-Sell Agreements   To provide for the possibility of a partner's death, a partnership agreement should include a buy-sell provision. Under partnership law, the death of a partner causes automatic dissolution unless state law or the partnership agreement provides otherwise. A buy-sell agreement may name either the partnership or partners who agree to buy the deceased partner's interest in the business. The agreement should be funded; that is, it should provide funds for the buyer to carry out his or her part of the agreement. Generally, insurance is used to fund a buy-sell agreement. Insurance may be carried by individual partners on one another's lives under a *cross-purchase plan*. Sometimes, the partnership owns the policies, pays the premiums, and acts as a conduit through which insurance proceeds pass to the estate of a deceased partner in exchange for the partner's interest. In either case, the premiums are not deductible. When there are several partners, the cross-purchase plan may be too cumbersome. Instead, insurance is used to fund a redemption of the deceased partner's interest. A buy-sell agreement should also fix the price of a partner's interest or provide a formula for determining the price.

Dissolution of the Partnership   A partnership is automatically dissolved when any of the partners is expelled, sells his or her interest, withdraws, dies, or is declared bankrupt. When partners cannot agree on dissolution, a court will dissolve the partnership in certain situations. A court will act if a partner has been guilty of misconduct that makes it impractical to carry on the business with the partner, or if the business can be carried on only at a loss. Also, a court will dissolve the partnership if a partner is shown to be of unsound mind or otherwise incapable of carrying on his or her duties.

How Partnerships Are Taxed   For some purposes, the partnership activities are attributed to the individual owners as if they were proprietors. For other purposes, the partnership itself is treated as a unit divorced from the individual partners. A partnership files a return on which it computes partnership income and loss. However, it pays no tax. Each partner reports his or her share of partnerhip income or loss. Finally, each partner pays self-employment tax for Social Security coverage.

INCORPORATING A SOLE PROPRIETORSHIP OR PARTNERSHIP

In time, you may find disadvantages in operating as a sole proprietor or as a partnership. Your personal assets remain at risk for business losses and liabilities. You may find it difficult to get long-term financing. To limit liability and to attract other financial support, you may want to incorporate your sole proprietorship or partnership. Further, a corporation offers these benefits, which are not available in a sole proprietorship or partnership:

- Fringe benefits in the form of accident and health and life insurance protection can be made available.
- Corporate retirement plans are generally less restrictive than plans available to the self-employed or partners.
- Beneficiaries of a stockholder-employee may receive tax-free death benefits up to $5000.
- Corporate form may facilitate saving income and estate taxes by gifts of stock to children.
- Members of a family may be stockholders without many of the burdens and restrictions of family partnership.

You can transfer your proprietorship or partnership assets tax-free. If you meet both of the following requirements, you may incorporate without tax:

- Assets are transferred to the corporation solely in exchange for stock and securities of that company.
- Immediately thereafter you (and your partners, if any) own 80 percent of the voting stock and 80 percent of all other classes of stock of the corporation.

In a tax-free exchange, the corporation takes as its basis for depreciation and resale the basis the assets had in the unincorporated business. This is so even if they are worth considerably more.

Securities received need not be proportional to one's interest in the unincorporated business before the exchange. However, although a disproportion between the value of the property transferred and securities received will not make the exchange itself taxable, part of the deal may be taxed as a gift or compensation.

Transfers of liabilities may result in tax. Often assets transferred to a corporation in exchange for stock are subject to liabilities, as, for example, a building subject to a mortgage. Whether the corporation takes assets subject to liabilities or assumes the liabilities, the tax-free nature of the transaction is not usually upset. However, you may realize taxable income on transferring property subject to liabilities when the transfer is part of a tax-avoidance plan, or when the liability exceeds your basis (tax cost) for assets transferred to the corporation.

ORGANIZING A CORPORATION

You create a corporation by filing certain legal papers. Once you have made out these papers, filed them, and paid fees to the state which has chartered the company, you have a corporation which is recognized by law as a legal entity separate from you, the owner.

As a general rule, you will set up a corporation in the state in which you will do all or most of your business. It is usually not advisable for a small business to incorporate outside of the state in which it does business. If you do, your corporation will be considered a foreign corporation and will have to pay additional taxes and fees. Sometimes there are advantages in incorporating in another state because of favorable state taxes and less restrictions on corporate powers and capital requirements. However, foreign corporations must pay a fee for a certificate to do business in states other than where they were incorporated. Failure to do so may prevent the company from taking certain legal steps in the state and subject the company to penalties.

It is advisable to hire an attorney to set up your corporation. Your attorney will file the necessary papers and organize the procedure of following corporate rules of doing business such as electing officers and directors and issuing stock. If you are interested in the details of a certificate of incorporation, you may buy a form from the state office that handles incorporations or from a stationer who sells legal forms.

Do not pick a name for the corporation which may be confused with the name of any other corporation doing business in the state. The state may reject your choice and delay incorporation. You can determine the acceptability of the name through the state office which receives certificates of incorporation or employ a service company to make the check.

After the company receives its certificate, the stockholders must meet to adopt the corporate bylaws and elect a board of directors who elect the officers who will run the corporation. Directors may elect themselves as officers.

Bylaws will cover such items as location of the principal office; time, place, and required notice of annual and special meetings of stockholders; quorum and voting privileges of the stockholders; number of directors, their pay, their term, elections and meetings; the election of officers and their duties and salaries; the issuance of stock certificates and transfers and the declaration of dividends.

In your choice of directors, remember that they have the power to run the business without interference from the stockholders. The powers of a director usually cannot be taken away by an agreement to act merely as a "dummy."

Directors and officers should know that minority stockholders have a legal right to injunction or damages in cases of the following:

- Fraudulent, illegal, or negligent acts of directors or officers
- Violation of their rights in reorganization, liquidation, merger, etc.
- Losses sustained through acts not authorized by the charter
- Wrongful withholdings of dividends

Restrictive Agreements Stockholders frequently enter into agreements restricting the sale or other disposition of their stock. There are many business reasons for doing this—to ensure continuity of control of the corporation, to prevent outside interests from becoming stockholders, to fix the price on disposition of stock after death of a stockholder, and to define the mechanics for disposing of a stockholder's interest.

There are difficulties in making these agreements. For example, the disposal price should not be set at a figure out of the reach of the survivor. Neither should it be set so low that it injures the family of the deceased. Unless the agreement is completely effective, a dissatisfied executor may contest it. Ask your attorney how restrictive agreements should be drafted so as to limit estate and gift tax valuations to the agreed price.

Multiple Corporations Business reasons may require you to form more than one corporation. For example, the owner of several restaurants may want to limit the liability of each one. The use of multiple corporations can also have these tax advantages:

- Corporations can use different tax years and accounting methods.
- The use of two or more corporations may facilitate the future sale of part of a business.

• The losses of one corporation can be offset with profits of another corporation, provided that the corporations are members of an "affiliated group" and file a consolidated return.

CAPITALIZING YOUR CORPORATION

An important step in setting up a corporation is proper capitalization. You can base your corporation's capital structure on common stock, preferred stock, and debt, such as bonds and notes. Not only legal and financial considerations but also tax consequences will influence your choice. For example, the Subchapter S corporation rules (discussed later in this chapter) limit an electing corporation to only one class of stock. This might be sufficient reason for a decision not to issue preferred stock despite other reasons in favor of such issue. If a Subchapter S election is not desired, the issuance of preferred stock is useful as an income-splitting or estate-planning device.

You may want to capitalize partially with long- or short-term debt. The corporation deducts interest paid on loans, avoiding the double tax on income paid to the stockholders on the debt. When the debt is finally repaid, no income is realized as usually occurs when stock is redeemed. However, there are tax restrictions to debt financing, as discussed later.

You may also want to use *Section 1244* stock which allows you to convert a long-term capital loss into an ordinary loss if the corporation fails.

ISSUING PREFERRED STOCK

Preferred stock stands midway between common stock and bonds. Although the preferred stockholder shares with common stockholders the risk that there may be no profits with which to pay dividends, the preferred stockholder is assured that any dividends must be paid to preferred stockholders before common stockholders receive theirs. Thus, in a sense, the preferred stockholder assumes the risks of an owner but enjoys to a limited degree the preferred status of a creditor. The preferred stock may be voting or nonvoting. It may be redeemable or callable at the will of the corporation, and it may contain a conversion feature, allowing the stockholder an option to convert the preferred stock into another class of stock, such as common.

Preferred stock can be used to implement corporate financial policy and tax-savings plans. By issuing nonvoting preferred stock the corporation can attract additional equity capital into the corporation without diluting the voting control. Preferred stock can also provide you with the flexibility needed for income splitting, bailing out corporate earnings, providing incentive for key employees, retaining an investment interest in your business if you someday decide to sell your controlling interest, planning for retirement, and keeping down your estate taxes.

Before organizing a corporation with preferred stock, you should consider its consequences on a Subchapter S election. One of the requirements for a valid Subchapter S election is that the corporation have only one class of stock. Since the most frequent use of the election is in the beginning years of a corporation's life (to allow the pass-through to stockholders of operating losses), you may decide to forgo the tax-planning benefits of preferred stock until the election is no longer required. At that point, you can terminate the Subchapter S election by recapitalizing the corporation with common and preferred. If, however, the new preferred is received in a tax-free distribution, such as a stock dividend or recapitalization, by persons also holding common stock, the operating rules of Section 306 stock must be considered. Gain on the sale of preferred Section 306 stock is taxable as ordinary income, not capital gain. Section 306 stock retains this undesirable tax "taint" until sale, redemption, or death of the stockholder who originally received the stock.

Income Splitting By issuing preferred stock in your children's names, you ensure that the dividends they receive are taxed at lower rates, resulting in an overall tax saving for the family. You can do this without relinquishing voting control by making the preferred stock nonvoting. If the stock is given at the organization of the corporation, there is little or no gift tax involved. Also, preferred stock issued at the inception of the corporation is not Section 306 stock.

If you do not wish to give preferred stock to the children upon incorporation, you can give it to them by way of gifts at some later time. However, at that time, the increase in the value of the corporate stock may give rise to a gift tax.

Bailing Out Corporate Earnings You can issue the preferred stock to your spouse. Later, when the business has grown and has accumulated earnings, your spouse terminates the interest in the corporation in a redemption of all of his or her stock, paying capital gains on the redemption profit. The redemption of stock initially issued to your spouse can be, for tax purposes, more readily redeemed than stock given to your spouse by you after the corporation is in existence.

Providing Stock for Key Employees   Key employees may want an interest in your corporation, but they may not be able to finance the purchase of common stock. If the value of the common stock is too high, a recapitalization issue of preferred stock would decrease the value of the common stock. In this way, the common stock can be placed within the reach of the key employees. At the same time, your substantial interest in the business is reflected by the preferred stock held by you.

Saving Estate Taxes   You can reduce the size of your estate by shifting from common stock to preferred. For example, if you foresee increased earnings and appreciation in value of the business, you can recapitalize the business, issuing the new common stock to your children and holding on to the new preferred stock. In this way, all the future appreciation in the business is reflected in the common stock. By residing voting power in the preferred stock, you retain managerial control of the business.

Retaining an Investment Interest in Your Business   If you anticipate selling your business to outsiders, but want to retain an investment interest to guarantee an income in your retirement years, you can accomplish this by selling the voting stock and retaining nonvoting cumulative preferred (or common) stock. Whether the buyers of your business will concede to this arrangement depends, of course, on the strength of your bargaining position.

ISSUING DEBT

There may be these advantages to setting up stockholder debt in structuring the capital of a corporation:

- *Deductions for interest.* This is preferable to payment of dividends which are not deductible by the corporation.
- *Tax-free repayment of debt.* If you are anticipating a future repayment of part of your capital, you may plan a tax-free distribution through a repayment of the debt. A repayment of debt is tax-free, whereas a redemption of part of the stock is generally taxable.

To achieve these advantages, companies have been set up with more stockholder debt than equity capital. However, the Internal Revenue Service resists attempts of businesses to set up substantial debt structures for the foregoing tax advantages and is aided by the tax law which sets down restrictions to the creation of debt obligations.

Stockholders may lend money to the corporation in proportion to their equity interests. However, the debt must be closely monitored. The debt must carry a reasonable interest rate, and interest must be paid currently. If there is a failure to pay interest in 1 year, the debt may be treated by the IRS as stock and a later payment of the back interest is taxable as dividend income. Where high interest must be paid, the IRS requirement to pay currently high interest may discourage you from issuing too much debt obligation unless the tax cost of receiving the interest is minimal.

Also under the regulations, stockholder debt, held substantially proportionate to stock, may also be treated as stock when (1) the debt is excessive, (2) the debt is not issued for money, or (3) the debt is payable on demand. However, even if loans initially qualify as debt, they may be reclassified as equity if the company fails to pay interest or principal when due.

Complex regulations set down certain permissible ranges of debt obligations to stock. These ratios should be discussed with an experienced tax practitioner who may decide whether and how much debt obligations should be issued.

ISSUING SECTION 1244 STOCK

If your corporation fails, your loss on your stock investment is treated as a capital loss. A capital loss deduction is not as favorable as an ordinary loss deduction. Ordinary losses are fully deductible from ordinary income. A capital loss is fully deductible from capital gains but is not fully deductible from ordinary income. If you do not have capital gains to offset your loss, you can deduct only up to $3000 of a capital loss from ordinary income. Further long-term losses are subject to a serious reduction. Each dollar of a long-term capital loss must be reduced by 50 percent before it may be deducted from ordinary income. Thus to claim a loss deduction of $3000 from ordinary income, you would have to have a long-term loss of $6000. In other words, a long-term loss of $1 is worth only 50 cents in terms of an ordinary loss deduction.

To avoid to some extent this capital loss limitation, you can designate stock as Section 1244 stock. If the stock meets certain legal tests and you do suffer a loss on the stock, you may claim an ordinary loss of up to $50,000 ($100,000 on a joint return). Losses in excess of these limits are deductible as capital losses.

To ensure that the designation of Section 1244 stock will be respected, make sure that the stock is common stock and that it is issued only for cash or property other than stock and securities. Finally, see that your attorney describes the issue as Section 1244 stock.

DIVIDEND DISTRIBUTIONS

The power to declare dividends rests with the board of directors, who can declare them only out of the firm's surplus funds. Know the law of your particular state on this point. Generally, past deficits from operations must be made up before a dividend can be declared. In most states, directors are personally liable to creditors if capital is impaired by declaration of a dividend not out of surplus.

These are some of the dividends that can be paid:

- *Cash dividend.* Paid in cash.
- *Stock dividend.* Additional stock that is issued to stockholders on a pro rata basis.
- *Dividends in property (dividends in kind).* For example, capital stock or bonds of the distributing company; other shares of stock or bonds owned by the company.
- *Liquidation dividend.* Paid out of the assets of the corporation upon dissolution.
- *Scrip dividend.* Paid in notes that are to be redeemed at a later date, usually in cash.
- *Consent dividend.* The stockholders consent to be taxed as if they had received a stated sum of money, but get no actual payments of any kind.
- *Elective dividend.* The stockholders may take cash or a stock dividend at their option.

CORPORATE TAX REPORTING

You have a choice of paying tax on corporate income in one of two ways:

1. The corporation which is treated as a separate taxpayer pays a corporate income tax on its taxable income. You pay tax on your receipts of salary, dividends, and interest from the corporation.

2. Under a Subchapter S election, the corporation reports its taxable income (or loss). On your tax return, you report and pay tax on this income whether or not you withdraw money or property from the corporation. If the corporation incurs losses, you deduct the losses in your tax return.

Corporation Pays Tax   Income which you do not withdraw in the form of deductible items, such as salary, interest, or similar expense, is subject to corporate tax, and when you withdraw the amount as a dividend, it is again subject to tax on your return. The Subchapter S election avoids this possible double tax by allowing you, as the stockholder, to pay a tax on corporate income directly.

Despite the possible double tax, you may decide not to make the Subchapter S election. You may make this decision where it is estimated that the corporate tax on current income, plus the potential tax due on the withdrawal of accumulated income, is less than the current tax you would pay on the income.

You may decide to accumulate earnings until you liquidate the corporation or sell out. At that time, you may pay only a capital gains tax on your gain. There is a limit, however, on the amount of earnings that may be accumulated. If this limit is exceeded, a penalty tax may be imposed. At least $250,000 ($150,000 for personal service corporations) of surplus earnings may be accumulated without subjecting the corporation to the penalty tax—perhaps more if you can show that you need the accumulation for a specific business purpose.

In a corporation subject to tax, drawing salary as a shareholder-employee is the usual and preferred method of reducing or avoiding the double tax. The corporation deducts the salary payments, which offset an equal amount when you report the salary on your return.

When you fix salaries, including your own, be aware that the corporation may deduct salary payments only to the extent that they are "reasonable" in amount. In determining reasonableness, consider duties, complexity of the business, pay in comparison with gross and net income salaries paid in similar businesses, and special abilities that make your services, and those of your executives, valuable.

Peg salaries at an adequate level from the beginning of the operation. Fluctuating salaries, high salaries in high earning years, and low salaries in lean years will attract a review of salary payments by the Internal Revenue Service. A charge might be made, for example, that the high salary payments were in fact payments of dividends.

If you anticipate losses in the beginning of your operations, you may first decide to start with a Subchapter S election. Under the election, you will be able to deduct the losses on your personal tax return.

Stockholder's Subchapter S Election to Report Corporate Income The election allows a business to operate in corporate form and yet not pay tax as a separate entity, thus generally eliminating the double tax on corporate operations. You may take advantage of the election as long as it benefits you, for as little as 1 year or indefinitely.

On your personal return, you report your share of corporate earnings and losses. Your share of corporate operating losses reduces your other income. You report your share of the corporation's long-term capital gain. However, you may not deduct capital losses incurred by the company; they are used by the corporation as carry-over losses to offset future capital gains. The corporation files only an information return, Form 1120S, instead of the regular corporate return.

To qualify for the election, your corporation must meet certain stock and income tests. Failure to meet all the requirements imposed by the tax law will invalidate your election and upset your tax planning. Consider the following points with your attorney.

Who can be a stockholder? You cannot make the election if a partnership, or other corporation, owns stock in your company. Only certain trusts are permitted to be stockholders. The beneficiary rather than the trust itself is treated as the stockholder. Stockholders may not be nonresident aliens.

What kind of stock can be issued? An electing company can have only one class of stock. It cannot have preferred stock.

Sources of company income? There are limits on the percentage of company income that can come from rents, royalties, dividends, interest, annuities, securities sales, and foreign sources.

How much of the corporation's losses can you deduct? You are limited to a deduction measured by the basis of your stock and your loans to the corporation. The stock basis of your stock is reduced by operating losses of the company which are passed through to you and reported on your individual return. If these reduce your basis to zero, further losses decrease any debts the corporation owes you. If your share of the loss exceeds both the basis for your stock plus the basis for outstanding debts owed you by the corporation, the excess is not deductible. Furthermore, you may not recover the loss deduction by making a new investment in your corporation in a later year. A shareholder who merely guarantees the corporation's debt is not considered a creditor of the corporation and does not increase his or her basis for deducting losses.

Electing Subchapter S Status An election may not be filed before a corporation is formally incorporated. A tax year of a new corporation does not begin until it has shareholders, acquires assets, or begins to do business. However, if under state law corporate existence begins with filing articles of incorporation, the first day of the tax year begins on the date of such filing, even though the corporation has no assets and does not begin doing business until a later date.

The election does not have to be renewed each year. It continues in effect unless it is revoked or automatically terminated. It may be revoked or automatically terminated under any one of these conditions:

1. All stockholders agree to revoke the election by filing a statement of revocation. If made before the close of the first month of the corporation's taxable year, the revocation is effective for that year. If made after that date, the revocation is not effective until the year following the year in which the revocation is filed.
2. A new stockholder enters the corporation and disaffirms the election. (To prevent a new stockholder from taking such action, you may consider putting a restrictive clause in the corporate charter preventing a new stockholder from disaffirming the election.)
3. The company no longer meets the stock or income test. Careful professional planning is required if you decide to form a corporation and elect Subchapter S status. You must be assured that you qualify for the election and that it is timely. Also, you must avoid investment transactions that will work on automatic termination.

6

CONTROL THROUGH ACCOUNTING AND RECORD SYSTEMS

Not only does good business practice dictate that you keep good records; current tax laws require you to do so as well. Further, the most direct and advisable way to initiate an accounting system for your business is to employ an experienced accountant. True, there are many small business owners who keep their own records. At the start, a do-it-yourself system may be adequate, but as the volume of business increases, you will find that there is no substitute for hiring experienced and professional aid.

There are two basic stages to a record and accounting system. One is *bookkeeping*, which involves the recording of income and expense transactions in journals and books of accounts. The other is *an analysis or an accounting of your books*. Keeping records is meaningless unless the data are organized and analyzed to inform you of the financial status of your business. At periodic times, a review or summary of accounts should tell you your profit or loss for the period, the amount of your cash, and your liabilities, costs, and other data relevant to your business. In addition, an accounting is also necessary to provide data for financial statements used to obtain credit ratings and for the preparation of tax returns.

BOOKKEEPING AND THE DOUBLE-ENTRY SYSTEM

You can keep a record of business transactions in a notebook or in commercially available record books designed for small enterprises,

but this manner of keeping records is often inadequate. Noting transactions in a book is insufficient. You must have a system that organizes
the entries of transactions to provide important data about the financial
condition of your business. Fortunately, centuries ago merchants developed a system of record keeping that has its own internal check
and provides a logical organization of data for accounting analysis. It
is called the double-entry system of bookkeeping. Under the double-
entry system, a business transaction is recorded twice, as a debit and
credit item. As a result, when you properly record both parts of any
transaction, your books are in balance. If both sides do not balance to
the penny, an error has been made, and you, your bookkeeper, or your
accountant is alerted to track down the discrepancy. Further, accounts
and adjustments are so arranged that various accounting statements
can be made periodically and systematically.

The following example illustrates the balancing feature of the double-entry system and a resulting simple balance sheet.

Example

You start your business with $50,000 of your own money and $20,000
of borrowed funds. Under the double-entry system this would be reflected as follows:

Debit side		Credit side	
Cash	$70,000	Capital	$50,000
		Liability	20,000

You buy merchandise for $25,000 and equipment and fixtures for
$25,000. You had to pay cash for these items.

Debit side		Credit side	
Merchandise	$25,000	Cash	$50,000
Equipment	25,000		

Entering cash as a credit item acts to reduce the cash account by
$50,000, and if you were to analyze your business, a balance sheet
statement would read as follows:

Debit side		Credit side	
Cash	$20,000	Liabilities	$20,000
Merchandise	25,000	Capital	50,000
Fixtures	25,000	Total credits	$70,000
Total debits	$70,000		

Although this example is a simplification, it reflects the principles and advantages of the double-entry system.

In actual practice, bookkeeping starts with sales and purchase invoices, register tapes, check stubs, and deposit slips. From these items, entries are made in journals, such as cash and disbursement journals or sales and purchase journals. Then the data from these journals are posted to ledger accounts, which in turn are adjusted and summarized periodically to give you various operating statements.

As you can see from this brief review, bookkeeping and accounting require technical training and experience. If you cannot at first afford a full-time bookkeeper, consider hiring a part-time bookkeeper. The cost of a bookkeeper may be repaid many times by the service and efficiency of an experienced hand.

HANDLING CASH

Observe these rules for cash transactions:

- Keep your personal cash separate from cash generated by the business.
- Use a bank account for your business funds and deposit all cash receipts in the account day by day.
- Record all incoming cash: the amounts, along with their sources and dates.
- Pay all business bills by check. Never make a disbursement out of daily cash receipts. Try to take advantage of bill payments that give a cash discount for prompt payment.
- Make a disbursement only when you have received a supplier's invoice or a receipted, paid-out voucher, dated and signed by the person who gets the check.
- Keep a check on all daily cash receipts and disbursements.

Petty-Cash Funds There are some expenditures for which you do not make checks. Some of these are postage, carfare, small entertainment expenses, delivery charges, etc. Thus, you open a petty-cash fund, which you keep in a special cashbox. You start the fund by making out a check from your general cash account to "petty cash." The petty cashier, or other person responsible for this fund, cashes this check and puts the cash in a cashbox. The size of the fund is determined by the amount of petty cash needed in a reasonable length of time. The petty-cash fund requires a neat and precise operation. Here is how it works:

1. You set up a fund, say, $50, by cashing the initial check.
2. You put this $50 in a cashbox.
3. When an employee requires a bona fide reimbursement or prepayment of an expense, say, carfare of $1.50, the employee will fill out a petty-cash slip or a voucher asking for this amount and sign it.
4. The petty cashier takes the slip from the employee and examines it for reasonableness. Then the cashier gives the employee the $1.50 and puts the slip in the box.
5. Thus, at all times the amount of cash in the box plus the amount of petty cash slips will equal the original amount of the fund, that is, $50.
6. When the amount of cash slips reaches a certain amount, say, $35, you reimburse the fund with a check equal to the amount of the petty-cash vouchers in the box. Thus you bring the amount of cash once more up to the $50 amount.

Bank Reconciliations The fact that a bank keeps an account of your cash transactions provides you with an important check of your cash records. A bank gives you monthly statements along with canceled checks, and reconciling your bank record and your own cash account should be done to check not only the accuracy of your account but also that of the bank. The actual procedure of reconciliation is straightforward, and this simplified example illustrates the general method of making a reconciliation. Let us say you have just received your bank statement. You see that it is larger than your ledger cash account. You proceed in the following manner:

1. Your bank has returned your canceled checks along with your statement. You arrange the canceled checks in numerical order.
2. You turn to the bank reconciliation as of the close of the preceding month and see if there were any outstanding checks noted in that bank reconciliation. If there were, these checks should have come through the bank during the current month and must be near the beginning of your canceled checks arranged in numerical order. Thus, you start "ticking off" (putting a checkmark next to) the outstanding checks listed in the previous bank reconciliation that have now come through the bank.

As you turn over each check and tick it off, examine it to see that it was properly endorsed on the back and that the amount on the front is the same as the amount you have listed on your books. When you finish ticking off the outstanding checks of last month, you may find that a few of them are still outstanding. Those that are still outstanding remain unchecked.

You then turn to the cash credit column of your cash disbursement book and next to each check that has been canceled put a tick mark. You proceed through them to the end of your canceled checks. Those checks which have not as yet gone through the bank, and are outstanding, will have no tick mark next to them.

3. You make a list of your outstanding checks, keeping them in numerical order.

4. In your cash receipts book you tick off your deposits listed on the bank statement. Also, you turn to the bank reconciliation made for the previous month to see if there were any outstanding deposits. If there were, the first deposit listed on the bank statement should be the record of that outstanding deposit. Perhaps you will find, near the end of the month, that there is an outstanding deposit not yet recorded by the bank for the current month. You know this because it is not ticked off in your cash receipts book. If, however, you find that you have a deposit listed on the bank statement and not in the cash receipts book or the previous bank reconciliation, you know that it has been deposited in the bank but has not been recorded on your books.

5. After you have done the above and have a list of all your outstanding checks and outstanding deposits, you proceed to make your bank reconciliation as in the following example.

Example

Your ledger cash balance is $72,000, and your bank statement shows a balance of $71,498. Your books indicate that there are two outstanding checks: no. 4856, issued for $780, and no. 4927, $460. In addition, the bank statement does not show a deposit of $1725 made after the date of the statement, and there is a bank service charge of $17 that has not yet been entered in your books.

BANK RECONCILIATION
March 31, 1982

Cash balance per general ledger		$72,000
Add: Outstanding checks		
No. 4856	$ 780	
No. 4927	460	1,240
		$73,240
Deduct:		
Deposit not received by bank	$1,725	
Bank charge not entered on books	17	1,742
Balance per bank statement		$71,498

REVIEW ACCOUNTS DUE YOU

When you provide goods or services on credit, bills should be sent out immediately. See that the bills list the date of purchase, items purchased, cost, down payments, if any, and balance owed. A bill should also list any overdue amount and the length of time the balance has been outstanding, along with a special request for payment of the delinquent amount.

Organize a procedure to age accounts due. At least monthly, list accounts that are current, those unpaid for 30 days, and those unpaid for 60 days and longer. Next review the list to determine why accounts outstanding for 60 days and longer remain unpaid, and then call the delinquent customers. Ask why there is a delay and get a new promise to pay.

OPERATING STATEMENTS
FOR DETERMINING
THE FINANCIAL POSITION
OF YOUR BUSINESS

Most businesses keep tabs of profit and loss by getting a monthly statement of income. This should be done about 10 days after the close of the month. At the same time a balance sheet should accompany the income statement. In addition to the balance sheet and income statement, some businesses also prepare a statement which shows changes in financial position and the sources and uses of cash and working capital.

Statement of Income   Profit is a major aim of business. To guide a business to profits, management must be able to make the correct decisions, based upon reliable information. No information is more important than the statement of income. Almost without exception statements of income follow the report form shown on page 59.

In following the report form, it is advisable to present information not only from the current period but also from a similar past period for comparison purposes (see table on page 60). Percentage figures for growth or decline indications give valuable clues on sales trends, cost of goods, and expenses. A percentage column based on net sales as 100 percent gives you the proportion of each dollar of sales that goes for goods purchased and for various expenses, and the amount remaining as operating income. Such percentage figures help you check efficiency trends.

THE CORPORATION
Statement of Income
For the year ended December 31, 19—

Gross sales			$ . . . . .
Less			
Sales Returns and Allowances		$	
Sales Discounts		. . . . .	
Net Sales		_____	. . . . .
Cost of Goods Sold:			. . . . .
Inventory, January 1		. . . . .	
Purchases	$		
Less: Purchase Returns and Allowances	. . . . .		
Freight In		. . . . .	
Goods available for sale		_____	
Less: Inventory, December 31		. . . . .	
Cost of Goods Sold		. . . . .	
Gross Profit on Sales			. . . . .
Selling Expenses:			. . . . .
Sales Salaries	. . . . .		
Store Rent	. . . . .		
Advertising	. . . . .		
Delivery Salaries	. . . . .		
Depreciation—Delivery Equipment	. . . . .		
Delivery Supplies Used	. . . . .		
Sales Supplies Used	. . . . .		
Freight Out	. . . . .		
Depreciation—Sales Equipment	. . . . .		
Total Selling Expenses	_____	. . . . .	
General and Administrative Expenses:			
Officers' Salaries			
Office Payroll	. . . .		
Bad Debts	. . . .		
Insurance	. . . . .		
Telephone and Telegraph	. . . . .		
Legal and Auditing	. . . . .		
Printing and Stationery	. . . . .		
Depreciation—Office Equipment	. . . . .		
Miscellaneous Taxes	. . . . .		
Total General and Administrative Expenses	_____	. . . . .	
Total Expenses			. . . . .
Profit from Operations			. . . . .
Other Income:			
Interest Income	. . . . .		
Cash Discounts on Purchases	. . . . .		
Dividends Earned	_____		
Total other income		. . . . .	
Other Expense:			
Interest Expense		. . . . .	
Other Income less Other Expense			. . . . .
Income before Income Taxes			. . . . .
Income Taxes			. . . . .
Net Income for Year			$ . . . . .

	January 1981	January 1980	Increase or decrease, percent	Percent of total	
				1981	1980
Gross sales	$50,000	$40,000	25.0	102.0	102.0
Less: Returns					
and allowances	800	700	14.1	2.0	2.0
Net sales	49,200	39,300	25.0	100.0	100.0
Cost of goods sold	34,100	28,300	21.0	69.3	72.0
Gross profit	$15,100	$11,000	37.0	30.7	28.0
Operating expenses:					
Selling	$ 4,500	$ 3,200	41.0	9.2	8.1
Administrative					
and general	5,475	3,400	61.0	11.1	8.7
Financial	140	100	40.0	0.3	0.3
Total expenses	$10,115	$ 6,700	51.0	20.6	17.1
Net operating profit	$ 4,985	$ 4,300	16.0	10.1	10.9

The technique of determining various ratios from an income statement is discussed later in this chapter.

THE BALANCE SHEET

Here is a listing, using the traditional account form, that is representative of most balance sheet statements.

Assets:
   Current assets
   Investments
   Fixed assets
   Intangible assets
   Other assets (cash in closed banks,
     subscriptions to capital stock)

Liabilities:
   Current liabilities
   Long-term liabilities
   Reserves (for contingencies, taxes,
     obsolescence, etc.)
Capital stock and surplus:
   Capital stock
   Paid-in capital surplus
   Retained earnings

The asset section of a balance sheet roughly follows in order the relative ease with which the assets will or can be turned into cash:

● *Current assets.* These assets can be or will be turned into cash within 1 year. They are liquid or quick assets, though the word "quick" is sometimes reserved for a special group within your current assets that includes cash, notes receivable, easily salable temporary investments, and possible, soon-to-be-collected, accrued income. Accounts receivable and inventory are also current assets, as are prepaid expenses and deferred charges such as prepaid insurance and supplies on hand. You set up these asset accounts to allocate expenses to the period in which they are used.

- *Investments.*
- *Fixed assets.* These assets include equipment, buildings, vehicles, and other assets used in the operation of the business. With the exception of land, they are your depreciating assets. If your fixed assets are in the nature of mines or timber forests, they are said to be "wasting" assets and are depleted as you remove the natural resources. Such depreciating and wasting assets are evaluated by allowance for depreciation and for depletion. You deduct these reserves from the assets they evaluate.
- *Intangible assets.* These are trademarks, goodwill, copyrights, patents, and leaseholds. The practice varies in evaluating these assets on the balance sheet. Generally, their values are difficult to measure and should be evaluated as conservatively as possible.
- *Other assets.* These assets you do not expect to be converted into cash or to be used as a working asset in the near future.

CONDENSED COMPARATIVE BALANCE SHEET
January 31, 1982 and January 31, 1981

	January 1982	January 1981	Increase or decrease, percent	Percent of total 1982	1981
Assets:					
Current assets	$15,380	$12,200	26.0	43.8	43.0
Fixed assets	18,000	14,100	27.6	51.2	49.6
Other assets	1,750	2,100	16.6	5.0	7.4
Total assets	$35,130	$28,400	23.7	100.0	100.0
Liabilities and net worth:					
Current liabilities	$ 6,000	$ 4,000	50.0	17.1	14.0
Fixed liabilities	10,000	8,000	25.0	28.5	28.1
Capital stock	10,000	10,000	00.0	28.5	35.2
Surplus	5,000	4,000	25.0	14.2	14.0
Reserves for contingencies	4,130	2,400	72.1	11.7	8.7
Total	$35,130	$28,400	23.7	100.0	100.0
Working capital	$ 9,380	$ 8,200	11.4		

You list your liabilities in classes. You distinguish between long-term and short-term liabilities and then list them in the order in which they will come due.

A comparative balance sheet should show the asset, liability, and capital figures at the end of two or more successive fiscal periods. It should, in addition, show the percentage change in each of the items. To guide your company, your main interest is the amount of the item on the latest report and the percentage change from the last statement, but 3 years or more may also be compared. The percentage figures for two or more dates enable you to analyze a statement more readily for purposes of determining the nature of changes in financial status. They will reveal whether current assets have grown or decreased in proportion to total assets over several years in comparison with similar proportionate changes in current liabilities.

FINANCIAL AND OPERATING RATIOS

A ratio is a comparison of one item with another on the balance sheet or operating statement. Compare two items from the balance sheet and you have a financial ratio.

For example, the current ratio $\left(\dfrac{\text{current assets}}{\text{current liabilities}}\right)$ is a financial ratio.

When a ratio uses one item drawn from the operating statement, it is called an operating ratio, as it relates to some phase of operations. An example is the inventory-turnover ratio:

$$\text{Inventory-turnover ratio} = \frac{\text{cost of goods sold}}{\text{merchandise inventory}}$$

Current ratio is a commonly used and important ratio for indicating financial condition. It shows the ratio or proportion of the current assets to current liabilities; for example,

$$\text{Current ratio} = \frac{\text{current assets}}{\text{current liabilities}} = \frac{\$15,380}{\$6000} = 2.56$$

In computing this ratio, prepaid expenses should be omitted from the current assets even though they are shown under that heading. Prepaid expenses usually cannot be turned into cash as can other current assets.

The figures you use to get the current ratio also give you the amount of working capital—the excess of current assets over current liabilities.

The working capital in the foregoing example is the excess of $15,380 over $6000, or $9380. Working capital reflects the ability of a business to finance its current operations after allowing for payment of its current liabilities.

The current or working-capital ratio for a store or a factory is ordinarily at least 2. This means that current assets should be at least twice current liabilities. This 2:1 ratio gives the business a margin of safety, as part of current assets may consist of slow merchandise not yet sold and of receivables which may be subject to discount for possible poor accounts.

A business which maintains current assets barely equal to its current liabilities will be in a weak financial condition if half or more of the current assets consist of merchandise and receivables. In an emergency requiring payment of all current debt, the merchandise and receivables would have to be sacrificed, and the assets turned into cash would not meet the payables. Therefore, the business might find itself in the hands of its creditors.

A current ratio of less than 2 may be satisfactory in some situations. A ratio higher than 2 should be maintained where the current debt is of an extremely short-term or demand character. Try to maintain a ratio similar to that kept by your particular industry.

Acid-test ratio is similar to the current ratio but shows cash capacity more sensitively. It expresses the relation between the quick assets (cash, collectible receivables, and readily salable securities) and the current liabilities; for example,

$$\text{Acid-test ratio} = \frac{\text{quick assets}}{\text{current liabilities}} = \frac{\$7350}{\$6000} = 1.2$$

Inventories, prepaid expenses, and longer-term investments are excluded from current assets in computing the acid-test ratio. When this ratio is 1, a business is considered in a satisfactory liquid condition.

Unless there is a special reason for accumulating liquid funds, such as paying off maturing debts, management should examine cash requirements periodically. Perhaps investment of some surplus cash in income securities or expanding operations is called for in order to put liquid funds to work.

Ratio of inventory to current assets serves as a check upon overinvestment of current funds in inventory and is obtained by dividing the inventory figure by the total current assets; for example,

$$\frac{\text{Inventory}}{\text{Current assets}} = \frac{\$8000}{\$15,300} = 52 \text{ percent}$$

Use this percentage along with the inventory-turnover ratio to determine a rational inventory policy in your business.

Ratio of liabilities to net worth reveals the relative proportions of business ownership belonging to all types of creditors, on the one hand, and to the proprietor, on the other; for example,

$$\frac{\text{Liabilities}}{\text{Net worth}} = \frac{\$16,000}{\$19,130} = 83 \text{ percent}$$

When computed for several successive periods, this ratio reveals the trend in proportion of debt to ownership. It shows whether a larger share of business assets is being held by the owner, or whether business assets are being acquired through borrowing from creditors.

In general, it is always preferable that business operations from year to year result in an increased proportion of ownership in the hands of the proprietor. This rule is subject to qualification. It may be changed as a result of temporary or periodic borrowing on favorable terms to meet specific situations.

Whenever a business retires some or all of its debt, this debt–to–net worth ratio is reduced. When, however, a concern finds itself sufficiently established in its field, it may prefer to increase its debt financing for expansion purposes. Then the liabilities will again bulk larger in relation to net worth. This situation may be particularly desirable if equity capital is unavailable, if surplus earnings are insufficient, and if borrowing can be done at favorable interest rates, leaving a considerable portion of net earnings for stockholders.

COMPUTING INVENTORY-TURNOVER RATIOS

The rate of merchandise turnover varies greatly with different types of businesses and with different degrees of management efficiency in terms of purchasing, inventory, and sales techniques. A new business should keep a record of this ratio on its operations for each fiscal period, preferably 3 or 6 months. It should watch closely any changes in the turnover rate. Then it can determine what the typical inventory-turnover rate is and whether it can be improved by careful management.

Merchandise turnover is computed by dividing the cost of the goods sold during a fiscal period by the average of the opening and closing inventories. This gives the number of times the average inventory has been "turned" during a period. For example, if the cost of goods sold was $120,000 and the average of the initial and ending inventories was $20,000, the merchandise inventory-turnover ratio would be shown thus:

$$\frac{\text{Cost of goods sold}}{\text{Merchandise inventory}} = \frac{\$120,000}{\$20,000} = 6 \text{ times turned}$$

The average age of the stock would be 2 months. This does not mean that every part of the stock has been sold and new stock purchased 6 separate times during the fiscal year. It does mean that the equivalent of this has been accomplished in terms of the total goods handled during a 12-month period. It is obvious that some parts of inventory stocks may not have been turned at all. Others would have been turned more than 6 times.

In the ordinary merchandising concern, the inventory turnover may be figured for all the merchandise combined. A separate rate of turnover should be figured by departments on main types of merchandise. It enables management to spot slow-moving goods that should either be pushed more aggressively by sales technique or be discontinued entirely. For this reason, every business manager engaged in distributing a variety of products should keep informed on the turnover trends.

In a manufacturing concern, inventories normally consist of raw materials, goods in process, and finished products. If the turnover rate is calculated for each of these classes of goods, the ratio is a good indicator for management. A lower-than-average inventory-turnover ratio is usually an unfavorable sign. The stock may contain so much old merchandise that sales of new goods are slowed up. An extremely high inventory-turnover ratio may sometimes be attained at the cost of a disadvantage. The company may be buying in quantities so small that the best prices are not obtained; or the company may be making excessive markdowns.

A valuable index of collections is the *ratio of net sales to receivables*, the ratio of net sales for a period to the amount of unpaid accounts and notes receivable at the end of that period; for example,

$$\frac{\text{Net sales}}{\text{Receivables}} = \frac{\$49,200}{\$5850} = 8.4$$

This means that annual rate of sales is about 8 times the amount of receivables on hand, or that the average period represented by unpaid accounts and notes receivable is one-eighth of a year's sales, or about 45 days' sales volume. This ratio is most valuable in a concern which makes sales exclusively on credit. In companies which do a cash, as well as credit, business, this ratio of receivables should be calculated in relation only to the portion of the sales handled on credit. In situations of expanding receivables, an annual or a quarterly ratio should be reviewed.

Ratio of net profit to net sales is one of the more significant ratios showing the number of cents of profit for each dollar of sales. This percentage reflects the efficiency of operation in terms of expense control as well as efficiency in purchasing goods handled by the business. The ratio is figured by dividing the net profit by the net sales; for example,

$$\frac{\text{Net profit}}{\text{Net sales}} = \frac{\$4810}{\$49,200} = 9.8 \text{ percent}$$

The variation in net profit per dollar of sales requires close study by management. Only by comparing operating statements for the last several periods can you detect facts accounting for these deviations. This ratio, coupled with the dollar sales volume, is the real measure of the efficiency of a business.

Since the ratio expresses the difference between the *gross-margin* percentage and the *expense* percentage of net sales, obviously either a high markup or a low expense will combine to produce a high net-profit ratio. Bear in mind, therefore, that a high markup may be depriving you of sales volume because your prices are too high. A too low expense ratio, on the other hand, might mean that you are not spending enough for advertising, promotion, care of stock, or selling to produce the sales volume that could be obtained at your location.

COMPARING STANDARD RATIOS

It is often instructive for a business to compare its data with those of other businesses in the same line of activity and of approximately the same size. Coded comparative data for a number of concerns are frequently available through trade associations and similar organizations. A necessary safeguard in making comparisons is that the businesses whose figures are used should have a standard or substantially uniform system of accounts. A comparison with an individual concern having different accounting forms would be entirely misleading.

Tables regularly prepared by organizations like Dun & Bradstreet of New York may be used to good advantage. They determine an individual company's operating position in comparison with that of a large number of concerns. Figures for certain trade lines may be found in publications of the U.S. Department of Commerce, available if you write to the nearest field office of the department. Check your telephone directory for the address.

BREAK-EVEN POINT

One of your first steps in inaugurating a business is determining your break-even point. This is the number of units of your product which must be sold for income to equal all expenses incurred in producing the merchandise. Logic dictates that, if you are in a high-rent area and need to sell half your stock of art objects each month in order to break even, you have started a losing business. (A restaurant would figure its break-even point by the number of customers it must serve in a month, or in a week, for its expenses to be covered.) Assuming your product or service is a worthwhile one, the control of your overhead is the key to your profit.

Overhead consists of fixed costs, such as rent, insurance, or payment on bank notes, which will not vary if your production increases. It also includes variable and semivariable costs. Variables mean such items as commissions to salespeople, purchase of raw materials, and other overhead, which increase in direct proportion to changes in production volume. That is to say, if a company which has been making 10,000 snow shovels per month, for example, doubled production to the 20,000 level, purchase of raw materials, sales commissions, and other expenses would also double. Semivariable costs will vary with volume, but not in direct proportion. The cost of lighting and power will increase with greater production, but will not necessarily double.

Each unit produced should provide some margin for fixed costs and profits. Or expressed a different way, at no point should the direct cost (not the fixed cost) of producing a unit be greater than its sales price. Your fixed cost per unit will vary inversely with changes in volume. Since your fixed overhead will not increase as a result of greater production and semivariable costs will increase by a percentage considerably lower than the rate of increased production, it follows that your cost per unit will lessen as greater quantities are produced.

The experienced entrepreneur uses break-even charts to indicate profit margins at a given rate of production. However, the chart is useful only when fixed costs remain the same, when variable percentages can be plotted with reasonable accuracy, and when a company produces only one item.

BUDGETARY CONTROL

A startling number of businesses attempt operations without a budget, trusting memory and luck to sort out the expenses and income faced in the months ahead. Occasionally, companies have survived without a written budget, but sooner or later the pressures on the manager become too great and the failure to organize relevant business data invites disaster.

The new business will probably be forced to feel its way along some dimly lit financial corridors for a time. Although the entrepreneur will know the capital on hand and most operating expenses, he or she will be able to make only educated guesses about sales. Cautious predictions at this stage are advisable. Certain arithmetical computations can and should be made such as how many units must the owner sell to reach the break-even point. The new operator should know all expenses and consider them against available capital. This sketchy budget will have to serve until 3 or 6 months' experience has given a basis for predicting receipts.

The purchaser of an existing business can base a budget on the company record if sales expectations cannot be reliably estimated. Allow a certain percentage of variation: Will some customers desert the company with the departure of its former owner? Were production and sales continued at an even rate during the negotiation and transfer of ownership? Has the same staff been retained at the same wages? All cash expenditures and debts should be enumerated and considered.

The sales forecast is the basis for all budgets. Whether you own a tool plant employing 40 workers or a retail shop with only 1 salesperson, your sales expectations will dictate your company's expenditures and income. If your operation is large, your department heads will prepare budgets for sales, production, purchases, costs of goods manufactured and sold, cash transactions, and cash flow. You will prepare the overall selling budget as well as personnel and administrative budgets. (You can decide whether you need the help of your accountant.) From these budgets, your master budget is composed.

Your master budget should then be broken down, preferably month by month, but at least by quarters, since seasonal sales usually vary. Do not base your budget on ideal conditions. Plan for 5 percent fewer sales than expected and 5 percent higher expenses. Your budget should itemize and classify costs by function, such as selling, administration, and manufacturing. Once you have formulated your budget, consult it frequently. Each month, compare your projected income and expenses with the actual figures to detect unexpected losses or to consider new or canceled orders. If any decided change should appear, alter your remaining budgets to make them meaningful.

Your Cash Budget Companies which are showing good profits may fail because of cash shortages. Their owners have theorized that cash on hand need only be sufficient to cover a month's rent, while they rely on day-to-day receipts to pay inventory expenses, maintenance, payroll, taxes, dividends, etc. Unexpectedly, a financial obligation descends upon them, and they are left embarrassed for cash, if not bankrupt.

Remember that cash to meet obligations is not provided by profits tied up in inventory or machinery. Your cash budget consists of cash on hand at the beginning of the month, plus collections expected from past and current receivables. Your cash receipts will be based on sales adjusted for collection. See the tables on pages 72 to 74 for an example of a cash budget setup.

The manufacturing budget will consider units needed to meet projected sales. Therefore, it will rely heavily on the requirements of the sales budget. It will include material for manufacturing components, purchased parts, direct labor, manufacturing overhead, tools, fixtures, and selling overhead. The manufacturer should isolate costs of production from marketing costs and costs incurred in general administration functions.

In planning production, consider the capabilities and limitations of your equipment. Make a methodical analysis of material requirements. Is your plant equipped to carry out these operations? Be sure your budget is not committing you to an output which makes unreasonable demands on your employees or equipment.

RETAIL-STORE BUDGET

The medium-sized retail store will require a separate merchandise plan or budget from each department. Your department supervisors can tend to their individual budgets. They are best-qualified to assess buying tendencies and merchandise turnover.

A retail establishment, even the one-person shop, has three ratios to consider: current assets to current liabilities, cash and accounts receivable to current liabilities, and equity capital to total tangible assets. As a general rule, your assets, including cash on hand, inventory, company-owned facilities, etc., should be twice your liabilities.

Your cash and accounts receivable should equal your current liabilities. For methods in finding these ratios, see pages 62 to 64.

BUDGETING CAPITAL EXPENDITURES

Capital expenditures should be planned as much as 10 years in advance. Your acquisitions should never deplete your working capital. Be sure you are financially capable of meeting long-term investments in equipment. Each year's budget should take into consideration the settlement of a long-term debt, not merely the payment of interest.

These budget-forecasting techniques involve extensive arithmetical work, but they are the necessary foundation for your company's present stability and future expansion. Your accountant can help you to determine the proper steps to take in designing your budget, but its actual completion and application are up to you.

CASH FORECASTS

Once you have devised a workable budget and satisfied yourself that you have employed every practical economy, you will want to consider using a cash forecast. You should always have enough cash available to meet a sudden shift in economic conditions or product requirements. On the other hand, too much cash on hand indicates that you are not alert to expansion opportunities. When your business is just starting, it is a good idea to keep your investments fairly fluid, to give you a quick source of cash when you need it. Should seasonal fluctuations result in cash deficits, short-term borrowing can tide you over.

Your cash forecasts will help stabilize the cash flow pattern for your business. They are your keenest tools for planning. Use them to direct new investments into growing lines and to withdraw capital from declining lines. By forecasting cash needs, a firm can determine the amount of excess cash which can be diverted to short-term investments. A sensible forecast enables an owner to plan for acquisition of new equipment or expansion of facilities.

In forecasting, use trends of the industry as a whole and the economy of the country in general to guide your thinking. Such statistics are available from the Bureau of the Budget, U.S. Department of Commerce, from the Brookings Institution, and from the National Bureau of Economic Research, among other agencies. If you have a fair idea of the percentage of the total market claimed by your company, use this percentage in forecasting.

CHOOSING YOUR
INVENTORY METHOD

Tax considerations govern the way you take your inventory. The regulations require the use of an inventory in every case in which production, purchase, or sale of merchandise is an income-producing factor.

Any inventory method that can be used under the best accounting practice in a balance sheet showing your financial position is all right for tax purposes.

Inventories should include all raw materials and supplies, as well as finished or partly finished goods, but they should not include the following:

- Raw materials and supplies which have not been acquired for sale or which will not become a part of merchandise intended for sale
- Materials ordered by you for future delivery, title to which has not yet been transferred to you
- Assets of a capital nature, such as machinery, fixtures, land, buildings, accounts receivable, cash, or like assets
- Goods received on consignment
- Goods (also containers) sold, title to which has passed to your customers

In inventorying your normal goods, a reasonably consistent basis of costing must be applied. Where you maintain perpetual inventories, inventory accounts are

- Charged with the actual cost of the goods purchased or produced.
- Credited with the value of goods used, transferred, or sold, calculated upon the basis of the actual cost of the goods acquired during the year (including the inventory at the beginning of the year).

The net value as shown by the accounts is accepted to be the cost of the goods on hand, but balances shown by perpetual inventories must be checked to physical inventories at reasonable intervals.

You treat other items as follows:

- *Operating supplies or property* not intended to be sold. Not required to be inventoried. You may classify it as a deferred charge to be deducted as used or consumed.

CASH BUDGET
Part I: Receipts and Disbursements
For 3 months ending September 30, 19—

	July		August		September	
	Estimate	Actual	Estimate	Actual	Estimate	Actual
Projected cash receipts:						
Cash sales						
Collections on accounts receivable						
Other income						
Total receipts						
Projected cash disbursements:						
Merchandise						
Payroll						
Rent						
Utilities						
Advertising						
Administrative						
Taxes						

Interest						
Miscellaneous						
Total disbursements						
Net cash increase or decrease (difference between receipts and disbursements)						

CASH BUDGET
Part II: Summary
For 3 months ending September 30, 19—

	July		August		September	
	Estimate	Actual	Estimate	Actual	Estimate	Actual
Expected cash balance at beginning of month						
Add increase or subtract decrease from part I						
Expected cash balance						
Required cash balance						
Short-term loans needed*						
Cash available for short-term investment†						

*If cash is less than requirements.
†If cash exceeds requirements.

- *Merchandise in hands of processor.* Inventoried by owner when goods are to be returned in kind, for example, goods to be dyed. But when a new product is to be returned (for example, refined copper for ore, or flour for wheat), then it is an exchange and is not inventoried.
- *Goods under contract of sale* but not yet segregated and applied to the contract. Include in inventory of seller; exclude from inventory of buyer.
- *Goods under a noncancelable contract of sale*, segregated and applied to the contract. Charge to the buyer, who includes these in inventory.
- *Merchandise, title to which has passed to the buyer.* (Title passes, usually, when the parties intend it to pass; local state law should be consulted.) Exclude from seller's inventory; include in buyer's inventory even if goods are in transit or buyer does not have physical possession.
- *Goods, including shipping charges, sent c.o.d.* Include in inventory of seller until payment and delivery are made.
- *Goods shipped on approval.* Include in seller's inventory until they are accepted.
- *Merchandise* sold and shipped according to contract but *refused by the buyer* because of a price decline. Do not include in seller's inventory.
- *Goods sold by sample*, subject to inspection and rejection within a given time. Include in inventory of seller if promptly rejected by buyer, even though the goods are not returned before the end of the year.
- *Goods rejected* because of defects. Include in seller's inventory, not in buyer's, if rejection is timely.
- *Goods sold and found unsuitable by buyer*, then resold to the same party in the following year with concessions from the original price. Exclude from seller's inventory from the first year when originally sold.
- *Goods shipped on consignment.* Include in seller's inventory until consignee sells them.

HOW TO INVENTORY
FOR TAX PURPOSES

You will wish to weigh the merits of all available systems before you choose your method of inventorying. Once you elect your method, it must be applied in later years, unless you can obtain authorization to change it from the Internal Revenue Service.

Cost, and cost or market, whichever is lower, are approved as proper methods for inventorying. To find cost, you may use the *first-in–first-out* (FIFO) or the *last-in–first-out* (LIFO) methods. How each of these works is illustrated by the following.

Method	Inventory at end of year is computed—	Therefore, cost of goods sold in year is—
Cost:		
First-in–first-out	1500 at $4	1000 at $2 500 at $4
Last-in–first-out	1000 at $2 500 at $4	1500 at $4
Cost or market, whichever is lower	1500 at $4	1000 at $2 500 at $4

Assume that the inventory at the beginning of the year was composed of 1000 units which cost $2 each. They had a market value of $2 on that date. Purchases in the year were 2000 units at $4. Sales in the year were 1500 units. Inventory at the end of the year was 1500 units. The market value was then $5. The effect upon cost of sales by the various methods of inventory is outlined in the following table:

Cost or market is used in inventorying by many businesses in a falling market. This enables you to choose the lower of the two figures for each individual item. In practice, your inventory records will show three columns of figures: cost of the item, its present market price at a typical volume of purchase, and the lower of the two. Thus, on several items, your choice will vary:

Units	Cost	Market price	Lower of cost or market
D	$ 5,000	$ 4,500	$ 4,500
E	6,500	6,800	6,500
F	2,000	1,900	1,900
	$13,500	$13,200	$12,900

What does "cost" mean? In the case of merchandise on hand at the beginning of the year, cost is the inventory price of such goods. In other cases, it is as follows:

- On merchandise purchased since the beginning of the year, cost is computed as invoice price less trade or other discounts, except strictly cash discounts. To net invoice price, add transportation or other necessary charges incurred in acquiring possession of the goods.

- On merchandise produced since the beginning of the year, cost is the sum of the cost of raw materials and supplies entering into or consumed in connection with the product, direct labor, and indirect expenses necessary for the production of the particular article, including probably a reasonable proportion of management expenses, but not including any cost of selling.
- For miners and manufacturers who, by a single process or a uniform series of processes, derive a product of two or more kinds, sizes, or grades, costs are allocated to each kind, size, or grade of product, which in the aggregate will absorb the total cost of production. Cost must bear a reasonable relation to the respective selling values of the diferent kinds, sizes, or grades of product.
- In any industry in which the usual rules for computation of cost of production are inapplicable, costs may be based upon an established trade practice of the particular industry.

What does "market" mean?   In ordinary circumstances, it is the current bid price prevailing at the date of the inventory for the inventoried merchandise in the volume in which it is usually purchased. This rule applies to goods purchased and on hand, to goods in process of manufacture, and to finished goods on hand. It does not apply to goods for delivery upon noncancelable sales contracts, at fixed prices below the market. These can be inventoried at cost. Or you can use the following rules:

- If no open market exists or if quotations are nominal because of stagnant market conditions, use evidence of a fair market price at the date nearest the inventory. Or use specific purchases or sales by you or others in reasonable volume and made in good faith. Or use compensation paid for cancellation of contracts for purchase commitments.
- When prices are falling, market may be your sales price, less what it costs you to make the sale. Correctness of this method is found by your actual sales for a reasonable period before and after the date of the inventory.

The use of last-in–first-out (LIFO) is not dependent upon character of a business. LIFO is generally the preferred method in inflationary times because a high inventory valuation minimizes profits for tax purposes. LIFO should not be used if prices are likely to decline in the years ahead. The LIFO method would leave you with high inventory valuations of the items acquired at high prices, while your cost of goods sold would be understated. If you use the LIFO method of valuing your inventory for some years and prices drop, see if it is to your advantage to apply to the Internal Revenue Service for permission to change.

Ordinarily, rent, repairs, taxes, depreciation, and other factory overhead expenses are charged to the cost of production. Such expenses would then be included in the value of goods manufactured during the year, some of which will remain in inventory. This conforms to accepted principles of cost accounting.

Storing Important Papers   Through regular weeding out and microfilming of records, the problem of storage space can be reduced, but while you may keep payroll records, canceled checks, invoices, vouchers, etc., on microfilm, you must retain your cash books, journals, voucher registers, ledgers, etc. It is important to know legal requirements. Your attorney will provide guidance.

The law may not require you to retain certain data for income tax record purposes more than, say, 4 years, but in certain circumstances you might be called upon by the Internal Revenue Service to produce documentation for earlier years.

Using Computers for Inventory Control and Record Keeping   With advancing technology broadening the types of computers, a small business can find a computer tailored to its needs and its pocketbook. The functions to which the computer can be put are almost limitless. See Chapter 17 for further discussion of the use of computers.

7

BASIC TAX MANAGEMENT DECISIONS

Several governments are silent partners in your business. Of these, the federal government probably takes the largest share of your profits through taxes, and, depending on the revenue needs of the state in which you do business, the state government can also siphon off a moderate amount of your income through taxes. Not too far behind, local tax authorities, city or county, may demand their share. In addition, the cost of keeping records and preparing returns adds to the cost of doing business.

The word "tax" is inadequate to describe the type of taxes to which businesses are subject. There are income taxes, payroll taxes, sales taxes, excise taxes, and property taxes. Major companies have special tax accounting departments just to keep account of tax liabilities and their due dates. In your own operation, if you cannot afford a special tax department, you must develop within your bookkeeping and accounting systems an organized pattern of meeting tax liabilities. Further, you must always be alert to tax consequences of your business transactions so that you can take steps to minimize tax liabilities.

Although the complexity of tax law makes professional advice essential, your awareness of tax problems is necessary so that you can understand and discuss them with your adviser. In Chapter 5 we discussed the tax aspects of choosing a business form. Tax decisions that affect current business operations are discussed in this chapter.

REVIEW OF TAX OBLIGATIONS
PLACED ON BUSINESSES

Income Tax Sole proprietors and corporations are required to pay income tax to the federal government and possibly city, county, and state governments as well. A partnership pays no income tax, but the partners themselves each pay their own income tax on their shares of income from the partnership.

In many states, income reported for federal income tax purposes is used as the base for computing state income taxes. The due date of income tax depends on the business taxable year chosen and the form of your business. Choosing a taxable year is discussed later in this chapter.

Employment Taxes Social Security (also known by its legislative initials FICA) must be withheld from the pay of employees except those who are considered self-employed, such as certain salespersons, contractors, and consultants. In addition, the employer must pay an equal amount of employment tax. The FICA withheld from the employees, the employer's FICA contribution, and the income tax withheld from employees' wages are reported to the IRS on Form 941.

The employment tax due on employees' wages is generally paid directly to a bank. The deposit is entered on Special Deposit Card 501, which is automatically issued to you when you apply for your federal employer identification number (which will identify your business the same way a Social Security number identifies an individual). More cards can be ordered by mail or telephone from the IRS. In an emergency, the IRS can accept deposits at the local office, but your only chance of having such a deposit credited correctly to your account is if the local personnel use Special Form 3244, the payment posting voucher. Otherwise, you would be liable for the penalties for late deposit.

Note that your own Social Security liability, if you are self-employed or a partner, is sent to the IRS as part of your income tax liability. Your personal Social Security obligation is not entered on Form 941, nor is it paid by Deposit Card 501, unless you are an officer-employee of the corporation. For a self-employed person, the rate of FICA contribution is greater than the withholding for an employee.

Unemployment Taxes Unemployment tax is paid to both the state and the federal government. The IRS gives a partial credit for unemployment taxes paid to the state.

First, you register with your state bureau of labor. The state then assigns your business an identification number (to credit your deposits to your account) and an *experience rate*. The experience rate determines how much unemployment tax you will have to pay. The rate can change, depending upon how often your business hires and fires employees. The higher your turnover, the more the demand is on the state unemployment fund, so the more they will want you to pay into it. The better you are at retaining your employees, the less employment tax you will be required to pay. Finally, the state will inform you how and when to deposit unemployment taxes with them.

The federal unemployment tax, also known as FUTA, will be smaller than the state tax. One month after the close of your tax year, you file Form 940 with the IRS to show how you calculated the unemployment tax that is due. The unemployment tax money is sent in with the Form 940 if the amount owed is less than $100. Otherwise, Special Deposit Card 508 is used to pay the tax to a bank. It usually takes three full-time employees before a business exceeds $100 in FUTA taxes. Procedures for obtaining Deposit Card 508 are the same as obtaining Deposit Card 501.

Excise Taxes   The IRS also collects federal excise tax. Currently, excise tax must be paid by manufacturers of coal, truck parts, tractors, firearms, tires, and lubricating oil. Excise tax is also imposed upon telephone services, carrying freight or passengers by air, and the use of international air travel facilities. Computed quarterly on Form 720, the tax can be sent with the form if the total tax is less than $100; otherwise, the tax must be paid to a bank with IRS Deposit Card 504.

Sales Taxes   If your state has a sales tax, contact the state sales tax department for instructions on how to register as a collector of sales taxes. You will then be informed as to which buyers are exempt from sales tax, which forms to file, and how to deposit sales tax monies you collect with the state.

If your business imports products or exports products, you may have customs duties to pay in the United States and abroad. Contact the U.S. Customs Bureau, a reputable freight forwarder, or the foreign embassies or consulates for the countries in which you do business for information about applicable fees and product restrictions.

Related Tax Obligations   Besides your duty to collect or pay the correct taxes, you may have an obligation to file other tax forms, even though no money is due. If your company has a pension plan, it may have to file a reporting form every year. You must provide a W-2 form to every employee from whose pay you withhold income tax or Social Security contributions. You must send a Form 1099 to other firms and individuals to whom you make payments. You must receive a W-4 form from each of your employees. Your accountant can give you further help in meeting these various tax-related responsibilities.

CHOOSING YOUR ACCOUNTING PERIOD

You compute your income taxes generally on transactions that have occurred during a 12-month period. If the period ends on December 31, it is called a *calendar year*; if on the last day of any month other than December, it is called a *fiscal year*. In any event, a reporting period (technically called a taxable year) can never be longer than 12 months unless a business reports on a 52–53 week fiscal year basis.

A taxable year can be less than 12 months in the year in which you start your business, or if you end your business before the end of your regular taxable year or if you change your taxable year.

In choosing your taxable year, you should weigh the following factors.

What is your natural business year?   Your first consideration should be the natural year of the business, that is, one which gives you an undistorted picture of your business. Selecting this period is especially important if you operate a seasonal business. It should cover your entire business season, and it should end when you have the minimum amount of incomplete transactions, for example, when your inventories and accounts receivable are at a minimum. This greatly facilitates the preparation of your financial statements and tax return.

Will there be any distortions of income or expenses in your first year of operations?   When you start your business, you may incur some unusual expenses or losses. If your operations have begun in the middle of a calendar year, it might be advisable to use a fiscal year that extends beyond December so as to include anticipated income that will absorb these losses. If the contrary is true and you begin with seasonal profits, you may want to extend the year to a period of off-seasonal losses. Sometimes, you may want to end an initial fiscal year just before anticipated profits are earned so that you can defer the payment of taxes. The freed funds can then be used during the year as operating funds. In considering these possibilities, do not let the initial advantages unduly influence your decision. Once you choose a fiscal year, you may find it difficult to switch to a calendar year without a good business reason.

When will your tax payments be due?   If your taxable year ends at a time when your cash reserves are low, you may find it difficult to pay your tax. In such a case, it may be advisable to end your taxable year when you have substantial cash on hand to pay your taxes.

How do you intend to operate your business?   Your freedom of choice may be restricted by the form in which you operate. If your business is operated as a sole proprietorship, you must use the same taxable year in which you report your personal income, but you may be able to change your personal calendar year to a fiscal year to meet your business needs. If you operate as a partnership, you generally may not adopt a taxable year other than that of all the principal partners unless a business purpose is shown for the choice. If a business purpose can be shown, the partnership may adopt a taxable year other than that of all its principal partners. If you organize a corporation, you have initially an unrestricted choice in selecting a taxable year for the corporation. When you file a return, you may adopt the calendar year or any fiscal period you choose, but again do not let the initial advantages unduly influence your decision. Once you choose a fiscal year, you may find it difficult to switch to a calendar year without a good business reason.

TAX ACCOUNTING METHODS FOR REPORTING BUSINESS INCOME

You can report on the *accrual* basis or the *cash* basis. If you have inventories, you must use the accrual basis. Otherwise, you may generally choose whichever method you prefer. You can change your accounting method, but you need the permission of the IRS to do so.

On the cash basis, you report all income in the taxable year that it is actually received. You take all deductions in the taxable year that they are actually paid. The cash basis has the important advantage of enabling you to control your income reporting. You can put off reporting income by postponing its receipt. However, you may not postpone reporting income that is credited to your account and subject to your control or set apart for you to draw on at will. Using the cash basis also allows you to postpone payment of expenses to a year in which their deduction gives you a greater tax advantage.

On the accrual basis, you report income that has been earned, whether or not you have actually received it. You deduct expenses that have been incurred in the tax year whether or not you have paid them. The accrual basis generally gives a more even financial report than the cash basis.

If you change from the cash to the accrual method, be careful that you do not report any income or expense items twice—or fail to include certain income items at all. When you adjust for a change in accounting method, an increase of taxed income in the year of adjustment will result.

If you are a retailer who regularly sells on the installment basis, you may want to consider a special *installment-sale election*. The installment basis is actually a combination of the cash and accrual bases. Instead of reporting your profit in the year of sale, you spread it proportionately over the year in which you receive the installment payments. That is, you report as income each year that proportion of the year's installment payments which the gross profit on the sales *for the year when the sale was made* bears to the total contract price. Expenses and other deductions (not included in cost of sales) are deducted in the year incurred if you use the accrual basis. They are not allocated to the years when the income upon the collection is reported.

You may decide to use installment reporting when you want to build up working capital in a current year by deferring the tax due on sales income to later years. However, when you are just developing an installment business, you may decide against a current election if you expect that receipts of deferred income plus increased sales may push you into a higher tax bracket in a later year.

TIMING INCOME AND EXPENSE DEDUCTIONS

By arranging your sales terms, you can sometimes control the year in which certain sales are to be taxed. In making your decision, you must consider your expected income and the tax rates for the 2 years involved. For example, if rates are expected to drop and your income will remain about the same each year, you may want to postpone some income of the current year to the next year. As a guide, note the following suggestions for your sales between now and the end of the year, if you want to bring more income into this year. If you want to postpone income until next year, do the opposite:

- Receipts of unrestricted advances and deposits give you income this year, even if the full cost of servicing or delivery comes next year.
- Consignment sales, approval sales, and layaway sales give income only when the sale is completed. If you want income in this year,

change your sales terms or offer discounts for payment or other incentives to close out these sales.

● Increasing prices now will change sales income this year. Setting higher prices for early shipment, with a declining scale as total shipments increase, will move some income ahead without an overall increase in price.

● Trade discounts on sales in this year reduce this year's income. Cash discounts reduce income when the customer takes the discount.

Timing Deductions   In high-income years, you should generally review what costs may be deducted currently rather than in later years when income may drop or be taxed at lower rates. You may gain by liquidating, in high-tax years, obligations that may ultimately have to be met, possibly in years of lower income. You get an immediate deduction if you settle:

● Bad leases that are likely to be a burden on you in later years.

● Contracts for services or materials that eventually will be expensive and difficult to carry in later years, or sales contracts which may be difficult to perform.

● Contingent liability. You might pay an employee's claim for damages for breach of contract of employment and claims for accidents, guarantee of lease, and breaches of contract.

● Assessments on state and local taxes. You should pay these amounts together with interest accrued. (You may file immediate claims for refund of the taxes and the interest paid.)

DEPRECIATION ELECTIONS

Depreciation is an expense deduction that lets you recover your capital investment in buildings, machinery, and other property used in your business. The law provides for rapid write-offs under the accelerated cost recovery system (ACRS). The law automatically fixes both the recovery period of each type of asset and the rate of recovery. For most purposes, property is classed as 3-year or 5-year property. For example, suppose you buy a car for business use in 1982. A car is within a 3-year recovery period for which the law fixes a specific write-off rate over the 3 years: 25 percent in 1982, 38 percent in 1983, and 37 percent in 1984. The entire cost is recovered; there are no salvage-value limitations. Real estate may be depreciated over a 15-year period.

Instead of adopting an accelerated depreciation rate fixed by law, you may elect to recover capital investments over longer periods of time, using the straight-line method of depreciation. In the case of 3-

year property, you may elect to use the straight-line method over 3, 5, or 12 years. In the case of 5-year property, you may elect the straight-line method over 5, 12, or 25 years. For realty, you may use the straight-line method over the regular 15-year recovery period or over 35 or 45 years.

In planning your use of the ACRS, remember that the total amount of depreciation for a piece of property remains constant; that is, total depreciation can never exceed the cost of an asset. Accelerated methods and shorter recovery periods for an asset give you an opportunity to advance the time of taking your deduction. This may be helpful where the increased annual deduction will give you cash for working capital. If you are starting a new business in which you expect losses or low income at the start, the acceleration of depreciation will probably waste depreciation deductions that could be used to offset income in later years. If you plan a program of regular replacement of equipment, an accelerated method of depreciation will probably be to your advantage.

Instead of claiming depreciation under the ACRS, you may treat part of your purchase as an expense write-off. In 1982 and 1983 you may take an immediate deduction of items costing $5000 or less. This election is limited to personal property, and, to the extent the property is treated as an expense write-off, no investment credit may be claimed. The portion of the cost not treated as an expense write-off is recovered under the ACRS. In 1984 and 1985, you may deduct up to $7500; in 1986 and years thereafter, up to $10,000 of costs may be deducted.

BAD DEBT DEDUCTION ELECTIONS

Although bad debts are deductible, not all bad debts are treated alike. The law distinguishes between two types of bad debts.

Debts that arise from usual business sales on credit. Here, an important election is available to businesses that are on the accrual basis. They can elect either to deduct bad debts as they arise or to charge to a bad debt reserve each year an estimated amount of bad debts based primarily on experiences of past defaults.

Debts that arise from loans made by you in your individual capacity. Here the law distinguishes between loans that you make in business transactions and those that you make in personal transactions. The distinction is important because business bad debts are fully deductible as ordinary deductions. In addition, you may elect to take a deduction for partially worthless debts. However, nonbusiness bad debts are limited deductions in the form of short-term capital losses. In one year, you can only deduct these losses against capital gains and $3000 of other income. You may not deduct partially worthless non-business bad debts.

Reserve Method to Charge Off Bad Debts Where you extend credit to customers, the reserve method is often the best way to account for bad debts. Through it, as a rule, larger deductions will be taken in profit years when most needed. The company elects to use the reserve method when filing its first tax return. If you are currently charging off bad debts as they arise and you want to change to the reserve method, apply for permission to change and give the reasons for the change; for example, the method you have been using does not enable you to state your net income or financial condition properly, or banks or credit sources have insisted that you make the change.

Permission to use the reserve method is limited. You cannot use it for the purpose of handling one specific debt. Once you adopt the reserve method, you must continue to use it unless you get IRS permission to change.

In the first year of a new business, try to base your reserve on your knowledge of the trade. If that is limited, perhaps you can form a basis from your competitors' experiences and credit reports. If you have changed over to the reserve method, you deduct in the first year an amount which covers bad debts currently charged to the reserve and fixes the reserve for the same year at a reasonable figure.

In making additions to the reserve, you are allowed to use reasonable judgment in weighing business conditions that will affect your customers' payments. This involves anticipating probable events that will alter your past reserve experiences.

Remember, the addition to the reserve cannot be a completely arbitrary amount. After each addition, the reserve should be your best estimate of what will probably become uncollectible out of the receivables then on the books. When debts become worthless, they are then charged to the reserve. The following are other adjustments that may have to be made:

- Deductions which both eliminate a deficit in the reserve and restore it to a reasonable amount for the next year. You include excess reserve in income in the year it is no longer required.
- Credits for recoveries of bad debts previously charged to the reserve. They must be credited even though you get no benefit from the addition to the reserve in the year the bad debt was sustained.

In using the reserve method, you may not do the following:

- Base your addition to the reserve on possible but unexpected losses.
- Increase the reserve retroactively when events of the later years show it was too small.
- Credit to the reserve recoveries of bad debts sustained before you started using the reserve method. These are included in income to the extent that the bad debt gave you a tax benefit.

Be sure to set up the reserve on your books and tax return. If you change to the direct charge-off method, you must close out the balance of the reserve and include it in your income, but you can exclude from income a final unused reserve balance, if you show that the deduction which made up the reserve gave you no tax benefit.

RESEARCH AND DEVELOPMENT EXPENSES

Research and development costs of producing a product can be either deducted in the year they are incurred or deferred and then amortized when the product is put into use in your business or starts producing income. If you elect to amoritize, you may elect a write-off period of 60 months or more. However, if property results from the research, the deferred costs are added to the basis of property and depreciated over the useful life of the property.

Deductible research and development expenses include the cost of management studies of production techniques, quality control systems, personnel training methods, efficiency studies, labor utilization, routing techniques, scheduling difficulties, waste control, and managerial control.

Your choice of how to deduct the research and development expenses will depend upon your projection of future tax liability. If you need current deductions, you may decide to claim the expenses as they arise. If you want to save the deductions for later years, you will elect to defer the deduction and accumulate the expenses until they may be amortized. Your accountant can help you in deciding which election to make by projecting your future financial position.

Once made, the election applies to all research expenses incurred in later years. If you elect to take immediate deductions and later want to change to amortization, you must ask for IRS permission to change. If you elect to amortize, and later abandon the project, the total accrued expenses can be deducted in the year the product is abandoned.

In addition to deduction or amortization for research and development expenses, a 25 percent credit may be taken for increased research activities. The credit is designed to stimulate new research and development activities and is figured on increases in expenses over an average base period. A year in which there are no research expenses, such as years before your business was in existence, is treated as zero in the base period average, but the average cannot be less than 50 percent of the current year's expenses. Any unused credit is subject to carry-backs and carry-overs.

DETERMINING COMPANY DISTRIBUTIONS

If you operate your business as a corporation, you should be aware of the tax consequences of corporate distributions. Dividend decisions will often be based on tax consequences. The following discussion applies generally when your corporation has *not* made a Subchapter S election. (In a Subchapter S company, most corporate earnings are currently reported by stockholders, but there are distribution problems not discussed in this book which, because of their complex nature, must be reviewed by an experienced tax practitioner.)

To determine whether a dividend is taxable, you must review earnings at two different periods:

- *Current profits as of the end of the current year.* A dividend is always considered to have been made from earnings most recently accumulated.
- *Accumulated profits as of the beginning of the current year.* When current profits are large enough to meet the dividend, you do not have to make this computation. Therefore, it is only when the dividends exceed current earnings (or there are no current earnings) that you match accumulated earnings against the dividend.

Current earnings are figured at the close of the year to determine the taxability of a dividend. This means that the amount of profits earned up to the date of a dividend payment made during the year is unimportant. Such profits are not reduced by dividend payments made during the year in determining the earnings at the end of the year. For example, the Jones Company had a $15,000 deficit at the beginning of 1981. In February 1981, it paid a dividend of $15,000. On December 31, 1981, it figured that it had made a current profit of $15,000. The dividend paid in February is taxed even though at the time there were no earnings and profits. Furthermore, the current $15,000 profit is not applied first against the deficit but against the dividend. That there is a prior year's deficit does not affect the taxability of the dividend as long as there are sufficient current earnings to meet it.

Current earnings and profits should not be confused with the amount of taxable income reported on the corporation's tax return. To determine the amount of current earnings available for dividends, you must adjust taxable income for items that did not enter into its computation, such as tax-exempt income and nondeductible expenses. Your accountant should prepare this figure for you.

In addition to paying dividends in cash or its own stock, a corporation can distribute property that it owns. These distributions are called *dividends in kind* and, when received by an individual stockholder, are taxed at their fair market values.

Dividends in kind can be a method of cutting down corporate taxes. If the corporation sells property and distributes the proceeds, the corporation pays a tax on the gain and the stockholders are taxed on the dividend received. But if it distributes the property directly to the stockholders, they pay only the one tax. The total tax cost is much smaller. In planning such distribution, be sure your dividend is in terms of property. Do not mention cash. If you do, you may be taxed as if a sale had been made to the stockholders. Be sure, too, that your corporation has no part in the sale of the property by the stockholders before they receive it.

The distributing corporation incurs no tax on dividends it distributed in cash, and, as a general rule, the distribution of appreciated property results in no tax to the distributing company. However, there are exceptions to this general rule. One, which may arise inadvertently, is when a corporation declares a cash dividend and subsequently decides to pay the dividend with appreciated property. Here, the IRS will contend that the company paid off a liability—the dividends payable—with property and thus consummated a sale. A careful drafting of the corporate resolution declaring the dividend to be paid in property with no inference of payment in a dollar amount avoids the possibility of tax to the corporation.

In an examination of corporate books, the IRS scrutinizes transactions between the corporation and its stockholders. Benefits accruing to the stockholders from the transaction can be taxed to them as dividends regardless of the lack of a formal dividend declaration by the corporation; for example,

- Excess payments to stockholders for salaries or rent on property owned by the stockholder.

- Corporate purchase at an excessive price of property owned by the stockholder.
- Loans to stockholders where there is no intention of repayment.
- Bargain purchases of corporate property by stockholder. The taxed amount is the difference between what the stockholder paid for the property and its fair market value.

TAX CONSIDERATIONS IN OPERATING A FAMILY BUSINESS

By making family members partners or stockholders in your business, you may reduce the overall tax on your business income.

Family Partnership You can split the partnership income by gifts of partnership interests if capital is an important income-producing factor. Where the partnership is essentially a service business, a gift of partnership interest to a family member will not shift partnership income unless the new partner actually performs services for the partnership.

A gift of a partnership interest is subject to IRS scrutiny. If you make a gift of partnership interest but retain control over the interest, the gift may not be recognized, and you will be taxed on partnership income allocable to that partnership interest.

No tax savings are possible if you make your spouse your partner since you will probably file a joint return. The overall family tax bill *can* be cut by making your children partners. A minor child will be recognized as a partner if competent to manage his or her own property and participate in partnership activities, or if the child's property interest is managed by a court-supervised guardian or placed in a trust.

Income Splitting with Corporate Stock You can make gifts of stock to your children without confronting the problems of similar arrangements in family partnerships. In a corporation in which stockholders have elected to report income, income can be shifted even after it has been earned. For example, a gift of stock in an electing corporation before the close of the taxable year can shift tax on that income to the new stockholder. However, here too, as in the case of gifts of partnership interests, the transfer must have economic reality. Dividend income paid to children should be placed in custodian accounts not under the control of the parent who made the gift of stock.

You may split income within the family by transferring property used in the business to your children. You might transfer to your children, or to a trust in which your children are the beneficiaries, rental property such as the building in which your store or office is located. If you lease back the premises, you split income by shifting rental income into the children's lower tax brackets while deducting rental payments as a business expense. The implementation of such a plan needs expert counsel since the Internal Revenue Service, if it examines the arrangement, may try to defeat it on the grounds that the gift and leaseback as a whole have no business purpose. Courts tend to allow the rent deduction where the following tests are met:

1. You do not retain substantially the same control over the property that you had before transferring the property to the trust. The trustee should be independent and the leaseback terms should be negotiated on an arm's length basis.
2. The lease is in writing and calls for a reasonable amount of rent.
3. You do not have an equity interest in the property.
4. The leaseback, but not necessarily the gift in trust, has a business purpose; for example, once the building is transferred to a trust, the leaseback and payment of rent are necessary for the continued use of the building for office space for your business.

To split income you must do more than make gifts of income. If your assignment is merely of income when collected, you are taxed. You avoid tax only by transferring the property providing the income. Take this example: A service-station owner gave his parents the right to collect rent from the station, notifying the tenant to pay rent directly to them. The son retained title to the property, paid the property taxes, and deducted depreciation on his own return. He did not report rental income on his tax return, claiming the income belonged to his parents. A court held he had to pay on the income; he had not transferred ownership of the property.

FRINGE BENEFITS

The law prohibits you from deducting most personal expenses, such as food, life insurance protection, your children's education, and vacations. With inflation pushing up the cost of living, it may be increasingly difficult to maintain the high standard of living you may have come to enjoy and expect. However, the burden of paying for some personal items may be shifted to your business, thereby freeing funds for additional investment or other things.

Owning a business enables you to take full advantage of several fringe benefits sanctioned by the tax law. "Fringe benefits" is a term designed to cover all benefits supplied by your company beyond salary. It includes such benefits as life insurance protection, discounts on company products, education plans to benefit your children, and medical benefits.

The main attraction of fringe benefits is that they come to the recipient partially or wholly tax-free. What this means in terms of dollars and cents depends, of course, on the tax bracket of the person involved. For example, say you are in the 50 percent tax bracket and own a corporation which pays $100 per year to provide you with group-term life insurance. If it did not provide the benefit and you wanted it, you would have to earn $200 to be left with $100 of aftertax dollars available for premiums payments. This assumes that the coverage could be obtained for the same cost as that paid by the corporation—not a likely prospect. Thus, you would have to earn more than $200 to be able to get the same life insurance coverage that a corporation can provide.

The major fringe benefit to consider is a pension plan. The amount that can be put into a plan depends upon whether the business is incorporated or not, but, regardless of how the business is organized, a qualified plan can be set up so that retirement monies can be credited, tax-free, to accrue, tax-free, to your benefit until such time as you withdraw the account. Again, depending upon how the business is organized, these pension plan payments may even be deductible for the business. Consult with your accountant for further details.

Of course, the availability of fringe benefits becomes meaningful only when the business is profitable enough to provide such benefits. In many cases, for the benefit to be a deductible business expense, the same fringe benefit available to you must also be available to your employees. Because the list of allowable benefits is subject to IRS policy changes, consult with a tax expert to find out what is currently available. At the time this book was written, among the more common fringe benefits were medical checkups, life insurance, educational assistance, meals that are provided in order that the employee remain at the job, uniforms, tools, courtesy discounts, and Christmas gifts.

HOME SPACE USED
FOR BUSINESS

You may operate your business from your home, using a room or other space as an office or area to assemble or prepare items for sale. To deduct home expenses allocated to your business, you, as a self-employed person, must be able to prove that you use the home area exclusively and on a regular basis either as a place of business to meet or deal with clients or customers in the normal course of your business, or as your principal place of business. For example, a woman operated a road stand a mile from her home and used her home to prepare items for sale at the stand. Although she used the home space for a business purpose, she was not allowed to deduct home expenses because her home was not considered her principal place of business. Her principal place of business was the road stand.

The exclusive-use test requires use of a specific section of a residence solely for the purpose of carrying on business. The use of a room for both personal and business purposes may not meet the exclusive-use test. The same rule applies to an unattached structure such as a garage used for both business and personal purposes.

Under the regular-basis test, expenses attributable to incidental or occasional trade or business use are not deductible even if the room is used for no other purpose but business.

The above tests will generally not present problems in deducting home expenses where the home area is the principal place of business. Problems may arise where you have a principal office elsewhere and use a part of your home for occasional work. If your deduction is questioned, you must prove that the area is used regularly and exclusively to receive customers or clients. For example, evidence that you have actual office facilities is important. Furnish the room as an office with a desk, files, and a phone used only for business calls. Also keep a record of work done and business visitors.

A deduction for home business use may include real estate taxes, mortgage interest, operating expenses (e.g., home insurance premiums, utility costs), and depreciation allocated to the area used for business. Household expenses and repairs that do not benefit that space are not deductible. For example, the cost of painting and repairs to rooms other than the one used as a business office is not deductible. However, a pro rata share of the cost of painting the outside of a house or repairing a roof may be deductible. Costs of lawn care and landscaping are not deductible.

Deductible expenses allocated to the business use of an area in your home may not exceed gross income derived from that use. Follow this order in deducting expenses:

1. Deduct allocable taxes, interest (and casualty losses, if any) up to the extent of income.
2. From the balance of income, if any, deduct operating expenses allocable to the office.
3. If a balance still remains, deduct allocable depreciation up to the amount of remaining business income.

The amount of taxes, interest, or casualty losses not allocable to the home office may be claimed as itemized deductions.

TAX PROBLEMS
OF A SIDELINE BUSINESS

A sideline business poses a special tax problem when it loses money. If your return is examined, deductions claimed for these losses may be disallowed on the grounds that you do not operate with expectation of making a profit.

If your sideline venture is running into the red, take your loss deductions, but at the same time be prepared to produce evidence of business or profit-making intentions. This may be evidence that your activity is in a field of personal expertise; you devote considerable time and effort to the activity; losses are due to unexpected events, such as casualties; you employ experts or consultants in the field; you run the activity in a businesslike manner, maintaining complete and accurate books and records; or the element of pleasure or recreation is not dominant. A reasonable expectation of profit is all you must show.

If your return is examined and your losses are questioned, there are special tax rules that may help you. If you show a profit in 2 or more years during a 5-year period, you are presumed to be in an activity for profit. The Internal Revenue Service may rebut this presumption. If it does, you must then show facts that support your claim of being engaged in an activity for profit. Similarly, if you do not show 2 profitable years in the 5-year period, you have to prove your case. If you anticipate profits in later years, you have this option: You may elect to delay a determination of the issue until the fifth taxable year from the year you first entered the activity. If you have by then realized at least 2 profitable years, the presumption of profit will apply to the loss years. In making the election, you sign a waiver of statute of limitations for the taxable years involved. The waiver keeps those years open to possible deficiency claims. In the case of horse racing, breeding, or showing, the presumption based on 2 profitable years is measured during a 7-year period.

REVIEWING STATE TAXES
ON BUSINESS ACTIVITY

If you are planning to do business across state lines, you must consider the state taxes that may apply to your business in each state in which you will do business. Each state has the right to tax, and a company doing interstate business will pay taxes to more than one state. In some cases, multiple state taxes can be as costly as federal taxes.

Check with your accountant and attorney. Tell them how you plan to handle sales, billing, accounting, and warehousing. Include any activities that may involve other states even indirectly. One trivial activity may subject you to tax liability. Your lawyer may seek information from a service company that will keep him or her posted on legislation and court decisions affecting businesses in each state. After a review with your counselors, you can decide in which states you will apply and qualify to do business.

Your books should reflect in which states income and expenses arose. Otherwise, you may have to pay state taxes on income that legally should escape. The way you render your bills may also affect sales tax liability.

Some states will hold you responsible for unemployment taxes and other levies if you use traveling sales representatives who solicit orders, even though final acceptance of the orders comes from the head office. One method of avoiding this type of tax is by limiting your sales in such states to independent agents.

If you sell equipment that requires installation or maintenance, you may be able to avoid tax liability in some states by turning the work over to local businesses and letting them handle it for their own accounts.

8

OPERATING THE
RETAIL STORE

Although the large retail chains must adhere to standardized methods of merchandising, the small, independently owned shop can concentrate on style, friendly atmosphere, and an individuality which make shopping there a pleasurable experience for its customers.

The independent retailer who feels overwhelmed by chain-store power and diversity may be encouraged to know that about 60 percent of retail-store selling is done by independent stores. There are close to 2 million retail firms in the United States and most of them are single-unit independent stores.

Instead of trying to serve the entire buying public, the small retail firm can thrive on specialization. Women's clothing boutiques, maternity and half-size clothing, health foods, upholstery, picture framing, greeting card and novelty items—these are some samples of lines ideally suited to small-store treatment. Patrons of these stores are in the market for specific items. If you can approach them with friendly, low-pressure help, your services can often draw them from department-store trade. Try to know your customers by name. Know their tastes and situations. Your individual attention may win their regular patronage.

APPEARANCE AND ATMOSPHERE

Ideally, your specialty shop should be the only one of its kind in the immediate area. However, if there is competition, your store can succeed if you capitalize on the principles or methods of operation in which competitors are weak. You might offer better selection in your merchandise, use more aggressive and intelligent sales promotion techniques, carry higher-priced quality goods or lower-priced lines, arrange better displays, offer more attractive packaging, and stress departments neglected by your competition.

It is good practice to clue the public in to the nature of your store by its exterior appearance, display, and advertising. Travelers, for example, are often attracted to chain restaurants on highways because they know what to expect. Your sign and your show windows should contain some indication of the store's price level and type of service. If you attract customers through misleading displays, their dissatisfaction may result in unfavorable publicity for your shop.

Try to arrange displays for dramatic effect. Set the season's mood. At very little expense, you can design simple decorations and arrange your store windows to represent a theme: school reopening, religious holidays, vacation time.

Arrange fixtures and tables so that your impulse items are stationed at the front of the store to attract customers who are shopping for more staple merchandise. The necessities can be kept near the back of the store. Beyond this sales area will be your stockrooms, which should be adequate to accommodate the items that cannot be easily stacked behind counters. If necessary, make arrangements for an alteration room or repair room. In a clothing store, you will need fitting rooms with good lighting and mirrors and with curtains for privacy. You will want a clean restroom for employees. Lockers should be provided for the protection of their coats, purses, etc.

Your front show windows can be open- or closed-back, depending on your preference, the size and nature of the merchandise, and the type of image you hope to create. With an open-back window, pedestrians on the sidewalks can look into the body of your store. If you want to give the impression of a friendly situation where shoppers are free to examine the merchandise without any purchase in mind, this style of storefront should set your tone. A closed-back window makes the display more prominent and is less likely to invite the casual shopper into your store.

The casual shopper's opinion of your store's merchandise and its quality, price, and style will be formed on the strength of your window displays. Arranging attractive selling displays is a challenge to any dealer. The money expenditure need not be great. You or someone in your family may have a talent for appealing window displays, or you may find a free-lance designer who works for several store owners in your vicinity. You may want to approach local schools which have good commercial art courses; arrangements are sometimes made for promising students to give part-time help in window display.

Try to make the exterior of the store distinctive in some way, whether by use of an attractive awning, a sign, or simply a fresh coat of paint on the trim and door.

The American Institute of Architects can direct you to the nearest architect to advise and aid you in design. Also, seek advice in lighting. Fluorescent lighting sometimes gives a washed-out look to merchandise. Use lighting which illuminates the true colors of the items. Such lighting reduces the return of merchandise by customers who have found that the colors did not look the same under normal lighting conditions.

Color is an important key in creating a mood conducive to sales. If your retail shop is large enough, you might try a different color scheme for each department: bright colors for children's wear or toys; perhaps a peppermint stripe awning or colorful wall decoration. For departments that draw chiefly male customers, brown, russet, tan, and other earth tones are often used, while departments that chiefly attract female customers are often decorated in pastels or bright colors.

Many times it is the atmosphere offered by a restaurant, not its food, that is the critical factor in determining its success. Darker lighting and muted colors give an air of intimacy and encourage leisurely dining. If you are relying on quick turnover of trade, bright lighting and clearer colors will probably fit your mode of service better.

BALANCING YOUR SPACE

In the majority of stores, the greatest volume of profitable sales is produced by well-balanced departments. Space cannot be added to one department without the proportionate reduction of another. For this reason, do not overdevelop one department at the expense of another unless you are convinced that total store sales volume will be increased.

Placement of departments is a major consideration. If you plan structures within the store that cannot be easily shifted, be sure to consult first with an experienced layout consultant or a trade association. Examine trade journals and visit stores carrying your type of merchandise to observe the effectiveness of their arrangements.

The amount of space to be given to a department often determines its location. Departments composed of a large percentage of bulky items and low unit sales are naturally forced to the rear of the store.

Departments made up of small items with a high unit sale come to the front. "Call" merchandise is displayed in the rear. Impulse items, whose sales depend upon display and visual suggestion, should usually be near the front.

To keep your premises attractive and in top condition, be sure the store entrance is kept free of litter, refuse containers, slippery substances, snow, and puddles. Do your part to ensure that the building harbors no rodents or insects. Stairways should be well-lighted and unobstructed, and shelves and display stands sensibly stacked. To eliminate fire hazards, keep the store cleared of excelsior, boxes, rags, paper, flammable liquids, and articles which may ignite from spontaneous combustion. Have heating equipment inspected regularly.

GIVING THAT EXTRA ATTENTION

The successful store owner cannot dictate policy to suit personal convenience. Because of the competition, the owner must generally cater to the tastes and requirements of customers. This may mean keeping one's store open on certain evenings, on holidays, or at other times when related stores are open.

The small store must answer customer complaints promptly and offer redress, when possible. Exchange on colors and sizes should be made willingly, and service on faulty merchandise should be given. With regular customers you create immeasurable goodwill by arranging accommodating payment terms on high-priced items. Some storekeepers win customer loyalty by making unscheduled deliveries for important occasions. Many firms create business by sending reminders, for example, for periodic car servicing, for tire replacements, for carpeting cleaning, or for reupholstering. Be conscientious about your reminders. Do not mail them before the customer's real need is likely to arise. Otherwise, the card will be tossed aside as just another bit of advertising.

Try to develop wide product-and-style knowledge about your merchandise. If you distrust your own taste, hire someone with keen selectivity. Be generous and honest with your advice to customers. Shoppers will remember the salesperson who recommends a lower-priced fixture because it is best-suited to their particular needs. The extra business this honesty brings you will soon compensate for any slight loss you suffer on one sale.

IMPROVING CUSTOMER RELATIONS

Certain attitudes and codes of behavior on the part of the sales staff help to establish an atmosphere of goodwill that makes a shop attractive to customers.

Are you considering service or credit rules that might seem oppressive? Be sure you avoid slighting one customer to the benefit of another. Express appreciation for customer purchases and prompt payments. Be pleasant to salespeople who come into your store. Your customers will be affected by your relationship with anyone who is in the store when they are. If possible, have a private, soundproof room available for discussion with customers or others, when controversy may arise and voices may be raised.

If your shop is losing customers, try to discover the reason. Were former customers alienated by your selling techniques, service, or credit policy? Evaluate your sales staff. Are they able, helpful, and well-informed about your stock? Does your advertising have sales appeal?

When you find out why you are losing a good customer, offer restitution promptly and pleasantly if you have been at fault. Even if the complaint seems unjustified, it is often best to give the customer the benefit of the doubt.

You might consider keeping the names of lost customers on file. Use every opportunity to send letters with a "news flavor"—new items, new policies, new personnel, new services, new floor space, etc.

In other words, build up a definite impression of progress and improvement. Be as ingenious and original as you please—you have nothing to lose and much to gain.

If the lost customer is a business house, watch for opportunities to be of unexpected service. Mail sales tips, clippings of articles, or news items which should interest the company. At times, a lost account can be picked up again by offering a bargain item from stock too limited for general sales.

SPECIAL PROMOTIONAL EVENTS

Special sales will attract many customers if the values offered are genuine. You may choose to promote a special line of goods which you obtained at bargain rates from your wholesaler. To this, you can add some other items of regular stock. However, check the overall results of this promotional gimmick. Sometimes it results in reduced patronage both before and after the sale. Does a long-range increase in customers become noticeable?

Many stores organize attention-attracting events to put their name before the public. Sometimes a contest, fashion show, raffle, celebrity visit, or other popular activity will help to stimulate sales. Food and toiletry distributors frequently make use of samples, coupons, and premium offers to gain attention.

ADVANTAGES OF
A SELF-SERVICE STORE

Self-service stores enjoy lower labor costs and higher sales from open displays of merchandise. Customers can examine items without the pressure of salesclerks. The open displays often lead to impulse buying.

Your savings on wages will be considerable. Customers make their own selections. Clerks are needed only to ring up sales and wrap the merchandise. Of course, some clerk assistance is needed in departments where a knowledge of the goods must be supplied by the store, or where sizes or fittings are in question. Expensive merchandise must also be tended by a salesperson.

Self-service in the small store requires special display stands for apparel. A service desk, equipped with a cash register, is needed for completing the sale and wrapping the goods. To protect cash more effectively, place registers behind a counter which isolates checkers effectively from customers when sales are rung up.

THE DISCOUNT STORE—
SPECIALTY AND DEPARTMENT
STORES

The specialty discount store usually focuses on one particular line of items or, at most, several related lines. These might be records, leather goods, small or large appliances, imported items, or exotic foodstuffs. Although shopping centers are often favored locations, the specialty discount store may be able to occupy low-rent quarters where occupancy costs are considerably lower than those of the department store of the same dimensions. Customer services are reduced or provided at an added charge.

The emphasis in the discount store is on fast-moving merchandise. Usually, the inventory turns about 7 or 8 times annually. Some items turn nearly twice that fast. Many discounters are franchised outlets.

The full-line department store has become a common form of discount retailing. If this is your area of interest, you might begin on a modest scale by opening a concession in an existing discount store. Your rental of department space may run between 5 and 14 percent of your sales, plus the cost of the fixtures you use. Usually your lessor will wish to control the advertising and will limit your maximum margin.

On the other hand, if you buy or build a structure big enough to house merchandise of department-store variety, you might lease out a number of departments to concessionaires and so reduce your own investment and management responsibilities.

PLANNING A BUYING PROGRAM

If you run a large store, you can hire an experienced buyer to formulate a buying plan, schedule trips to domestic and foreign markets, check on delivered items, set prices, and plan advertising and promotions. The small-shop owner will have to assume most of the responsibility for these tasks.

Real buying skill comes from practice. As you start out, adopt the price lines most suited to your customers' pocketbooks. You will have to keep abreast of trends in your line of business and subscribe to upcoming styles even when they do not coincide with your taste. Recognize the point at which trends change. This will not necessarily be dictated by media reports of new fashions. Customers often resist, or even reject, fads. Let sales tendencies guide you.

At first, you may not want to risk being the trendsetter in your town. You might get ideas of local preference by watching displays and advertisements of other stores. Get the advice of suppliers' salespeople. They will usually tell you of any market likes and dislikes which may be based on the effects of climate, social influences, or traits of nationality. Listen to the requests of customers.

Your stock should be balanced between nationally advertised and private brands. The nationally advertised brands attract customers who are constantly reminded of their quality, durability, and general value.

They require little selling effort. Because of the manufacturers' promotion, these brands can usually be merchandised at a narrower profit margin.

Your private brands may often boast a greater value than the comparable nationally known brands. Sometimes it is possible to obtain exclusive local distribution of a brand. Then the store is able to reduce the margin of profit and offer the items at attractive prices. This exclusive right to merchandise, when it is fairly priced and in good taste, often gives the retailer the individuality needed to attract patrons.

When buying a large assortment of items, guard against selecting merchandise that is too similar in quality and price. The similarity will slow customer selection. Intelligent buying requires a thorough knowledge of terms offered by the seller. You must know how goods are packed by quantity and assortment. Sometimes the manufacturer or wholesaler will prepare well-balanced assortments that sell out completely. Often, however, assortments contain end sizes and less desirable colors and styles.

Although the manufacturer's packing of an item is referred to in quantity units, you should always think of merchandise in units of time: a week's, a month's, or a season's supply. Stock of the safe-and-sure volume items on hand and on order should be gauged for a longer time than stock maintained on items needed to add variety, to complete assortments, to build customer interest, or to increase markup.

Before setting up your buying program, study these common practices of manufacturers:

1. Advanced datings are sometimes granted to induce buying prior to actual needs. This alleviates the pressure that sellers experience when goods must be produced and shipped to all buyers at the same time. In such cases, you are not obliged to begin payment until the advance-payment date listed on the invoice.
2. Some manufacturers will sell on a consignment basis. This sales method provides for payment after the sale, sometimes at a regular monthly rate. The advantage in consignment buying is that you do not have to invest your own money in the goods you purchase.
3. Job lots, sample lines, and closeouts can be profitable purchases if you know the quality of goods before you buy. Speculative buying is a form of gambling to be indulged in only with money that is not required for the normal operation of a business. It is a dangerous risk for the average merchant with limited funds.
4. A good buyer will risk reasonable purchases of untried items. Some of them will prove highly profitable; others will not. Here again,

experienced judgment and sufficient money are necessary. Advance buying on a rising market is considered conservative merchandising for experienced merchants. The merchant who has bought in advance can either mark up goods on hand to agree with the increasing market prices or maintain former prices based on the lower cost and thus undersell competitors.

DEALING WITH
THE WHOLESALER

The progressive wholesaler puts as much effort into serving as into selling and can give practical advice and information on many phases of retail selling. Some of the larger wholesalers help their customers select a location. They may even supply, build, or help to choose the equipment. They may also give suggestions on financing, record keeping, and store operation.

Your wholesaler's salesperson can suggest what merchandise you should stock. He or she knows the price ranges that will be profitable for your particular location and type of store and can give good advice as to how much money you should invest in inventory and in store fixtures and equipment.

Your wholesaler may be willing to overlook your credit problems for a time. Your credit rating will be a big factor in your relations with sources of supply during critical times, and to a lesser extent in good times. When goods are scarce, the choicest and most needed merchandise naturally goes to the retailers who pay promptly and buy the most.

Another source of buying is the *drop shipper* who acts as a manufacturer's agent or broker. A drop shipper's function is to sell the merchandise but not to warehouse or handle it in any way, except in the credit and billing. The manufacturer ships directly to the retailer. Specified minimum quantities must be purchased. The manufacturer pays the drop shipper's commission.

USE OF BUYING OFFICES

Many proprietors who are unable to make frequent trips to the market affiliate themselves with a buying office. These offices maintain a staff of experienced buyers, each specializing in certain merchandise. The buyer can line up good sources and lines for the retailer and schedule advance showings of goods, enabling the retailer to accomplish perhaps an entire year's buying in a few days' time. Normally, buying might entail several trips a year and weeks of work.

Some buying offices will handle a store's complete buying program. Most of these offices serve only one store in a given area or city, ensuring the retailer an exclusive line of goods. For a certain percentage of your store's most recent annual sales volume, you can get lower merchandise costs, better selections, and increased profit. Generally, you will need to sign a 1-year agreement. Monthly installment payments can usually be arranged.

Some buying offices also supply their clients with advisory and bulletin services dealing with store operations. They might let you know what goods to dispose of and how to do it, which markdowns to take at certain times, and how to operate on a turnover basis.

You may also become affiliated with a *commission office*, which charges the manufacturer, rather than the retailer, a commission percentage for selling. *Listing offices* are another important buying-service setup for some stores. In return for a uniform fee, the retailer receives a catalog listing various types of merchandise with prices, sources of supply, and minimum-order requirements. The merchant places orders directly with the listed factories at the prices quoted in the catalog. These buyers have searched the market for fast-selling merchandise, with values and prices that enable the independent variety store to compete with the large chains.

Usually the listing office or other types of buying services are used along with the services of the regular wholesaler. Most buying offices do not supplant the services of a regular wholesaler.

STOCK CONTROL
IN THE SMALL STORE

Your stock control system should keep you aware of the quantity of each kind of merchandise on hand. An effective system will provide a guide for what, when, and how much to buy of each style, color, size, price, and brand. It will reduce the number of lost sales resulting from being out of stock on merchandise in popular demand. The system will also locate slow-selling articles and indicate changes in customer preferences.

The size of your establishment and the number of people employed are determining factors in devising an effective stock control plan.

Your accountant will be able to advise you. Can you keep control by observation? Or should you use "on hand, on order, sold" records, detachable ticket stubs, checklists, or a physical inventory?

The observation method, unless you have an unusually alert sense of quantities, fails to keep a satisfactory check on merchandise depletion. It means that you record shortages of goods for reorder as the need occurs to you. Without a better checking system orders are usually placed only at the time of the sales agent's regular visit. Such a haphazard plan often results in lost sales.

Detachable stubs on tickets placed on merchandise afford a good means of control. The stubs, marked with information identifying the articles, are removed at the time the items are sold. The accumulated stubs may then be posted regularly to a perpetual inventory.

A simple checklist, often provided by wholesalers, is another effective counting device. The list provides space to record the items carried and the selling price, cost price, and minimum quantity to be ordered for each. It also contains a column in which to note whether stock on hand is sufficient and when to reorder. You might also keep a chart on slow-moving merchandise, listing each brand and item which begins to lag in sales.

Regardless of how effective your stock control system is, much of its value will be lost unless you do your buying on budget. Usually the buying budget covers a 6-month period, but it could be limited to 3 or 4 months. The main consideration should be the peak selling period. After the sales estimate is completed for a given period, you can prepare the buying budget.

MAINTAINING AN ADEQUATE SUPPLY

Until you have experience on which to draw, you may find it difficult to determine how much stock to carry and how many times yearly your stock must turn to give you a satisfactory return on inventory. Perhaps your wholesaler may be able to advise you at first. To find how rapidly your stock has turned, you divide the dollar amount of sales during a given period by the average of the beginning and ending inventories valued at retail prices for that period. You might choose instead to obtain your ratio by dividing cost of goods sold by the average of beginning and ending inventories figured at cost.

Your turnover rate is governed by the nature of the goods, the sources of supply, and your buying policy. Merchandise should be bought in quantitites that can be sold within a reasonable length of time. The longer the goods are held, the greater the danger of depreciation and obsolescence. Beware of overstocking items that are perishable or have a limited shelf life.

Try to give substantial depth to your standard, essential items, and keep a smaller sampling of your less important or limited-demand items. The latter will add variety to your assortment, though customer demand for them will be sporadic, and you will not lose many sales if you lack certain colors or sizes. You might want to purchase four or five units of your standard items for each nonessential item.

FIGURING OCCUPANCY EXPENSES

Labor and maintenance costs rise when goods are held. Money must be spent for rent, heat, and light for storing or displaying them. In buying larger-than-normal quantities to secure extra-quantity discounts, weigh your quantity discounts against the additional costs of carrying the goods on an "overtime" basis. You may wisely figure that an item carried in stock twice the average length of time is unprofitable unless you can successfully add a higher margin of profit.

Always be sure you do your ordering well in advance of the peak season. This gives you ample goods for large displays at the time when buying interest is intense. Delay in ordering may result in overbuying and late deliveries. Failure to meet demand on time leads to the accumulation of unsold stock.

Take stock once a month to find sales trends. You must take a physical inventory at least once a year in order to prepare your profit-and-loss statement. This inventory involves counting the quantity on hand of each item in stock and determining its value. The total represents the value of the entire stock. Strictly speaking, the physical inventory is not a means of controlling stock, but it gives you a good indication of shortages and oversupplies. For more information on selecting an inventory method, see Chapter 6.

HOW TO PRICE YOUR MERCHANDISE

Profitable pricing of merchandise by the retailer is an indispensable ingredient of success. Prices so low that they do not cover costs, or so high that sales volume suffers, can quickly put a retailer out of business.

What governs markup? Some stores attempt to solve the pricing problem by merely following competition. Better sense says decisions on prices must be made on a more definite, day-by-day basis. Use these principles:

- Markup is essential to cover your operating expenses. It must be large enough to do it.
- You buy to obtain value, but value is determined by what customers consider good. Their idea of value is relative. They compare your prices with those of other stores. Customers will judge your markups as fair or out of line by your prices on items that can be compared from store to store, such as brand goods.
- The greatest purchasing power for retail stores falls in the middle range of income. Therefore, in the nonluxury store it is advisable to have price levels that will appeal to the thrifty or value-conscious segment of the well-to-do class, the large middle-income class, and the upper level of the low-income class.
- If the store is located in a high-income neighborhood, it is probably advisable to offer credit and delivery. You may assume that customers are willing to pay for these extra services.
- If the store is located in a medium-income neighborhood and offers no special services or types of goods to differentiate itself from its competitors, prices will probably have to adhere rather closely to the general level of competitors' prices.
- If the store is located in a low-income neighborhood where many customers require credit and you provide credit service, you are justified in charging more than your cash-and-carry competitors.
- Distance from competitors is an important factor in determining the prices that can be charged. If you own a small grocery store, for example, you would be foolish to attempt to compete on a price basis with a supermarket five or six blocks away. You will have to content yourself with the fill-in, pickup, and "off-hour" business. You may legitimately charge higher prices than competitors who do not render these types of service.

In addition to the problems of location and competition, you must consider three factors: selling price, sales volume, and expense.

If you offer merchandise at a low price, you may enjoy a large sales volume but perhaps not realize sufficient revenue to cover the cost of selling the merchandise. On the other hand, if you have a high selling price, your sales volume may be so low that you will be unable to meet your operating costs.

Clearly, the best prices are those which yield the most dollars after all costs are subtracted. This does not mean the highest possible markup on each unit or a price that will yield maximum sales. It means that prices should be fixed at the point where markup per unit multiplied by the number of units sold will yield the maximum gross margin over operating expenses.

The guiding principle should be that each item will cover its own extra costs plus whatever other contribution it can make to the general overhead and net profit. If demand for some items is small because competitors' prices are lower, an attempt to use the average markup would only make matters worse. With the price for these items higher than that of competitors, sales will decline. As a result, there will be even fewer dollars of gross margin to contribute toward overhead expenses.

Only experience can teach you the feel of the market. If you are to succeed in making up for the things that you are forced to sell at low markups or even at cost, you must learn which items you can sell at higher markups.

FIGURING PROFITABILITY

The average merchant limits the examination of profit to a fairly simple routine. Assume it is winter and you are selling children's gloves and mittens in navy, brown, and multicolor at $5 a pair. This year, youngsters favor the multicolored; conservative brown and navy move at a moderate rate only. You have been paying $36 a dozen for all styles. This cost is low for the selling price; you could pay more and still realize a profit. Sales volume for the dark colors is satisfactory, but you think you could sell more of the favored multicolored gloves and mittens.

Reviewing your overall selling pattern, you decide that you will continue to pay $36 for brown and navy, but for $42 you could get a greater variety in better multicolored gloves and mittens; you will promote this favored seller. You explain your sales strategy to the staff, knowing that the results of the promotion will help you decide what to do next season.

To simplify the example, assume the cash discount equals the freight charges on the gloves. During the previous season, 75 pairs of multicolored gloves and mittens were sold.

$36 per dozen = $3 per pair

$5 − $3 = $2 markup per pair

75 × $2 = $150 gross margin on multicoloreds

This season, 110 multicolored pairs were sold.

$42 per dozen = $3.50 per pair

$5 − $3.50 = $1.50 markup per pair

110 × $1.50 = $165 gross margin on multicolored

$165 − $150 = $15 increased gross profit

The increase is not startling. New lines often are slow to win acceptance. You will need to weigh all factors before deciding whether to continue buying this higher-priced stock. You might continue with the better gloves and mittens because you think the increase in sales will continue. Or, you might consider the effect of this individual item on the business in general. Increase the sale of any line in the store, and all lines usually benefit. A higher volume of sales raises your expenses at a modest rate in comparison with the added net you will realize.

As your sales volume increases, the profit percentage of each new sales dollar increases. This is because the portion of sales volume that represents fixed costs (rent, insurance, etc.) is decreasing. Likewise, as sales volume declines, the percentage of your sales volume that represents profit also declines because your fixed expenses cannot be cut.

Storewide, an increase in profit from larger sales volume is not much. It may be the difference between 3.1 and 3 percent. However, sales volume is the name of the game. The more you sell, the more your profit adds up. Calculate turnover time, the period it takes to ring up sales equivalent to the entire inventory of your store. A retail store should turn over inventory several times a year.

THE INVENTORY TRAP

Sales volume and turnover time are more important than percentage of profit. For example, the owner of a hardware store normally buys 60 heaters every year, each heater costing $50. The heaters sell for $100, thus generating $3000 on the $3000 investment. This 100 percent profit is the same as the store owner makes on all inventory, which the store owner typically turns over once a year.

The supplier offers the hardware store owner a deal: 500 heaters for $7500, a cost per heater of only $15. The hardware store owner can then lower the retail heater price to $90, selling 50 percent more heaters, while making a profit of 500 percent.

The hardware store owner should decline this offer. Keeping cash tied up in unsold heater inventory actually costs the business money. If 75 heaters a year are sold at a price of $90, it takes almost 7 years to sell all the heaters. Total profit on the heaters is $37,500, or about $5350 a year. Had the $7500 been invested in regular inventory, it would have been subject to the hardware store owner's normal 100 percent markup, generating a yearly profit of $7500.

Therefore, it would be a blunder for the hardware store owner to put a large amount of funds into unsellable heaters. Although the percentage of profit was greater in the special deal, the resultant sales volume was too little and the turnover time was too long, so the owner actually loses money on the deal. Had the heaters been priced at $40 retail and sold out entirely in a year, the owner would have profited because the percentage of profit would be greater than normal while the turnover time would not. High sales volume usually does more for profits than inventory bargains.

There are certain special factors to consider in setting your prices.

Leaders and loss leaders.   A leader is an article given a special price, usually below that charged by other merchants. The margin is less than normal. It is offered as a promotional item to increase store traffic. Leaders can be sold at a profit or at a loss. A loss leader, in its simplest terms, is one that is sold below its cost. It may be priced below its cost plus the estimated expenses involved in handling it. If the invoice cost of an item is 31 cents, and if the expenses are 18 cents and it is sold for anything under 49 cents, it becomes a loss leader. A good leader sells itself. It should need no promotional effort. Items that are in everyday use, that are bought frequently, and that have a well-established value make good leaders.

Staples.   Staples have a higher-than-average cost because the markdown expectation is below the average. They are sold on value and price. Higher-price lines will cost less in proportion to the lower-price lines. The lower-price lines sell faster, are in the store a shorter time, and cost less to handle. Low-price lines should give value. People are more likely first to sample low-price lines. If these are found satisfactory, the same persons may later become steady users of both the popular and high-price lines. Staple volume depends on store traffic. Unless there is something distinctive about such merchandise, it does not benefit from promotion.

Novelties.   Novelties that catch on show a good markup at the start and as long as they continue to be popular. Soon, however, other manufacturers come into the field. The price is then reduced, and customers begin to look for new items. To cash in fully during the popular stage, you must anticipate your needs. If you are overstocked on novelties in the initial period before the price is reduced, your profits will be reduced by the necessary markdowns. If they sell out and must be reordered, the reorder may not arrive until after everyone has purchased elsewhere.

Extremely fashionable goods. These are in the same class as novelties. The fad may involve a color or a design, but its appeal depends on novelty. The markup is high. So are the markdowns at the end of the season.

Fast-selling items. These usually carry a lower-than-average markup. This is only fair. Their rapid turnover reduces the handling expense. It is important to have competitive prices on fast-selling items. Customers are familiar with their prices and values and are critical of small price differences on fast-selling, popular goods. Slow-selling merchandise should have a higher-than-average markup, under the presumption that it is normal for the item to sell slowly. If the item is not a normal slow seller, it may have become unattractive to purchasers because of its quality or price. First, check how your competitors are handling the item. They may be causing your slow sales by a more aggressive pricing policy. You may have to lower your markup in response. If the product is not selling normally anywhere, you may have to slash your markup to get rid of it. Consider dropping the item in the future.

Prices fixed by manufacturers. Pricing sometimes is not left entirely to the discretion of the merchant. State and federal laws governing retail selling should be checked with your supplier.

SIMPLE FORMULAS
TO FIND PROFITABLE MARKUPS

To understand the relation of costs, markup, selling prices, and gross margin, it is necessary to restudy some retailing mathematics. You may not make constant use of the formulas and calculations which follow, but you should understand them. They are the ABCs in the language of the retailer.

● *Cost of goods.* Cost of goods is the freight-inclusive cost at the store. It is expressed in dollars or as a percentage of sales. The cost divided by the selling price is the cost percentage. Thus, if an item costs $1 and sells at $1.50, the cost percentage would be:

$$\frac{\$1.00}{\$1.50} = 67 \text{ percent}$$

- *Initial markup.* Initial, or original, markup is what is added to the cost to get selling price, or the difference between cost price and selling price. It is expressed as both a percentage of sales and a percentage of cost. Thus, in the case of a $1 cost and $1.50 selling price, the initial markup would be 50 cents. That is 33⅓ percent of selling price,

$$\frac{\$0.50}{\$1.50} = 33\frac{1}{3} \text{ percent}$$

or 50 percent of cost price,

$$\frac{\$0.50}{\$1.00} = 50 \text{ percent}$$

- *Retail reductions.* Retail reductions cover all reductions of the original retail price, including markdowns and shrinkage. They are expressed as a percentage of final selling price or as a percentage of cost.
- *Additional markups.* Occasionally, it is discovered that an item has been priced too low in error, or for some reason it is found desirable to raise the original price. Increases after the original markup has been taken are called additional markups. Downward revisions of the retail price are also common.
- *Markdowns.* A markdown is a reduction of an original selling price. After a retail price is established on any item (by adding a markup to its cost), the price may have to be reduced for any one of a number of reasons, such as
  - For special sales to stimulate volume
  - To clean out remnants, leftovers, poor assortments, and damaged goods
  - To get rid of poor buys
  - To meet sudden changes in the market price
  Early markdowns are the smallest. The sooner you discover that merchandise is not moving and start taking markdowns, the smaller your loss will be. The time to sell is when people want to buy and not at the end of the season after everyone has bought. When you start to mark down, it is best to forget all about cost and continue marking down until the goods are sold.
- *Gross margin.* Gross margin, sometimes called realized margin, gross profit, or maintained markup, means the amount realized after all retail reductions—the difference between the final selling price and

the cost of goods. It is expressed in dollar amounts and also as a percentage of sales.

It is easy to determine the *selling price* if you know the cost and percentage over cost by which you are marking up prices. The formula is:

Cost × markup percentage = markup

Cost + markup = selling price

Suppose all the items in the store get marked up 30 percent. An item costs you $1.50, 30 percent of which is the 45 cent markup, or profit. Adding markup to cost determines the price. Here, 45 cents plus the $1.50 cost becomes the $1.95 sale price of the item.

The average markup for the store is composed of numerous rates of markup for the different goods handled.

Some goods will have to be sold at a close margin, either because they are competing in price with merchandise in other stores, or because they are used as leaders to bring in trade. Other items will be sold at about the average markup sought. Still other articles will carry a long profit markup. Then there will also be variations in relative sales of the goods at different markup rates.

A little arithmetic will show how to arrive at the average total store markup under such conditions.

Let us assume for simplicity that there are three items, or three departments, with sales and markups as follows:

Department	Sales	Maintained markup, percent
A	$20,000	20
B	10,000	25
C	5,000	35
Total	$35,000	

The gross margins then would be

A	$4000
B	2500
C	1750
Total gross margin	$8250

Average store markup $= \dfrac{\$8250}{\$35,000} = 23.6$ percent

If the average maintained markup is not sufficient to allow for a net profit after expenses are deducted, then the sales volume must be increased to lower the expense percentage, expenses must be reduced, or some revisions in the lines must be made so that more goods are sold at a higher markup. Margins cannot usually be increased by arbitrarily raising selling prices.

The next problem is to calculate an initial markup to establish original retail prices, making due allowance for markdowns and shrinkage, which are known as *retail reductions*. If goods are priced at the outset at the markup which is desired as a final maintained figure, and if markdowns or shrinkage occurs later, you may find that the realized margin is far below the total you had planned to cover expenses and profit.

The retail reductions will apply more to some lines than to others. Some staple lines in steady demand, with little or no spoilage, breakage, or theft and on which no cut-price sales are made, are seldom subject to reductions. The initial markup on such goods may be counted on as a maintained markup.

But on merchandise having a style or use obsolescence on which markdowns must be anticipated, or on goods subject to deterioration, pilferage, or other shrinkage, the initial markup will have to be higher than the planned, maintained, or realized markup.

At the start, you will have to make some rather arbitrary allowances for such anticipated retail reductions. As you gain experience, you will know more precisely what goods will be subject to the reductions and how much the reductions will usually amount to.

One object of good merchandising is to reduce markdowns to a bare minimum. This goal involves improvement in practically all phases of the store's operations, but principally in buying, selling, stock care, and pricing.

However, you can plan a markdown when setting the original price; thus, when you mark down the item later, you still end up with the amount of profit you intended. The formula for setting the original markup to take into account a subsequent markdown is as follows. (Note that these percentages are figured on the sales price, not your cost, because a sale advertised to shoppers as "10 percent off" refers to a discount from the sales price.)

Markup percentage on sale price

$$= \frac{\text{percent gross profit desired } + \text{ markdown percentage}}{1.00 \; + \; \text{markdown percentage}}$$

Example

Percent gross profit required = 40 percent

Markdown percentage = 5 percent

The markup percentage on the sale price would be calculated as follows:

$$\frac{0.40 + 0.05}{1.05} = \frac{0.45}{1.05} = 0.4286, \text{ or } 42.86 \text{ percent}$$

If a markup of about 43 percent on the sale price is required, the percentage by which the cost price would have to be increased would be approximately 75 percent; that is,

1.00 (selling price) − 0.43 (markup) = 0.57 (cost)

$$\frac{0.43}{0.57} = 0.7544, \text{ or } 75.44 \text{ percent markup on cost}$$

Many goods are bought to sell at a designated retail price in accordance with competition and with your analysis of what price lines will sell best. When you are buying goods to advantage so that you can sell at the desired prices, the initial markup is automatically set by the cost price.

Suppose that you want to carry a $1.95 line of toys and that the quality you want will cost $17.40 a dozen, or $1.45 each. The initial markup is set at $1.95 less $1.45, or $0.50. Thus, the initial markup would automatically be 25.6 percent of the selling price. Excessive retail reductions would bring the realized margin dangerously low.

If allowance must be made for markdowns and shrinkage, two questions arise:

- At a given initial markup and an estimated shrinkage, as a percentage of sales, what will the realized gross margin be?
- In order to realize a planned gross margin with a given initial markup, how much can be allowed for retail reductions?

The calculation for the first situation is as follows:

Cost of goods × percent retail reductions = cost reduction

Initial markup − cost reduction = maintained or realized markup

INITIAL MARKUP TO PRODUCE SPECIFIED GROSS PROFIT, ALLOWING FOR STATED RETAIL REDUCTIONS

Gross profit to be realized, percent	Ratio of retail merchandise reductions to net sales, percent					
	5	6	7	8	9	10
	Gross markup required, percent					
25	28.57	29.25	29.91	30.56	31.19	31.82
26	29.52	30.19	30.84	31.48	32.11	32.73
27	30.48	31.13	31.78	32.41	33.03	33.64
28	31.43	32.08	32.71	33.33	33.94	34.55
29	32.38	33.02	33.64	34.26	34.86	35.45
30	33.33	33.96	34.58	35.19	35.78	36.36
31	34.29	34.91	35.51	36.11	36.70	37.27
32	35.24	35.85	36.45	37.04	37.61	38.18
33	36.19	36.79	37.38	37.96	38.53	39.09
34	37.14	37.74	38.32	38.89	39.45	40.00
35	38.10	38.68	39.25	39.81	40.37	40.91
36	39.05	39.62	40.19	40.74	41.28	41.82
37	40.00	40.57	41.12	41.67	42.20	42.73
38	40.95	41.51	42.06	42.59	43.12	43.64
39	41.90	42.45	42.99	43.52	44.04	44.55
40	42.86	43.40	43.93	44.44	44.95	45.45
41	43.81	44.34	44.86	45.37	45.87	46.36
42	44.76	45.28	45.79	46.30	46.79	47.27
43	45.71	46.23	46.73	47.22	47.71	48.18
44	46.66	47.17	47/66	48.15	48.62	49.09
45	47.62	48.11	48.60	49.07	49.54	50.00

Example

Percent initial markup = 40
Percent retail reductions = 5

The maintained markup would be calculated as follows:

1.00 − 0.40 = 0.60 (cost of goods)

0.60 × 0.05 = 0.03 (reductions at cost)

0.40 − 0.03 = 0.37 (maintained markup)

Suppose, in the case of $1.95 toys, that you estimate the retail reductions to be 5 percent. What would the realized margin then be? The calculations follow:

1.00 − 0.256 = 0.744 (cost of goods)

$0.744 \times 0.05 = 0.0372$, or 3.72 percent reductions at cost

$0.256 - 0.037 = 0.219$, or 21.9 percent maintained markup
or gross margin

If the 21.9 percent gross profit is lower than you want, just what retail reductions may be taken to leave you the minimum realized margin (say, 23 percent)?

Those calculations to arrive at this answer follow:

Initial markup percent − percentage of gross margin desired
= percent of reductions at cost

Reductions at cost ÷ cost of goods
= percent reductions allowable at retail

For example,

$0.40 - 0.37 = 0.03$

$$\frac{0.03}{0.60} = 0.05, \text{ or 5 percent allowable retail reductions}$$

Let us apply this calculation to the $1.95 toys where the initial markup is set. You want to know just how heavy a retail reduction they will stand to give you a final stipulated gross profit, in this case 23 percent. You know that the initial markup will be 25.6 percent of sales, and you know the desired gross margin. Let us see in this practical example how far you can go in markdowns and shrinkage reductions.

$0.256 - 0.230 = 0.026$

$$\frac{0.026}{1.000 - 0.256} = \frac{0.026}{0.744} = 0.0349, \text{ or 3.49 percent retail reductions}$$

You know that at the cost and selling price of these toys, you can afford to take retail reductions of only 3.49 percent if you want to realize at least 23 percent gross profit.

KEEPING A RECORD OF CUSTOMER SALES

Well-trained sales personnel are essential to successful retail selling. Chapter 15 gives some valuable instructions on the training of your sales staff. Other aspects of selling your product, including advertising, are dealt with in Chapter 18. Another ingredient necessary for maintaining smooth store-customer relations is good records management. Often the retail store can keep adequate records without an undue amount of paperwork. Your customers' sales slips, filed vertically, can be used as a sole record of customer accounts. Once a month, you can total these slips, or, if it is more convenient, post each sales total to a monthly statement immediately after it is made. If storage of these records becomes a problem, you can reduce the amount of space needed by microfilming your records. Consult the yellow pages of your telephone directory for the names of agencies from which you can rent one of these devices.

CUTTING DELIVERY COSTS

Your delivery service might be limited to employing a youngster on a bicycle carrying office supplies, medical prescriptions, or some other small, easily handled item. Some stores use motorbike delivery. A proprietor might use his or her automobile or station wagon to provide this service. On a larger scale, the store may use its own truck, hire a service which delivers for several companies, or mail merchandise parcel post. Check with delivery services for rate quotations, which are generally computed by weight and time. In some states, rates are governed by regulations. Some delivery services charge a set fee.

Your first job is to compile a factual study of the advantages and disadvantages to your store of various methods of shipping. Will your business benefit from a cash-and-carry policy? Or should you require a minimum purchase from customers before delivery is made available? Perhaps charging a reasonable fee will satisfy them and at the same time enable you to realize an adequate profit on the sale.

9
PROFIT POINTERS
FOR THE
WHOLESALER

Operating on your own, you need to promote a bold marketing program which will gain the attention of manufacturers and retailers. Your services must appear unique and superior. At the same time, you will need to observe techniques that reduce the expense of handling your goods and that protect your gross margin rates.

SERVING THE RETAILER

Your value to the small retailer lies in your ability to combine a vast number of orders from your customers so as to obtain reduced rates from manufacturers. This enables the retailer, in turn, to offer merchandise at a price competitive with large outlets. Many manufacturers compete with wholesalers by offering their merchandise directly to retailers, but small manufacturers must rely upon wholesalers because they lack the sales personnel necesary to move their goods themselves.

Even in the face of competition with manufacturers, wholesalers have the resources to enable them to do business. The size of a wholesaler's order entitles the wholesaler to price discounts not extended by manufacturers to retailers. Also, in computing discounts, manufacturers consider the reduction in shipping costs that results from sending a large amount of goods to one place. Wholesalers can thus profit if the addition of their overhead expenses to the cost of merchandise still permits them to charge the retailer a lower price than the retailer could have gotten from the manufacturer.

In choosing with whom to do business, the retailer considers the extra services the wholesaler performs. Wholesalers sort goods, grade them, and break the goods down into manageable quantities. When retailers try to reduce their on-site inventory to get better effect from their cash flow, their wholesaler becomes, in effect, the holder of their inventory, which strengthens the relationship between wholesaler and retailer. Wholesalers also get involved in the promotional advertising of products, even advising retailers how to display their products. Probably the most important service of the wholesaler is the extension of merchandise credits to the retailer, easing the retailer's cash problems and hopefully enabling the retailer to move more of the wholesaler's goods. The retailer's financial picture also can be improved if the wholesaler takes back inventory that the retailer is having trouble moving in return for credit toward other merchandise.

You may offer other assistance. Many wholesalers compose accounting forms for use by the retailer, offer financial aid, or maintain real estate files to inform business people of available store locations. The range of cooperative efforts is wide. Remember, your business depends on your retailer's success above all else.

Help the retailer anticipate demand. Since you cover many outlets in the market, you know which items consumers are buying and which they are not. When a price increase is likely, tip your customers off in advance, enabling them to order quickly at the lower rate. Your sales personnel can further help customers by relating to them the good practices of the efficient merchants in your clientele. They can instruct retailers on good merchandising techniques, encouraging them to enhance their image with attractive storefronts, more effectively designed and illuminated interiors, and attention-arresting advertising campaigns.

When losses from fires or floods, or acute cash flow problems such as those encountered during recessionary times, threaten to put a retailer out of business, the wholesaler should take every possible measure to keep the retailer from bankruptcy. The loss of a retailer causes a wholesaler to suffer in two ways: an outlet is lost for the wholesaler's merchandise and the wholesaler loses money on the items the merchant has taken but not yet paid for. If your cash flow will allow it, aid a troubled retailer by extending the repayment period or easing credit terms.

If possible, maintain showrooms where retailers can bring their customers to examine goods and installations which they do not have in their stock. If you are an efficient wholesaler, your warehouse will be a stockroom from which the retailer can draw goods at the times needed and in the quantities required.

Wholesalers usually offer prompt delivery on small quantities. The retailer does not wish to risk the acquisition of large quantities of goods which may not sell and may order unknown goods in sample quantities until the demand for them has been established. Dealing with a wholesaler enables the retailer to keep stock supplies small. This means you will have to have facilities for storage of heavy, light, bulky, odoriferous, rapidly deteriorating, and many other types of product, depending on the lines which you supply.

Trading with a wholesaler instead of directly with the manufacturer reduces the retailer's task of buying. You must keep the retailer posted on price changes and new lines of merchandise. Your service is valuable to the retailer since it eliminates much of his or her accounting and clerical cost.

Today, a wholesaler who runs a computerized operation is able to help a retailer maintain inventory automatically. For example, a wholesaler might use pressure-sensitive labels on products; on making a sale, the retailer strips off that label and pastes it on a card. The wholesaler receives a batch of cards, runs them through a computer, and ascertains the retailer's requirements in terms of profitable merchandise.

Retailers with sound pricing policies help lower wholesalers' operating expenses by creating a predictable volume for their goods. If you know the nature, quantity, and frequency of retailer's orders, you can plan operations so as to reduce selling, billing, recording, shipping, and storage expenses.

Many independent wholesalers have set up a procedure for assisting retailers in pricing their merchandise. The retailer must know how to meet competition by varying markups on individual items and finding the markup which results in the largest volume of sales, giving the best profit.

PLANNING YOUR PHYSICAL OPERATIONS

Most of the nation's wholesalers use electronic equipment of some kind in their operation: computers for inventory and billing or machines to read the labels on cans and cartons. Modernization can increase your profits by reducing your operating costs and increasing the volume of merchandise your facility can handle.

It may be difficult to keep your prices competitive, as the transportation costs of moving your goods great distances rise with the cost of gas and the deteriorating condition of our highways. The alternatives to buying your own trucks are few: railway freight, air delivery, and contract trucking. If you wish to open up a new branch of your business to be nearer to some of your customers, plan the location with an eye toward minimizing your transportation costs. Some wholesalers combine to share distribution centers, thus reducing the expenses of opening a new branch.

Although your customers may prefer delivery at a specific time, they will understand if you plan the deliveries so as to cut fuel costs in the serving of *all* your customers. If you can keep to an established schedule of sales calls and deliveries, loading your trucks and routing their stops efficiently, your organization will establish a reputation for reliability that your customers will appreciate.

CHOOSING YOUR TERRITORY

If you extend your territory too widely, you will probably increase your operating cost out of proportion to the volume you can hope to obtain. You will thus dissipate profits realized in areas which you can more legitimately serve. On the other hand, if you do not extend enough, you may forfeit desirable trade. How do you determine the dimensions of the territory you may profitably serve? You can approximate the boundaries by comparing the cost of serving each questionable district with the gross profit to be secured from it. Since all costs, other than selling and delivery, can be charged to outgoing merchandise on an equal basis regardless of destination, you can determine the profitability of a given area by adding selling and delivery costs. Then compare the result with the gross profit which the area yields.

Before opening a new territory, scout your direct competition to see whether other companies have built up a big following on their own brands. Is there a retail-owned wholesale house in the territory? At what price is your type of merchandise selling in that territory?

Do not refrain from entering a new territory just because competition is there already. If it appears as if you have reached agreement with another wholesaler to respect each other's markets, you may both be prosecuted for violating antitrust law. Also illegal are arrangements with manufacturers or distributors to fix prices or to prevent customers from buying an item unless they also purchase other, less desired goods.

EXPANDING SALES VOLUME
WITH CASH-AND-CARRY
OUTLETS

Many wholesalers find it profitable to have a cash-and-carry branch. Select your location carefully. Be sure it is outside the area covered by your own sales force. After all, you wish to draw your trade from competitors, not from your own sales force. When a branch is opened, send circulars to every prospective customer in the region. List the staple merchandise they can obtain from your outlet at low prices. Later, send a second circular to the retailers in the vicinity who are not patronizing the branch.

Cash-and-carry branch prices should be high enough to cover all cost plus a fair profit. Close any branch which constantly shows a loss. To be most effective, the outlet should be geared to handle only fast-moving items which can be stocked in a small area and readily assembled for customers. Do not stock it with every item carried by the parent house. If you find a profitable location in an area covered by sales agents, be sure the outlet does not carry the long-margin items for which you have the exclusive agency and on which you rely for much of your profit.

When possible, have the manufacturer drop-ship merchandise to the branch. This eliminates several handlings and greatly reduces cost.

HOW MAIL-ORDER SALES
INCREASE PROFITS

You might consider extending your market by using mail-order wholesaling to reach locations outside your convenient delivery area. In these transactions, your customer should pay delivery costs. If feasible, terms should be net, cash in advance.

The price sheet is your only contact with the mail-order customer. It should contain all items offered and all terms, allowances, and discounts. Every price on the sheet should remain in effect until either an amendment or a new sheet is mailed out. Note that it is illegal to quote different prices to different customers without some adequate economic justification.

Be sure that your mailing list does not include any customer who is contacted by your sales personnel. Avoid mailing price sheets to customers in direct competition with a good customer who is being served by your sales force.

Begin your mail-order program by sending price sheets to prospective customers. To those from whom you get no response within 3 months, say, send a friendly letter reminding them of the range of your services and products and stating that they will be continued on the mailing list for a further limited period. Perhaps they have not looked at the price sheets that were sent to them. Request that they examine them. After a further period with no response, a final notice that as they have not taken advantage of your offers, their names will be removed from your mailing list at the end of 30 days. If no business results, strike their names from the list.

CONTROLLING COSTS

Because of the narrowing gross margins, rising expense levels, and increased merchandising of controlled brands, you will need an effective system of cost control to operate on a profitable basis.

Keep a constant surveillance on your sales force for checks on sales and margin analysis. Ask for a written report on sales volume obtained by each salesperson in the various departments and on the volume of each product, class, or brand. It is also revealing to check the dollar gross margin of each salesperson, minus direct expenses for which he or she is responsible, as a means of finding the salesperson's effectiveness. Evaluate the records of the total or departmental sales to each customer. Keep close control over the credit-granting powers and collection activities of salespeople, using records to disclose current conditions in the outstanding accounts of each salesperson's customers. These policies and more stringent credit can speed your collections and reduce your bad-debt losses.

What method should you use in compensating your sales force? Many wholesalers base commissions on dollar gross margin, but this in itself may not provide a sufficient incentive. Try extra awards for expense reductions and increased volume. You might institute an annual contest to reward enterprising salespeople. Since many find the recognition of their peers and the thrill of competition to be as satisfying as monetary incentives, a contest with a reasonable prize may pick up sales volume and boost office morale simultaneously.

Net profits are a result of two variables: *dollar gross margins* and *dollar operating expenses*. Net profits may be changed by a shift in either or both of the variables. You can get an increase in net profits by eliminating unprofitable customers, even though such a move reduces the total sales volume. Your savings in operating expenses will exceed the loss in dollar gross margin.

Try to make an account profitable to you by inducing the customer to increase his or her order size. This cuts credit, delivery, and selling expenses.

Look beyond the dollar gross margin when determining the relative profitability of different brand groups. Be sure to weigh the actual dollar contribution the brand group makes to the net profits of the business. For example, one brand may carry a high gross-margin rate, but because of small sales volume, it contributes little to the dollar gross margin of your business. Another brand may have a low gross-margin rate, but because of large sales volume, it contributes a large part of your dollar gross margin.

GOOD ACCOUNTING NEEDED
FOR CONTROL SYSTEMS

Constant vigilance and guidance of financial position are essential to the successful wholesaler. Annual statements are revealing, but current control demands that the manager be guided by detailed records and reports on daily, weekly, and monthly operations. You will require a sales and gross-margin analysis to determine your most profitable commodities, customers, and brands, from the standpoint of dollar gross margin. Your inquiries will disclose slow-moving and duplicate items and brands which should be eliminated. With careful daily or weekly analysis, you can find the gross-margin rates on individual items needed to obtain a satisfactory average gross margin for the business as a whole. In addition, your salespeople will be kept alert if their sales and gross-margin attainments by commodity, departments, customers, and brands are regularly reported.

How do you proceed with your analysis? Find the cost of goods and gross margins by items or by totals on each invoice. Classify by departments, sales personnel, or customers. Your totals should aid you in making policy decisions.

A simple way to arrive at your figures is by columnar analysis of invoices, yielding volume of sales, cost of goods sold, and gross margins of individual commodities or departments. Enter the current cost of each item on the office copy of the invoice and extend it to obtain the cost of goods sold. Then subtract this from the extended selling price to obtain the gross margin for each item.

Some wholesalers enter only the cost extensions on the invoices. Then they total the sales price figures and the cost figures of the items listed and deduct the cost total from the sales price total to get the gross margin only for the invoice as a whole, disregarding sales and gross-margin analyses for each commodity, but making such analyses for the sales force and for the entire business.

Where the wholesaler's only interest is in total sales gross margins for the house and for each salesperson, the invoices are first sorted according to salespeople. If figures for sales and margins are needed by individual commodity departments, the invoice items can be resorted by commodity departments.

To proceed with the columnar-analysis method, prepare an analysis sheet with a column for each department and post the amounts of the invoice lines into appropriate columns. Add these columns daily, semiweekly, or weekly and transfer the totals to summary sheets. If you want a departmental analysis by salespeople, sort their invoices and use a separate columnar sheet for each salesperson. Total all these to secure house totals.

Finding the profit and loss by customers, commodities, brands, departments, and territories is as important as gross-margin analysis. To do this you must allocate all expenses of operations.

You may be able to locate weakness in your profit structure by making comparisons with the costs and revenues reported by sample segments of the wholesaling field. Use the methods developed by the U.S. Department of Commerce for allocating unit costs to individual customers and to commodity departments or lines. Your accountant can readily install these for you with the aid of the booklets issued by the Commerce Department.

Your need for control is particularly great if you operate on a principle of low gross margin with high turnover.

WORKING FOR GOOD
INVENTORY CONTROL

Inventory represents a large proportion of your capital. Your success often depends on your instincts for maintaining a suitable quantity of each item you sell. Data provided by your inventory-control system should call attention to the need to reorder when an item approaches the predetermined minimum stock level. Avoid an oversupply of any item, whether staple or seasonal, and thus increase the rate of turnover. Inventory control discloses slow-moving items and permits you to reduce purchase quantities and to set minimum stocks at lower levels.

Today, the management and control of inventory can be computerized. You may want to explore this type of application in relation to your business, but as a small, independent wholesaler you may not be ready for the complexities of the computer. In this case, you may turn to your accountant for advice on the most satisfactory system of inventory control for your business. Although there are many variations of detail, the inventory-control systems fall into three classes: (1) observation methods, (2) periodic stock-count methods, and (3) perpetual inventory control.

The ideal inventory-control system furnishes a measure of the actual amount of stock on hand of each item and its value at any time. It also shows the rate of movements, or sales, of each item.

The *observation method* is simplest and least expensive. But it is generally the least satisfactory because heavy reliance is placed on judgment and memory. It gives you no record of the rate of movement or quantity on hand of any given item. There is no information on which to base minimum and maximum stock points, ordering points, and economical purchase quantities. It is not really an inventory control.

The *stock-count method* is an improvement. A regular periodic count gives you some indication of the rate of movement, as well as of the quantity on hand. It also furnishes a written record of your experience with any item. Its principal disadvantages are opportunity for error, lack of data between counts, and concealed errors in the calculated rate of movement.

The *perpetual inventory-control method* furnishes the most complete information, although it involves a greater investment of time and money. But the cost is moderate in view of the controls it gives. Under this system, you record complete data on every item of merchandise. Enter each purchase, receipt, sales, and return on this record. This procedure eliminates the necessity of taking physical count. You will have the previous inventory balance, plus receipts, minus sales, to equal the quantity on hand. Occasionally you will want to take a physical inventory to check *actual* count against *book* count.

On small items, you might consider the use of a container as a reorder reminder. With this system, you fix a point at which your supply will need replenishing, allowing for gaps in ordering and delivering time. This "cushion" amount is placed in a separate container. When the regular source is exhausted, you will be alerted to the need to reorder.

To gain a true perspective on your merchandise, you might keep a file box containing cards for every item in stock. List the number sold annually, cost per unit, and total expected value. Arrange all cards in the file box from highest to lowest according to sales quantity. This enables you to evaluate the relative profitability of each item in stock and decide which should be culled from your lists.

A similar system of inventory control can be set up on a small business computer. However, there can be problems in computer-assisted inventory control using automatic reorder points. The correct timing of inventory purchases often hinges upon complex variables not programmable into the computer. For instance, if the manufacturer will be offering special deals because of a very successful production run, you may alter your inventory purchase pattern to get a good buy. An automatic reorder may also fail to take into account a revised sales forecast for the next period. If a new product is altering customers' needs for other products (for example, a new engine with less need for lubricating oils), you want flexibility on reorders while you determine what the pattern of new customer demand will be. Finally, automatic reorders will not benefit customers who expect a great deal of personal service.

The computer is most valuable for rapid sorting. It can scan your items to pick out those not in stock. A computer can quickly point out all the items furnished by one of your suppliers. Also, it can automatically inform you when your goods fall below the reorder point. Traditional methods will do the same but can never equal computer speed.

A good perpetual inventory-control system will reduce the amount of goods you need to carry in stock. Expenses will be reduced. Purchasing fast-moving merchandise in diminishing quantities to achieve a high turnover may merely result in increased buying, receiving, and other expenses. It may give you a higher cost of goods and an increased risk of out-of-stocks, without compensating advantages. By reducing inventory, you can often reduce financial charges on your investment (interest, insurance, taxes) as well as space costs. If you have space to fill, try eliminating slow-moving items and replacing them with goods having a higher turnover rate. Your investment costs will be the same, but the increase in total dollar gross margin should leave larger net profits.

Another recourse is to increase sales volume without proportionate increase in inventory. This results in a larger dollar gross margin without increasing the finance and storage expenses of inventory.

10
SERVICE FIRM MANAGEMENT

A common complaint among consumers is the lack of qualified service people to fix items ranging from a small appliance to a furnace in the basement. Many communities need the services of skilled and reliable service people. If you have the skill and training, a service firm may prove a profitable investment of time and money. Even if you decide to set up in a community which already has established service firms, you may be able to distinguish your firm above others in the community. There are techniques to attract and hold customers.

Quality work at a reasonable price is one success formula for the service firm. Your reputation from satisfied customers will bring others to you. From the start, let people know right away of your desire to excel. Post the industry code of ethics and standards in your shop along with a poster of your standards which exceed the norm. For example, have a longer warranty period than your competitors and offer service repairs for a greater range of problems. A more liberal credit policy or acceptance of credit cards may be sufficient to differentiate in the minds of customers your business from competitors. The goodwill you create will enable you to keep your customers and create new ones. The word-of-mouth recommendations of satisfied customers are the greatest force in expanding a clientele.

ORGANIZING THE OPERATION

Many service firms suffer from poor management stemming from inexperience and inadequate training. Fine trade skills alone usually do not sustain the service firm. Mastery of good bookkeeping methods is needed as well. Although the inventory control of materials and supplies may be fairly simple, you will still need to adhere to orderly storekeeping procedures. Customers become irritated when their goods can be located only after an extensive search. An identification system for work in progress is essential.

Service firms such as beauty parlors, travel agencies, and investment counseling firms of course rely on glamorous surroundings to win customers. If your type of service requires no customer visits, you will be able to locate in a low-rent building and can create a friendly impression with magazines, radio music, or perhaps television in the waiting room.

Be honest with your customers. If an appliance can be repaired at a reasonable rate, do not try to pressure the customer into buying a complete replacement. High-pressure tactics betray themselves quickly and your reputation suffers. If you run a repair shop, try to keep customers informed on the status of their appliances. Will the repair take longer than you forecast? Is the bill going to be significantly higher? Let your customer know before proceeding with the work. For example, an automobile repair shop should tell a customer that the radiator which seemed repairable needs to be replaced. Obtain a phone number so that you can keep your customer posted. If you can supply a substitute while an item is being repaired, you will win a large measure of loyalty from the customer.

Can you offer extras for services which run over a certain amount of money? Some service stations, for example, offer a free car wash after expensive repairs. In some service businesses, such premiums as glassware, simple toys, or lollipops are given to children. How much more friendly an atmosphere is created when the preschool tot is given a toy to play with while waiting for a first haircut. And a lollipop at the end will leave a positive impression. The child is likely to urge his or her parents to return to your shop for the next haircut.

The popularity of do-it-yourself repairs would seem to threaten the existence of service shops. However, this has not proved true. The do-it-yourself project often leads to complications which drive the amateur to the repair shop for solutions. Do not hesitate to offer advice to the householder who is trying to cope with home plumbing, carpentry, or mechanical problems. Sooner or later you may be paid to do the job that is too complicated for an amateur's untrained skills.

Some service firms thrive by directing their appeal toward a small segment of the total market. For example, a service station might try to attract taxis or truck drivers. An employment agency may specialize in placing engineers, office help, or domestics. A laundry could emphasize the cleaning of slipcovers and rugs, and attract the singles trade with special advertising and low rates on shirts and blouses.

BUILDING A CLIENTELE

What steps can you take to attract customers when you are opening your shop? Advertising in your daily paper, perhaps with some discount offer, may make your community quickly aware of your presence. Perhaps the newspaper will carry a brief article about you and your shop. The yellow pages of your telephone book will keep the town continually aware of your location and services.

Keep your advertisements simple, clearly stated, and consistent. Do not alter your style from day to day. Your makeup should be easily recognizable. You can continue developing your business by announcing your services to new markets, which you can identify from news stories about newlyweds, newcomers to the community, purchases of houses, births, deaths, departure of daughters and sons for college, promotions, and hobbies. You can make your shop especially welcome if you contribute time, money, or personal effort to community drives. You might lend some item of equipment to a parade or fair or devote a space in your front window to posters. Usually credit is given, either verbally or by program, to merchants who aid in welfare drives. Your name is once again placed before the public, and in a favorable light.

If you run a general repair shop, demonstrate your overall expertise when discussing your services so the customer will be aware that you can deal with other problems besides the one you are attending to. For example, when the customer picks up repaired storm windows in February, you or your helpers can point out that a lawn mower or hedge trimmer may need overhauling by spring. A motel operator can inform departing guests of special attractions in the coming off-season. A locksmith might also discuss the need for a burglar alarm. Quality work is the best way to build sales, but it can be enhanced by a schedule of added inducements.

TYPES OF SERVICE BUSINESSES

If you are planning to start a service-type business and have not settled on a particular line, take time to consider the skills needed and your experience. There is no trade in which you can succeed without having training or background or at least the full-time assistance of someone who has. Learning the tricks of the trade as you go along is a big handicap to overcome. If you still want to enter a field where you are not skilled already, consider a franchise investment. The training program run by the franchise company may overcome your initial handicap. Know the skill requirements of a business and don't enter it without suitable preparation.

What are the areas of service in which a business person might make a successful livelihood? Your district Small Business Administration office will assist you in assessing your opportunities. Moreover, the SBA publishes a series of pamphlets which give many important details on operating various types of service firms. Read all the available literature before you make a decision.

As in other types of small business, consider any economic crisis that would affect a new enterprise. A recession could reduce the chances of a new furniture store, but when money is tight and people delay the purchase of new furniture, the skills of a good upholsterer may be more in demand to keep older pieces in service.

Motel ownership is attractive to many couples. The advertising of new opportunities is often designed to appeal to retired people. However, this line of work requires physical stamina and wide skills—among others, a flair for plumbing, mechanics, accounting, and interior decorating. It is possible that a couple may enjoy the bustling activities of the traveler and tourist trade. However, it is a full-time, demanding job.

Nursery schools have become a popular enterprise. Private preschool enrollments now outnumber public preschool enrollments by more than four to one. A factor stimulating the nursery school industry is the growing number of families where both parents work. Also contributing to the growth of the nursery school industry is the federal tax credit given for dependent-care expenses. Many people have acquired expertise in handling small children through their own experiences as parents and grandparents. Nursery schools require little in the way of operating expenses. Some people, for example, supplement their income by looking after other people's children at the same time that they watch their own.

Skilled automobile mechanics no longer look to invest in service stations; they open up repair shops instead. Mechanics with the highest skills open up foreign car repair shops. The time consumed by pumping gas detracts from profitable major repair jobs. Most service stations are now opened by competent mechanics who desire the gasoline income to supplement the money earned on small repairs such as tune-ups, tire changes, and brake jobs.

Before investing in a service station, find out why it was abandoned by the former lessee or owner. The station might be located too far from the beaten path or it might be too close to another station selling the same brand of gas. Sometimes changes in an oil company's policies, for example, revised gasoline allocations or increases in the wholesale price of gas, drive an operator out of business.

Dry cleaning is another enterprise that attracts many individuals and couples. There is a good deal to learn before engaging in such a business. This knowledge can be acquired by studying dry cleaning in a technical or trade school, taking a correspondence course, or working in a dry cleaning plant to gain experience. The dry cleaner needs four types of knowledge: mechanical, electrical, industrial, and power plant. Up-to-date machines will help the business to compete. The latest pressing machines will do 100 shirts an hour, sorters can now fold 1000 mixed-sized towels an hour, dryers now handle 100-pound loads, and conveyor systems can transport the clothes between the steps in the automation process. The latest machinery requires a large capital investment but eliminates the need for costly labor. The long-term risk of the dry cleaning business is that the new clothing fabrics of the distant future will make dry cleaning obsolete.

Also check state and local regulations that control your activities. Investigate zoning and the licenses you will need for special equipment. Some states insist that your cleaners, spotters, and finishers be certified as qualified technicians. Consult with city hall, your attorney, and the state board of dry cleaners before acting.

A hair salon may offer you prospects of a profitable venture. A salon may specialize in women's hair, men's hair, or unisex styling. Once you decide on your specialty, you must pick a location. Do you want to attract a well-to-do clientele interested in the height of fashion, a trendy crowd desiring the latest style, or a more conservative clientele seeking a perpetuation of the look to which they have become accustomed? Is the area of your shop sufficiently populated to provide you with clients?

You may consider buying a franchise in a chain of beauty shops. Your franchisor will design the salon in the area you select. They help find your staff and work with you to formulate a realistic budget of expenses. The parent company will continue to provide advice and consultation as styles change. The franchise fee may be $10,000 to $30,000, with an additional percentage of your yearly gross also going to the parent company. In addition, you have to invest in equipment and fixtures for your location. You may need an initial outlay of $25,000 to $75,000 to cover licensing, insurance, advertising, phones, security, equipment, salaries, and rents.

If you have a warm, outgoing personality, your expertise and enthusiasm may give you a successful start in the beauty business. However, before you get your business under way, you will need to know the numerous regulations that restrict and guide you. For example, your job applications must comply with federal antidiscrimination laws and the fair employment practice laws of your state. Most states will also require operating licenses of some kind. You may need additional certification to expand your basic business to services such as saunas, exercises, massages, and facials. Some states, for example, still have laws forbidding cosmetologists from working on male clients. Consult with a local lawyer to discover what the law in your area permits.

There are risks in service firms as in so many other types of small business. The need to which they cater may decline because of changes in a specific neighborhood, unfavorable general economic conditions, or unexpected governmental edict. Some thriving businesses go bankrupt. But again, the knowledgeable and adaptable self-employed individual may have an advantage over the employee who is laid off by a large corporation when hard times come. Such an individual may find another way to cater to new needs and to render services for which there is a sudden demand.

11
A BASIC GUIDE TO FRANCHISE OPERATION

The lure of a franchise operation is the prospect of starting a local business with the goodwill of a widely known product or trademark.

Franchising developed around the turn of the century. The automotive industry, in which dealers were financially aided by the car companies, signaled the way for gas-station dealerships. Then came the franchised drugstore and distributorships in bottled soft drinks. In the early 1950s, franchising in "fast foods" led the way to the multiple enterprises of today that have generated many new-style stores and businesses and put many old "mom and pop" retailers out to pasture.

The types of franchises available range from the ubiquitous ice-cream parlor to tax-preparing services. Franchised enterprises include restaurants, hotels and motels, travel agencies, health food stores, recreation services, business colleges, paramedical schools, auto transmission repair shops, beauty salons, various types of rental services, child care centers, nursing homes, and a host of opportunities from real estate investment to "make spare cash at home" offerings.

Franchised businesses acquire the standard symbols, equipment, and products of all others in the chain, although they are actually owned by individuals to varying degrees depending on the contract. In some, the franchisor owns the real estate; in others, the owner-manager may have to buy or lease the premises. The investment entitles the franchises to use the master company's name and system of operation under certain conditions and restrictions. The enterprise may be highly profitable; it is equally vulnerable to loss.

How does the individual franchisee fare under the system? Some franchises are so potentially rewarding that investors compare the return against the yields on stocks and bonds. A typical McDonald's in 1979 returned a profit of $70,000 on an investment of $275,000, after paying a royalty fee of 11 percent of sales back to the parent company. For the typical U.S. retailer, the average return on investment is 28 percent; many franchises exceed that. To decide if you can do business better as a franchisee, you must thoroughly understand what you are getting into. Some individuals have more to gain by putting their capital into a totally independent business. However, when comparing the return on a franchise investment with that of another small business, keep in mind that 80 percent of small businesses eventually fail, compared with only 5 percent of franchise outlets. The comparative safety of a franchise investment is as much of an attraction as yield.

SHOULD YOU BECOME
A FRANCHISEE?

An analysis of yourself is as important as a thorough investigation into all aspects of franchising. Do you have the personal qualifications called for in the particular type of franchising that interests you? Can you work within the system? Some franchising companies employ psychological and other tests through which unsuitable applicants can be eliminated. Before you get as far as approaching a specific company, you can evaluate yourself, your aims, and your potential success in a franchise. By so doing, you protect yourself and, at the same time, eliminate the types of franchise unsuited to your personality and abilities.

Do you work well under supervision?   Some franchisors, in effect, keep a tight rein on their franchisees. Others do not, and the area adviser supposedly available to you is conspicuous by his or her absence. Can you go it alone, if need be? Know the facts about yourself before you investigate the franchisor's attitude.

What is your business experience?   Some franchisors advertise "no experience necessary." Even if the franchisor offers an extensive training program, you should still thoroughly evaluate the total background you can bring into any enterprise. Can you handle personnel? Have you experience in buying, selling, and accounting? Can you cope with government paperwork? While some individuals have succeeded in totally unfamiliar lines, knowledge of the business you propose to undertake could be a lifesaver.

Are you genuinely enthusiastic about the franchised line you are contemplating? Lukewarm interest is unlikely to generate profits or to carry you through difficult days. Enthusiasm is important since most franchise owners put in very long hours of hard work.

Would it be to your advantage to be a "silent investor"? Some franchises are geared toward the silent investor who can hire a manager to run the business. The silent investor just drops in from time to time to check the books and observe the operation. The silent investor may be comparing the yield on a managed franchise operation against the yield on Treasury bills, bonds, or equities. People with money to spare for investing and little time of their own to spend on a business can find franchises available where a reasonable profit can be attained even though a manager must be employed. Silent investors then do not need the business expertise expected of owner-operators (although useful experience in a business similar to the franchise may help in combating employee theft). Typical of the franchises encouraging the passive investor are the Sheraton Inns.

OBTAINING INFORMATION ON FRANCHISES

Advertising of franchise opportunities appears in the business sections of such newspapers as *The New York Times* and *The Wall Street Journal*. Also, franchise brokers provide information and offer choices of different franchise investments. If a national franchise that interests you is not advertised among the current openings, write to the main office of the company to inquire about new franchises.

The book, *Franchise Opportunity Handbook* (available from the U.S. Government Printing Office, Washington, D.C. 20402), alphabetically lists various types of franchised operations, companies doing business under those categories, and general information. If you are interested in, say, fast-food operations, you can look up a number of companies and check what equity capital is required; what, if any, financial assistance, managerial assistance, and training are provided; how many franchises are in the operation; and how long the company has been in business. In addition, this valuable government booklet offers useful guidance to the potential franchisee and sources of further information.

You can obtain further information from the International Franchising Association, 1025 Connecticut Ave., N.W., Washington, D.C.

20036. Also available are the *Directory of Franchising Organizations* from Pilot Books, 347 Fifth Ave., New York, N.Y. 10016, and the *Franchise Annual* from Info Press, 736 Center St., Lewiston, N.Y. 10942.

You should be alert to current articles and news items on franchising in reliable magazines and newspapers. Your public library will be of assistance to you in looking up publications and in guiding you to books on the subject.

If you live near a city, you may be able to attend a franchise show. Here, you can talk with representatives of franchises and pick up their pamphlets and perhaps a simple copy of their contract. But beware of pressure tactics to sign up at once and any "this is your last chance for this profitable location" deals. Gathering information is your present objective; getting caught for a heavy financial commitment before you can assess the situation is not.

If your interest has narrowed to one or two franchisors and to establishing yourself in a certain location, you can launch inquiries at a better business bureau, the chamber of commerce, and the local bank. In that way, you may learn of any negative factors about the franchisor and whether there is already an overload of similar businesses in the immediate area.

In each state the law on franchises varies. Be alert to press reports of changes in the law on local and federal levels and to regulations issued by the Federal Trade Commission.

AVOIDING THE GYPS

In the past, many entrepreneurs were reluctant to court franchises because of the shady operators permeating the field. Gyp schemes have succeeded because the would-be franchisee is often gullible and greedy. The investor is enticed by a "come-on" advertisement offering quick profit for small effort and low investment. The franchisee may be promised training and is usually told that prior experience is not necessary. Whatever reluctance the investor has when the promoters ask for an investment is overcome by the confidence of the gregarious, charming personalities associated with the scheme. The investor's psychological desire to be like these people, in both attitude and prosperity, is further impetus to make the commitment. Details on the scheme will vary, but they all hinge on promising much and returning nothing of value. The hopeful franchisee gains no more than an expensive lesson on fraud.

The most common frauds are *"Ponzi"* schemes and the *pyramid* promotions. In a Ponzi scheme, the promoter pays old investors with the money garnered from new investors to give the appearance of a successful business and encourage more new investors. A pyramid franchise requires each franchisee to find other people to whom to sell new franchises. Again, only the first investors will see a return on their money. In either case, the promoter will have absconded with the bulk of the investments. As a general rule, if the promotion appears "too good to be true," it usually is. Few fortunes are made in the real world without having to do some good, hard work. If, in seeking a franchise, you become aware of a shady deal, it should be reported to the United States attorney's office or to other such authorities.

EVALUATING THE FRANCHISOR

Having selected the type of business that most interests you—and to which, it is hoped, you can bring a useful background of experience— you will note the names of several franchisors. Famous names may be on your list. Nevertheless, your investigation of each enterprise should be thorough. In the course of checking out each company, they will provide you much valuable information about their franchise, as required by law.

Federal legislation has given the investor a much better chance of evaluating potential propositions. Of course, the services of a lawyer and an accountant are still instrumental in evaluating any business opportunity, but the increased information now available to the potential franchisee greatly reduces the chance of making a blunder.

Federal Trade Commission legislation of 1979 requires the franchisor or franchise broker to provide an investor with a disclosure statement at the earliest of three possible dates: 10 days before any term of the contract must be executed, 10 days before a payment must be made, or at the first personal meeting between the investor and the franchisor. The disclosure statement is not required when the franchise fee is less than $500 or the franchise arrangement is in the nature of an oral contract.

The Federal Trade Commission law provides two other protective measures. First, the franchisor must provide the investor with a copy of the actual franchise agreement at least 5 days before the agreement is to be executed. Then the seller must provide the potential buyer with an earnings claims document anytime the franchisor makes a statement, written or oral, as to what sort of return a buyer might expect on his investment.

The earnings claims document must be updated every 90 days by the franchisor to reflect the latest income statistics. The data in the report must be based on substantial numbers, not estimates, so that the raw figures can be provided to the investor upon reasonable notice. Like the disclosure statement, if the material in the earnings claims document is false, the franchise owners are punishable by civil law.

These documents give the investor a lot to study, but even if they make the franchise appear to be a good investment, don't sign the contract until the terms have been reviewed by your lawyer. Statements as to the legitimacy of the business often fail to indicate crucial restrictions in the operation. Although the various statements are providing you with more background information than you would receive from the seller of a small business, the financial viability of the setup might be designed for an area with a different cost of living or where people have different spending habits.

The basic disclosure document should contain twenty categories of information:

1. It must provide the name under which the franchise does business, its trademark, and the name and address of the parent company.
2. The directors of the franchise and the franchise's chief executives for marketing, service, operations, and training should be identified by name, and their business experience and previous employment during the last 5 years should be revealed.
3. The operators should state the length of time they have been selling the franchise. If the parent company has been selling other franchises, the names of these franchises and the length of time they have been sold must also be revealed.
4. The franchise owner must reveal and describe the history and settlement of any court actions for felony convictions, embezzlement, restraint of trade, injunctions, and civil actions that have been made against any of the franchise operations of any of the franchise owners.
5. The disclosure statement must reveal the bankruptcy history of any of the franchise directors, officers, or executors, including reorganization due to insolvency.
6. The franchise business, the product line, and the probable market for the product must be fully described.
7. There must be a listing of the initial funds required to be paid to the franchise or its affiliates, such as down payments, rents, inventory costs, and other fees.
8. The periodic payments the investor must make to the franchise owners should be fully listed, such as leases and rentals. If some of these fees are expressed as percentages of the outlet's volume,

estimates must be provided as to what the percentage fees may amount to.

9. The purchaser must be provided with a list of persons with whom the operation will be required to do business, and the affiliation these people have with the franchise.

10. If the purchaser is required to do business with certain people, the disclosure statement must give a basis for calculating what revenue the franchise receives from these people (thus disclosing rebates and kickbacks).

11. The purchaser must be given a list of materials he or she is required to lease or purchase. If the materials must be purchased from a specific person (including the franchisor), the names and addresses must be provided.

12. Financing arrangements provided directly or indirectly by the franchise must be disclosed, including the names of lenders, amounts to be lent, percentages charged, collateral necessary, and the default provisions.

13. The franchisor must state any limits as to what products may be sold, whom they may be sold to, where they may be sold, and what sales territory is protected.

14. If personal participation in the franchise is required of the investor, a description must be provided of the duties he or she is expected to perform. This may indicate that silent investors are not wanted.

15. The disclosure statement must spell out the terms by which either the purchaser or the franchisor can terminate, cancel, or renew the contract to run the franchise. Also to be revealed are any obligations that might exist after termination or expiration: whether the investor is allowed to sell the operation; what the rights of the purchaser's heirs are; and, should the purchaser leave the franchise, what would be the nature of a covenant not to compete.

16. The disclosure statement must include statistics as to the number of franchise operations, the number voluntarily terminated, the number terminated by the franchisor, the number for which renewal was refused, and the number of operations canceled by the franchise in the middle of the agreement. The franchisor must also provide the owners' names and addresses of the 10 franchised locations nearest to the one being purchased.

17. It must be stated whether the franchisor must approve the location of the site of the purchaser's operations. If so, the statement must specify the range of time between the signing of the franchise agreement and the site selection, and the usual length of time between the signing of the franchise agreement and the opening date for a purchaser's location.

18. The minimum amount of training required of a franchise operator must be indicated as well as the type and cost of training offered by the company.
19. If a public figure is involved in the promotion of the franchise, the statement must reveal that person's investment in the franchise, his or her remuneration, and what the celebrity's obligations to the franchise are.
20. The franchisor must provide the investor with a balance sheet and income statement for each of the last 3 years.

At this point in your investigation you should evaluate both the information you have received and the company's willingness to provide it to you. There are certain facts you need to know.

What do present franchisees say about the organization?   From a list of franchisees in your prospective area, arrange to interview these people and find out how they rate the company. Can they get advice when needed? Are they too heavily supervised? Have they any financial grievances? Do they have complaints about the contract? Are advertising arrangements satisfactory? How is business? Is profit measuring up to expectations? Did the franchisor quote reasonably accurate figures on the costs of setting up operations, on actual operating expenses, and on profits? Be observant while on the franchisee's premises; if possible, spend a day at a franchise. When possible, also see franchisees whose names were not supplied by the company. You want to make sure you are talking freely with unbiased people.

Are you pressured to sign a contract?   A bad sign is the overeager approach on the part of the franchisor. The legitimate company wants to check out potential franchisees and will urge that the franchisee have a lawyer go over the contract and other details of a commitment. The franchisor who evades investigation is to be avoided.

Questioning the Franchisor   By mail or in person, there are some questions you should ask a franchisor:

What training and assistance are given to franchisees?   You want specifics on the type of training you get from your franchise, for how long, at whose expense, and whether it would be sufficient to prepare you for owner-management. The training provided by some franchises has proved to be totally inadequate. Is there an area supervisor or troubleshooter regularly available? What kind of help does he or she provide? Is that person (or team) designated solely to work with franchisees? Some area personnel are actually salespeople for franchises and render little help to those who have already bought.

How are differences between company and franchisees settled? Find out if the contract calls for arbitration of disputes and if both parties are bound to accept.

What is the extent of territory protection? Your company or its subsidiaries might set up other franchisees in the same or a similar line too near for your profit. Find out what restraints are operative.

What is the potential profitability for the franchisee? You and your accountant need a precise breakdown of figures involved in a particular enterprise. Quite apart from the difference between going into business as a dry cleaner and running a motel, there may be many financial variations within a particular franchise organization; for example, costs differ from one location to another and in a new enterprise against one taken over from another owner-manager.

The costs should be spelled out in the disclosure statement. Note that some outlets may take more than a year to reach a cash flow break-even point. Until this point is reached, a franchise will drain your finances just as any other small business would.

Many franchises are profitable almost immediately. These command the highest prices. Some of the more famous can cost as much as $1 million to start. The market value of these outlets rises as the popularity of the product increases, or as the location of the outlet becomes more desirable.

A McDonald's hamburger stand once cost only $11,000. You can see how a chance to get in on the ground floor of a growing field can be an excellent investment. If the management is sound, the franchise will prosper as the whole field grows. Profitable prospects for the 1980s would appear to be personal computer stores, computer service agencies, energy-saving devices, and video equipment.

THE FRANCHISE CONTRACT

Before the contract is signed, go over every clause with an attorney who is experienced in this area of the law. Analyze each commitment and the possible repercussions. A franchise contract not weighted heavily in favor of the franchisor is a rarity indeed, but, given a reputable company and a knowledgeable franchisee who knows what must be lived with, the system can be worked to mutual profit. Some essential points are discussed below.

Franchise fees, royalties, payments for equipment, etc.   Determine whether the franchise fee is a one-time payment or recurring. What are you getting for it? You may also have to pay royalties in a specified amount or as a percentage of gross sales. Will you gain certain financial advantages as a franchisee to help balance any such constant payment? Your investment may cover such items as inventory, licenses, and permits. Establish just what it does cover and what you need in addition. Do you have to buy trucks, fixtures, or equipment? Must you buy such essential items from the franchisor? Could you buy elsewhere for less?

Sales and prices.   You may have to fulfill a certain quota within a specified period. What happens if you fail to meet the requirement? Failure may allow the franchisor to terminate the contract. Prices may be set by the franchisor. Will this limit you in meeting competition? The franchisor may stipulate a limit to the amount you can withdraw as your personal management fee. If so, is this a reasonable and businesslike arrangement?

Financial details, accounting, and banking.   Franchisors may prescribe all details of bookkeeping and banking, and may stipulate their own access to financial details. Are you willing to go along with all their requirements?

Advertising and promotions.   Some contracts call for the franchisee to make a specified contribution to national advertising and to follow company directions on local advertising and promotions. To what extent will you benefit from this advertising? Will it provide some of the fanfare for your opening? Must your advertising be approved?

Business premises and repairs.   The franchisor may demand final say in the building or alteration of your premises, require certain standards of maintenance, set time limits on painting and repairs which are done at your expense, and be free to send supervisors and inspectors at any time. Are the stated terms reasonable? Could you be put out of business if you fail to fulfill any of them?

Employees.   The franchisor may want final say on hiring and firing, employee uniforms, company-sponsored training courses, and wages and fringe benefits. Check that you, as the employer, are satisfied with the conditions.

Insurance.   The insurance company may be picked by the franchisor, who decides on the coverage for which you must pay. Do you have alternative plans you think should be considered?

Products, inventory, and supplies.   Clauses in the contract relating to these matters are vital. The franchisor may attempt to curtail your right to add lines to your inventory, insist you carry all, or only, franchise products, or require that only certain suppliers provide the ingredients for your line. The courts have ruled favorably in a number of cases where franchisees have shown that they could obtain supplies at better prices from other sources. The Federal Trade Commission has also forced companies to rewrite contracts so that any suggestion that franchisees are compelled to purchase from specified suppliers is eliminated. Review your contract to see if unwarranted limitations are being placed upon you. However, the franchisor may legitimately demand that the standard of the franchise product be maintained.

Hours, pricing, and conduct of business.   The contract may set your opening and closing hours, set prices, and require conformity to all company policies and regulations in the conduct of business. Can you accept this standardization?

Territory and location.   A clear definition of your territory, or a map showing it, should be part of your contract. Has the company reserved any rights to curtail your territory? In some circumstances, a company may need freedom to change, expand, or meet new demands. Your area might be able to take more franchises without undercutting your business. The location of your store or service should be entirely to your satisfaction because inferior location may spell failure even to the best-run business. Large franchisors usually have experts investigate a location before a new outlet is opened and, because they can pull some weight, obtain sites not available to the small business owner alone. Conduct your own survey of the location; you may want to retain the right to turn down a spot allocated to you. Return on your investment hinges on the right location.

Termination, transfer, or renewal of contract.   Your failure to fulfill any one of a number of conditions named throughout the contract may be named as cause for cancellation. You and your lawyer must review each clause specifically to see where the company has retained re-vocation rights. The threat of termination might hang over, say, the failure to fulfill a sales quota. Or, in the event of the franchisee's death or disability, the family might be ousted from the business with less than just recompense. Some franchisors eventually want to take over highly profitable stores or eventually want services to be company-owned and run. The contract may provide an option for the company to repurchase the business. Has the means of establishing a fair market value been set in the agreement? Sometimes a provision is included which states that the repurchase price should not exceed the amount originally paid for the franchise. In consequence, the franchisee stands to lose the results of many years of building up the business. Check also provisions relating to transfer, renewal, or sale of the franchise. The franchisor may demand to approve a buyer proposing to take over your franchise. Your right to sell and make a profit may not be ques-tioned, but the company wishes to keep a control on selection of its franchisees—and perhaps to make sure that some competitor is not trying to take over through an intermediary.

THE DECISION TO BECOME
A FRANCHISEE

If you have opened up negotiations with a franchisor who you believe is reliable and you are confident that you can make a success in that type of business, you are now weighing the final decision. Shall you sign up or go it alone?

In favor of franchising.   A good franchisor has already solved many of the problems which beset small businesses; the company has the know-how newcomers need to get on their feet quickly. The product or service may be nationally known; it may almost sell itself. The franchisee may benefit from national advertising and the well-known signs and symbols of the franchisor instead of being an unknown, struggling to make an impression. The franchisor will set the guide-lines for your operation, the hours, the prices, and the procedures. They research new products, develop marketing programs, and test the viability of every phase of operations—something you could only do by the expensive process of trial and error. If you work hard and follow instructions, you receive heavyweight support.

In favor of venturing alone.   An individual small-business owner holds the reins on his or her investment; no part of the profit is paid out in the form of royalties or other ongoing fees, and the owner does not have to adhere to rules, regulations, or regimentation. The person with a strong sense of identity and many ideas to be put into action may be too restricted as a franchisee.

12
MAIL-ORDER BUSINESS

Mail-order catalogs of a century ago still fascinate consumers; if they cannot order products from them, they can still enjoy turning over the pages of those catalogs, newly reprinted, for their historical and entertainment value. Despite the change of consumer buying habits, new products, and giant shopping malls, American consumers enjoy perusing and selecting items from catalogs in an unhurried atmosphere; in their own homes, they are free of the pressures of sales personnel and of other shoppers. Thus, mail-order business continues to grow, enjoying a significant rise in popularity in recent years. Even though closed-circuit television may eventually allow viewers to buy items from lists appearing on their television screens, mail-order buying from catalogs, publications, and direct-mail advertising will probably continue to claim consumer interest.

CHOOSING A PRODUCT

Consider marketing a product that is already being sold successfully by mail. The market may be big enough for another vendor of the same established product. A retailer usually faces the same choice. A wineshop can find a clientele ready to buy the same vineyard products as other liquor stores sell, but the business would probably fail if it relied on selling intoxicants fermented from dandelions and elderberries.

Most successful mail-order ventures are based on the promotion of good sense items. Home aids are popular. They appeal to the vast number of people who feel overwhelmed by the gadgetry offered in their local hardware store (and pressured by the salesperson). The mail-order ad explains the function of a formerly mystifying gadget, usually with a picture of the item actually operating in a domestic setting. A reader made aware of the item's appealing qualities may be tempted to send away for it.

Mail-order businesses have been founded by individuals for the marketing of items that they themselves have made. If you, or perhaps a friend, has a special skill—in candlemaking, leathercraft, ceramics, or beaded ware, for example—you might test your possible success with a tastefully produced magazine advertisement. Rare or sometimes eccentric acquisitions often attract the reader's attention. Recent energy and fuel shortages and expenses have led to a plethora of heating devices, from foot warmers to old-fashioned potbellied stoves, which appeal to the frugal homemaker. Often these items are not readily available in department stores or are not conspicuously displayed. Your advertisement can awaken the interest of a customer who had previously never given a single thought to the item that you are advertising.

If you are looking for something out of the ordinary to sell by mail, look through foreign magazines for items sold abroad that have not yet reached this country. A similar technique is to read decades-old magazines, looking for items that could be coming into fashion once again or that might now be marketed on their quaint or chic appeal. When supply is a problem, you might be able to find a manufacturer who could develop your product.

In choosing a product, beware of advertisements that purport to offer you the secret of a successful mail-order venture. These promotions claim to provide you with a marketable mail-order product and advice as to how to sell it. They ask you to invest in certain business tools necessary to make, market, or mail the product. It is very unlikely that this sort of an advertisement will lead to your enrichment. If the product were marketable, the company would be selling it instead of trading the idea to you.

Publications dealing with the mail-order industry will acquaint you with techniques at less cost than you would pay for a "magic success formula." There are no mysteries to mail-order business—success depends upon the usual applications of time, persistence, know-how, and money. It is not unheard of for mail-order businesses to go from $5000 in sales to $10 million.

If your item proves successful, expect competition. Most mail-order businesses shift from product to product as the demand for an item tapers off. They milk the maximum from a product and then come up with a new one to sell. Businesses can stay with a single item only when they are fortunate enough to control the source. When you buy the item you sell from a manufacturer, you must accept the fact that you may be able to sell it profitably for only a limited period of time before the competition enters the market.

MAILING YOUR LETTERS
AND PRODUCTS

The customer programs division of your post office can provide you with booklets of information concerning all postal rates, regulations, and requirements that might affect your mail-order business. If your local post office has no such program, write to the Customer Programs Division, U.S. Postal Service, Washington, D.C. 20260. The amount of presorting you do to the mail (grouping it in bundles of similar zip codes) can lower your postage rates. Business-reply cards and envelopes must be approved by your postmaster. Permits for bulk rates (a fraction of the cost of first-class mail) must be applied for with the appropriate postal form and the payment of annual fees. Postage meters allow you to prepare mail in the office and earn you reduced rates because the post office can process the mail more quickly.

Postal rates have been rising rapidly. Mail-order shippers should compare the fees for parcel post and express mail with those charged by competing delivery firms, such as United Parcel Service. As cutbacks are made in the U.S. Postal Service, the use of these private firms will become more advantageous.

Your product must not be so bulky that it cannot be sold easily through the mails. Fragile products may encounter problems as well, and returned broken products decrease your profits. If you anticipate having problems with the mails, consult with your postal authorities and with competing shippers about packaging, parcel insurance, and other aspects of special handling.

In addition to postal problems, your product may be subject to other restrictions that reduce the effectiveness of a mail-order campaign. Foods may perish on shipment. Drugs may lose their potency between the time they are bottled and the time they are shipped, if they are stored for significant periods of time. Items such as toys that must be shipped disassembled might prove difficult for consumers to reassemble. Such problems can get your business in trouble with the Federal Trade Commission, the Food and Drug Administration, the Better Business Bureau, or postal authorities. You can consult with a lawyer as to your responsibilities to the purchaser. There are also organizations that will, for a fee, aid mail-order businesses. For example, the Direct Mail/Marketing Association, Inc. (6 E. 43rd St., New York, N.Y. 10017) will sell you a book summarizing current legal responsibilities.

WORKING WITH YOUR SUPPLIERS

If you do not make your own mail-order product, then you must find a supplier who manufactures items which interest you. Many manufacturers are wholesalers and will not sell their products in small amounts. You may need to find an intermediary who will obtain the quantity you need. Or, more simply, you may be able to obtain the items you need by examining mail-order directories at a library. These will tell you where you can obtain a wide selection of suitable items. One such directory is the *Mail Order Business Directory* by B. Klein and Co.

For best possible profit, purchase your goods from primary sources. Secondary sources will need to tack an extra margin onto the manufactured price in order to realize their profit. If possible, obtain an exclusive right to the merchandise.

You do not need to mail the product yourself. You can have the supplier drop-ship the product directly to your customer. This means that you accept the customer's order with payment and then send a payment to your supplier with a mailing label for the customer; the supplier then sends the product directly to the customer. This eliminates your need for storage quarters, but you must rely on the integrity of the drop-shipper's mailing practices. It is a wise practice to obtain from your suppliers a written agreement that they will not copy your customers' names for their own future solicitation.

Be certain that your products fill all their manufacturers' claims. You will be held legally responsible for any misleading or false data about the merchandise offered in your advertisements.

SELLING YOUR MAIL-ORDER PRODUCT

Daily newspapers often carry mail-order advertising, but their appeal is, in general, too broad to claim maximum customer attention. If newspapers do suit your product, the regularity with which you can present your advertisement may prove an advantage over monthly publication advertising. The Sunday magazine or classified section of a newspaper often provides an excellent opportunity for mail-order advertising. Interested mail-order customers have made it a practice to peruse these pages for new and interesting offerings.

Monthly, bimonthly, quarterly, and biannual publications are productive outlets for mail-order advertising. You can direct your appeal to a specific readership—homeowners, hobbyists, gardeners, car owners, etc. The readers of the publications you choose should be the logical customers for your merchandise. Do not necessarily be deterred by high advertising rates. The return per dollar on your advertisements determines their profitability.

Your advertisement may contain a complete description of the merchandise and include an order blank, or it may give a few particulars about the products and ask interested readers to send for complete details. This system is recommended for higher-priced items.

Schedule your advertising strategically. Nonseasonal items sell best from advertisements placed in magazine issues in fall, winter, and early spring. Items which may be purchased as Christmas gifts should usually be advertised in October and November issues. The length of time it takes to get results varies from one type of publication to another. From newspaper advertising, you will receive about 70 percent of your orders within a week. Items placed in the magazine section of newspapers usually pull about 40 percent in the first week. With monthly magazines you can expect to get only 10 percent of your orders in the week after the issue reaches the stands. During the following 2 to 6 months, you will get the full flow of orders.

COMPOSING THE ADVERTISEMENT

Your advertisement should convey clearly all the pertinent information about your product: what it is, how it is constructed, what it does, and how it does it. What are its exclusive qualities and advantages over other makes of the same type of item? What are its cost and payment terms? Where can the customer order it? You may get good results by offering your merchandise on installment terms, with a discount provided for all customers who make payment in full on receipt of the merchandise.

The actual design of the advertisement or blurb is usually left to commercial artists, typographers, and advertising agencies. Tests have shown that illustrated sales copy is read by more people and produces more orders or inquiries than purely verbal advertisements. A photograph of the product will prove more valuable than a drawing. Readers may question the accuracy of the drawing.

An aid to help the reader respond, such as a coupon, will increase the response to an advertisement. A direct mailer can increase responses by enclosing a business-reply card or envelope.

DIRECT-MAIL SELLING

Direct mail means selling your product through the mails by means of advertising, specifically addressed. You work from mailing lists of likely customers for your product. If buyers have already responded to your advertising in publications, you have the names of these customers for a direct approach in selling new merchandise. You may wish to continue advertising in various publications at the same time as you begin direct mail. The list of names you build up can profitably be rented or exchanged.

A typical mail-order package for your direct-mail list consists of a sales letter, a descriptive circular, an order form, and a business-reply envelope. Experienced firms have found that they will get 15 to 20 orders from each 1000 mailings. At times, second and third mailings will get additional results. Experimentation will show you the possible gains in repeated mailings.

Even if you get your customers from classified advertisements, you will want to prepare a direct-mail campaign to alert known buyers to your next offering. Repeat business opportunities cannot be ignored. The most valuable mailing list you will have is the carefully maintained list of your former customers.

OTHER MEDIA

Your advertisement can be placed upon billboards, passenger buses, placemats, or in programs for cultural or sporting events. Matchbook advertising can be effective depending on how much you are willing to spend to reach a wide audience. (Consult the Universal Match Corporation, 3401 La Cienega Blvd., Los Angeles, Calif. 90016, Atlas Match Corporation, 1000 E. Ave. H, Arlington, Tex. 76011, or the Diamond Match Division, Diamond National Corporation, 733 Third Ave., New York, N.Y. 10017.)

Television and radio are also effective forums for a mail-order campaign. While the listener or viewer may have difficulties writing down the particulars, the use of a toll-free 800-area-code phone number can overcome this hurdle. The potential customer, by remembering one phone number, can get in touch with your sales personnel. The cost to you per hour of use ranges from almost $50 an hour initially to $2 an hour for extended use, depending upon the area being served. If your sales personnel talk to 20 customers an hour, 3 minutes for each, the cost per sale can be very low.

SOME MARKETING HINTS

1. October is generally recognized as an excellent month for a mail-order advertisement.
2. Some publications make editorial mentions of new products. Prepare a publicity release of an innovative product, and send it to a publication whose readership would be appreciative.
3. Direct-mail campaigns are better than the use of classified advertisements when you want to shield your product from potential competitors.
4. The most important single word in your classified advertisement may be "guaranteed."
5. Your initial classified advertisements should provide a relatively complete description of a product so that the consumer's lack of information won't retard your sales. Once you have determined that the product can be marketed successfully by mail, you can prune your ads to eliminate unnecessary words.
6. Make your original deal to enter the marketplace at a slight loss if you can run a good profit on the repeat business you generate.
7. If your product cannot be easily sold by mail, use your classified advertisement to establish contacts. Then have sales personnel visit the prospective customer to try and close the sale. The sales personnel can demonstrate the item being sold and deal with the customer's questions. The sales agents have a better chance of making a sale to the respondent of a classified advertisement than to a potential customer solicited out of the blue. This combination of mail order and sales agent is employed by many businesses, the sellers of vacuum cleaners, encyclopedias, and insurance policies, for example.

OBTAINING MAILING LISTS

Any published directory is an obvious source of lists of names. Some examples are city directories, telephone directories, voting and tax lists, and users-of-utilities lists.

Some firms, such as list brokers, specialize in the compiling of lists of names, which the mail-order company may purchase at a price per 1000 names. The price will vary upon the degree of selectivity needed. For example, a list of the general population will cost far less than a list of, say, pharmacists, real estate brokers, or interior decorators. It is estimated that a general list will yield a 2 percent return, whereas one that is directed to a specific market will realize sales of 5 to 10 percent of the total mailing. The Small Business Administration can provide you with a list of mailing list houses. The classified pages of the telephone directory may also be a valuable source of special-list names.

Usually a mail-order business rents a list of names through a broker on a one-time basis. Sometimes the firm which provides the lists will prepare the mailing and send the advertisements for you. Lists are usually sold by the thousands. Often a minimum of 5000 names is required if a one-time test sample advertisement is being mailed.

Sometimes magazine publishers will rent out lists of their subscribers. These might point you toward a group of, say, homemakers, world travelers, sports fans, or theatergoers.

As a result of publication advertising, you may have developed a good customer mailing list of your own. This list of satisfied customers has far more potential for your business than rented lists, however selective. Besides notifying your customers of new products, you are in a position to rent your list to other businesses or to a list broker. The broker's commission is 20 percent of the fee charged to renters of the list. Very often competitors will exchange mailing lists, saving the money they would have spent had they bought each other's lists through the services of the list broker.

Be sure the list of mail-order customers you receive is kept up to date. It has been estimated that 200 to 300 addresses in every 1000 mailings become inaccurate in a year's time. Mailing lists should be verified at least twice a year. One method of checking addresses is putting a "return requested" label on each envelope so that those that are undeliverable will be returned to you. When the postmaster returns a mailing piece to you, you can cross that particular address from your list.

The post office will correct a list of names, submitted on cards, at a charge of 25 cents per name. Each name and address must be presented on a separate card, about the size of a postcard. Carriers will verify names and addresses for you, though they cannot guarantee correct name spellings and titles. Such names imprinted by stencil can be sent third or fourth class depending on the weight, but handwritten or typed cards will require first-class postage. First-class mailings may be address-corrected by the post office at no charge.

EMPLOYING AN ADVERTISING AGENCY

Mail-order houses work with advertising agencies which specialize in this type of business. Some handle both mail order and direct mail; others, one or the other. Watch the competition. Your chosen agency should not be handling another client whose product is similar to your own.

If you operate from a small town, you may have to find a mail-order advertising agency in a nearby city. While not so convenient as a local agency, a moderate-sized-city agency can serve you very well through mail and telephone contact and the occasional conference. The volume of return would have to be considerable to make it worthwhile for the agency to work with you on a commission basis. A fee basis is more likely.

PRINTING YOUR LITERATURE

In mail order, you will need various types of advertising circulars, catalogs, brochures, perhaps printed or mimeographed instruction sheets, and letters to your customers. In direct mail, the need for attractive printed material is vital since it has to sell your goods.

Offset is generally cheaper than letterpress, but since you may need both types of work, you should seek a printer who can provide both. Your printer will supply the paper and advise you on the size and quality needed for the job. Select a firm with which you can work satisfactorily. You may require a company that can handle more than a print job. Addressing and mailing are services offered by some. If you launch your business on a small scale which does not include the use of an advertising agency, your printer may be able to help you in such matters as design.

You can give your printed sales letter a hand-typed quality through the use of a photographic reproduction procedure. In direct mail, addressing the reader as a member of an elite group may be an effective approach—for example, "Dear Art Lover," or less elite, "Dear Car Owner." Large mail-order concerns sometimes use computerized mailings so that potential customers are addressed by their own names, e.g., "Dear Mr. Goldman."

The direct-mail business owner who has developed a worthwhile enterprise should check into the costs of installing a small photo-offset printing machine on the premises. With a camera, such as a platemaker by Itek or 3M, plates can be produced at reasonable cost for runs on offset machines. The Addressograph-Multigraph Corporation of Elk Grove Village, Illinois, is well known for its Multilith offset machines; these and other printing methods should be studied.

MAIL-ORDER TECHNIQUES

Usually, the printing of descriptive direct mail can be done more cheaply by hiring out the task to a professional printer. This is especially preferable during the formative period of the mail-order endeavor when failure would leave you with a large investment in printing and mailing machinery. The advantages of having printing machinery in your own shop are better quality control over the printed product and a greater ability to ensure that the material goes out on time. The larger the business gets, the more sense it makes to set up your own printing facilities. The overhead cost will become a relatively small part of the cost of the goods sold. Other machinery that will pay for itself once the business gets off the ground is electronic letter openers and automatic letter inserters.

Your responses to customers should also become "mechanical" through the use of form letters. Business-reply cards are a sort of form letter. Form letters used to respond to customer complaints enable you to be consistent in both civility and legality.

EXPERIMENTING WITH
YOUR MAILING LISTS

To find your most profitable market, you might try sending out literature to names taken from three separate mailing lists. Mail to at least 1000 names from each list. Send all advertisements on the same day to allow for psychological differences that might result from day-of-the-week delivery. (Are customers more susceptible to sales pitches at the busy beginning of the week or at the end, when they anticipate a day or so of relaxation?)

The successful mail-order firm is constantly testing to ascertain its most favorable products, selling techniques, and locations. Should you decide to conduct such a test, allow only one variable per mailing. If you permit several variables, you will not be able to discern which was responsible for the difference in buying patterns.

MAINTAINING GOOD CUSTOMER RELATIONS

Slow mail deliveries often impede the mail-order firm's early progress. If merchandise is late in arriving, many customers, fearing they have been duped, appeal to government agencies for restitution. Your best response is to quickly send another shipment to the same customer, requesting return of the original shipment when it arrives some time later. Notify the post office of the missing package. Thus, you will give satisfaction to your customer before your firm becomes the victim of unfair publicity.

Always replace damaged goods immediately after the package is returned, and never carry on a long-distance quarrel with a customer over a product which does not satisfy him. Make a refund as soon as a refused item comes back. The time you waste in justifying your product can be spent far more profitably seeking other sales. Reluctance to refund payment to dissatisfied customers can give your firm a bad name.

The Federal Trade Commission, a state attorney general's office, or city authorities may investigate a concern which fails to fulfill orders and may put it out of business. The operation might have started as an honest enterprise, but demand outpaced staff and facilities, or suppliers failed to meet time schedules. For the reputation and stability of your concern, see that orders are filled promptly. When a wait is necessary, notify the customer—and see that the order is kept under the close attention of your staff. The customer may demand a refund or substitution of other goods in cases of prolonged nondelivery of an order. Be aware that the Federal Trade Commission has ruled that a customer has the right to cancel any order not received through the mail within 30 days of order.

Misleading "free offers" and order forms, substitution of shipments without customer authorization, and failure to offer refunds, as well as dubious collection practices, have been condemned by the Federal Trade Commission. The Federal Trade Commission is in a position to issue cease-and-desist orders against offending mail-order firms.

Some consideration should be given to the reception your merchandise will receive from the customer. It must meet the customer's expectations or you will be plagued with return problems. Even if your advertising is not meant to be misleading (such as selling children's toy kites under the name "Ben Franklin Electrical Unit"), the reader of the advertisement may indeed get the wrong impression. Dissatisfaction with the product or a poorly conducted return program can cause enough bad will to ruin your business reputation or simply destroy your profit margin in extra postage and handling charges.

Know the effect your product will have on its users. Will cosmetics cause rashes on some customers? Can clothing be expected to fit? Will auto parts be effective when installed in any car? Will toys break almost immediately under the normal stress provided by a 5-year-old user?

COMBINING RETAIL AND MAIL ORDER

Many retailers conduct mail-order campaigns to supplement store sales. One retailer recently found that his store operations returned 12 percent profit while his mail-order campaign yielded about 21 percent.

Mail-order customers have greater confidence in doing business with a firm that also maintains a retail outlet. Some of the eventual mail-order sales are generated by walk-in traffic. A customer sees an item in the store, perhaps even handles it or tries it on, and later makes the decision to purchase the item by mail. Mail-order customers also feel more secure when they know they can return an item in person. The reputation of the retail outlet serves to attract mail-order business; well-known specialty shops routinely list the procedures for ordering by mail in their magazine and newspaper advertising. Many retailers find that computers ease the problems in adding a mail-order line. If the store uses a small computer to handle its regular inventory control, the computer can handle the mail-order inventory as well. The computer is also useful in updating mailing lists and processing orders.

A retail store must make a large investment to ready its goods for sale. The largest expense of a mail-order business, on the other hand, is the cost of the goods to be sold.

13
HOW TO OPERATE AN EFFICIENT PLANT

No book can give you the know-how of running a factory. Experience comes from years of work. What we can suggest are those phases of plant management which, in the press of activity, tend to be overlooked. Good practices in running a plant lead to greater safety for employees, a better community image, and more efficient operation.

DESIGNING THE LAYOUT OF YOUR PLANT

It is a mistake to rent or construct plant space first and then go about trying to utilize the available space. A more efficient approach is to detail your space requirements carefully and then build a plant that encompasses the design. Prepare a paper or blueprint schematic diagram that shows the entire material flow for the plant from the unloading of supplies to the shipping of the finished product.

If you are building your own plant, consider incorporating a lobby or leisure area into your design. This area will give your odd-duty employees a pleasant place to relax, while also serving as a place for customers to wait. The decoration of this nonproduction area should make for a more pleasurable working atmosphere and a better selling environment.

Keep the plan as clear-cut and as uncluttered as possible. Ideally the raw materials enter your plant at one end and the finished product emerges at the other. The flow need not be a straight line. U-shaped patterns, parallel flows, or even a zigzag that ends up with the finished product back at the shipping and receiving bays can be functional. Backtracking is to be avoided; when some parts and materials are moving contrary to the overall flow, personnel and paperwork can become confused, parts can be lost, and coordination is difficult.

Investigate the possibility of using conveyor belts, cranes, hoists, and industrial trucks to keep the materials moving. It can be less costly to have materials moved by machine than to lose time by having employees moving to production areas. Take care that your building plan allows sufficient aisle space or ceiling height to accommodate the means of conveyance.

One goal of a processing plan is to reduce the need for machinery by improving handling or coordination. Having employees who are performing related tasks work near each other minimizes the distances materials must be moved.

Wide aisles are essential along all traffic lanes in a well-managed shop. Their actual dimensions will depend on the size of trucks which must travel down them, the size of the loads, and the frequency of trips. Check on danger points. What types of machines will border the aisles? Shafts, housings, pillars, braces, or other dangerous projections which extend into the aisle space should be painted in attention-compelling colors. Yellow and black bands painted on such obstructions will help to prevent collisions. Use yellow striping also to mark the edges of open pits, elevator wells, etc. Reduce the possibility of accidental injuries by placing potentially dangerous structures and machinery away from the flow of employee or visitor traffic.

You need ample space for receiving and shipping. The size of entrances must be adequate. The entrance bays should allow the largest truck driven by your suppliers to be driven inside for unloading. Loading ramps and platforms attached to the outside of the business can ease in handling materials. Try to minimize the hand labor required to unload large castings or machinery. If the delivery door for trucks cannot be opened easily by one employee, have a smaller door by which people can enter and leave.

Storage facilities should take advantage of all possible vertical space. Place on the higher shelves items that are used infrequently, such as duplicate parts needed to repair your machinery. Skids and pallets can also be used to increase storage space. When planning your need for storage, compile a parts list. Such a list will help you know what storage to provide for. You should also list the sources, costs, and specifications of each component to aid in your overall planning.

Most plants will require a shop for maintenance operations. Repair of tools and equipment is a regular task and should interfere with manufacturing processes as little as possible.

Your need for inspection space depends upon your product, but almost any item requires some sort of inspection before it is ready for customers.

If a laboratory or other room is needed for research and testing operations, isolate it sufficiently from the heavy workload area.

Like the reception room, your general and sales offices should be located near the front entrance. To create an air of authority, keep executive offices separate. Accounting and bookkeeping offices should be situated near sales offices so that stored records can be easily consulted. If production control and timekeeping procedures are necessary in your operation, locate these offices handy to production so that production personnel will not have the inconvenience of trailing through other offices. A window opening between production and control areas often serves as a step saver and, if your product creates dust or grime, will aid in keeping offices cleaner.

Even the location of the lavatories should be carefully planned. One manufacturer thought to save money by designing one huge lavatory to be used by the entire work force. Later the manufacturer realized that the extra expense of building two small lavatories instead would have more than paid for itself because of all the work time lost by employees making a longer trip to the one main lavatory.

USING THE RIGHT MATERIALS

Too much glass in industrial and business edifices has led to accidents. Be sure that only safety glass is used in areas of danger when glass is necessary. However, windows are important in an industrial structure. If windows and skylight areas take up less than the equivalent of 30 percent of the floor area, the daylight inside the room is insufficient. Be sure that windows are located handily for cleaning. It has been demonstrated that windows lose their efficiency as a light source if left unwashed for 6 months.

A concrete floor is satisfactory for an industrial structure. Wooden floors, whether of planks or blocks, are not as strong, durable, stable, or level. Although wood is softer and less tiring to the feet, it is likely to become oil-soaked and then extremely inflammable.

Check the thickness of the concrete floor. You can drill a hole through it if it can be measured in no other manner. You will not be able to trust heavy loads on it unless it has a safe margin of strength.

Consult with a construction engineer to find the ratio of thickness to weight needed for a given load. Choose a ground floor location if possible. It gives better foundation for machinery and is more accessible for shipping purposes. Level, nonsagging floors, rarely found in upper stories except in steel or concrete buildings, are needed for maintenance of close tolerances for welding heavy assemblies.

If the ceiling has exposed steel beams, you may find them useful for mounting a chain block or hoist. A hoist can facilitate the unloading of equipment. It should hang from a beam strong enough to carry safely any load it will be called upon to support.

A light-colored paint on ceilings and upper walls helps to reflect the light to working spaces and makes the entire shop look more efficient and well-planned.

LIGHTING THE PLANT

When all the plant equipment is installed, you will be able to see the effect of what natural lighting there is upon your factory. You and your lighting specialist (or the local power company) can then plan to provide the rest of the lighting necessary during the daytime and the additional lighting necessary at night. A badly lighted workplace may save on utility bills, but production will suffer for it. However, you can see to it that no more lighting is used than necessary by gradually turning on more lights as conditions grow darker. Some lighting systems make this adjustment automatically by using a sensor to detect the natural light available at any given moment. By choosing the right combination of lighting—mercury, vapor, or fluorescent—you should be able to avoid glare and provide for optimal working conditions. Recent research has shown that the closer artificial light approximates actual sunlight, the healthier the atmosphere it creates for workers in the plant.

HEATING AND VENTILATION

In addition to exploring the cheapest method of heating, try to find ways to reduce the need for heating:

- If different departments have their own storage facilities, combine the separate storage facilities into one storage area that need not be heated.

- Proper use of skylights and southern exposures makes maximum use of natural heat to supplement expensive heating systems.
- Ventilation used to cool areas made overly warm by machinery can recycle this hot air to heat other parts of the plant.

Consider the following points, also, in heating and ventilating your plant:

- Temperatures which should be maintained for efficient working conditions are approximately as follows: machine shop, 65°F (18°C); welding shop, 50 to 60°F (10 to 16°C); and office, 65°F (18°C).
- Provide for proper circulation of air in summer and winter. Ventilation cannot safely be left to chance alone, especially when there are noxious fumes in the air.
- In some places, such as engine and boiler rooms, the air has to be changed every few minutes. In the average shop, about 1200 cubic feet of air per person per hour is needed to provide proper air sanitation.
- Installation of a hood and blower to eliminate dust and fumes at their source may provide sufficient air turnover for the whole shop. Humidity is best maintained at 50 percent but can range safely from 35 to 80 percent in ordinary shops.
- Have a thorough inspection and cleaning at the end of the cooling season and arrange needed repairs before another season. Keep dampers closed in the off-season.

If you content yourself with poor ventilation in order to "save money," you lose the price of good ventilation many times over in lessened output by your employees and an increased amount of spoiled work and scrap. Usually, natural ventilation through doors, windows, and skylights is not dependable. In the absence of a full-fledged air-conditioning system, ventilation should be supplemented with exhaust fans and, if necessary, with ducts which will reach the bad spots.

There are many economical moves you may take to maintain good working temperatures. For example, spraying water on the factory roof after exposure to a very hot sun sometimes gives relief at low cost. Air conditioning can often be attained simply through the use of exhaust fans to remove bad air and intake fans to draw in fresh air. In some situations, normal air currents, aided by windows, louvers, and ducts, will suffice. If your process requires controlled air conditions which call for special handling, study the problem with the manufacturers of the needed equipment. They will supply full information about the fully mechanized temperature-control systems available.

ORGANIZATIONAL EFFICIENCY

Personnel, machines, supplies, work in process, finished products, and deliveries must all be coordinated if your plant is to be successful. Production effects must be judged by time, cost, quantity, and quality.

An efficiently run plant will keep employees and machines constantly busy. There will be a steady flow of raw materials and good coordination among departments. Adequate provisions will be made for emergencies and rush orders. Inspection ratios will be examined daily for any serious and costly discrepancies.

Regardless of the size of your potential output, you will have to be guided by your customer orders. An increased production rate is no advantage if it means you will have to provide storage for large masses of unwanted merchandise. Also, consider the effect of speeded-up production on your labor force. If you complete orders too rapidly, what will workers do with the extra time? Are there other tasks to which they can apply themselves, or will a layoff be necessary? Like your budget, production schedules should be geared to sales.

In an organization chart, you should outline each step in your operation: purchasing, manufacturing, supervision, sales, and shipping. Define each function thoroughly, avoiding any overlapping of duties and authority.

Your need for a separate supervisor for each department will depend on the size of your operation. In a small plant, one individual might be able to serve as foreman, receiving agent, and maintenance engineer. As the plant grows, you will need to hire a different person for each job. Try to keep the size of your departments balanced; otherwise, you will have excess costs in certain seasons when one department may be very busy while another is idle.

Don't be afraid to delegate authority. Authority should equal responsibility in any job. If properly structured, your firm should be able to function successfully without your constant intervention. Meanwhile, you will be freed for planning and policy decisions.

Helpful Charts   An *operation* process chart can plot all the steps in the operation, the time allowances, and materials required. A *flow* process chart can plot the steps taken in a given process in greater detail. A *Gantt* chart can break down each step in the assembly of the finished product to give the time required to perform each operation. This helps in planning the use of employees and supplies. Machine or operation time can be scheduled by hours, days, or weeks; each machine can be graphed separately, and the need for parts can be planned by the time it takes to perform the entire assembly, or any fraction of it. A PERT chart (project evaluation and review techniques) can plot a series of interconnected production activities which mesh to complete a common goal. Efficiency, productivity, and quality control are stated as probabilities, giving the plant manager a realistic appraisal for determining output and production time. These various manufacturing charts help incorporate maximum efficiency into production.

INDUSTRIAL RESEARCH
AND QUALITY CONTROL

In the effort to keep its product competitive, the small plant must make some provision for research and quality control. Larger concerns experiment constantly to find better, more economical ways to create their products. Some plant owners may refer their problems to university research bureaus or hire private research agencies. Your trade association may have a research program which will aid you. You may also hire a member of a university faculty as a consultant.

Provisions should be made for quality-control investigations. To maintain a high degree of excellence, your product must stand tests to be sure that raw materials, intermediate items, or finished products are up to specifications. Very often, this testing can be handled adequately by your production manager. It is usually a short-time activity. Quality-control investigations may involve something as simple as a sifting apparatus to sort out units that do not meet the proper requirements, or they may require very specialized viewing equipment and a qualified technician to observe units under specific conditions of temperature and stress.

USING AUTOMATION

Progressive automation may include feeding mechanisms, such as rotating hoppers and vibration bowls that sort and feed small parts into a process, or loader and unloader conveyors that transport components from one workbench to another. The latest automated device to have an impact on the industrial scene is the robot. A pick-and-place robot, controlled electronically, ranges in price from $5000 to $30,000. Robots can be designed for specific assembly jobs. They can be computerized to have artificial sensing abilities. They can be programmed to memorize a sequence of movements.

If you do utilize automated operations, plan, if possible, for a backup system of production to circumvent a trouble spot when automated equipment breaks down. Repairs can be expensive and time-consuming. Have your lawyer check to see if the contract to purchase the equipment clearly stipulates the vendor's responsibilities on repair. Make sure you have business interruption insurance so that your business is not hurt by production delays.

BUYING YOUR MATERIALS
AND SUPPLIES

Your relationship with your suppliers can prove a decisive factor in the success of your business. The small firm is frequently at a disadvantage in dealing with its suppliers. In periods of shortages, manufacturers are apt to favor larger customers who can, with one order, buy out an entire stock. Thus, the small firm must exert special efforts to maintain its relationship with suppliers.

If you can achieve a cooperative relationship with your supplier, you will find the firm a valuable source of management advice. Suppliers may be able to provide repair services on their product, extend credit, and quickly apprise you of discount offers. (As you gain experience, you will find that it is often advisable to secure a bank loan to take advantage of discount prices.)

Usually you will find that the salesperson follows certain schedules and counts on making calls at fairly definite and predictable intervals. Your cooperation will work to mutual advantage. The salesperson can often advise you on the status of a manufacturer, a product's quality, and business integrity. The information carried from one plant to the next may alert you to new trends in the industry.

Plan for a rapid turnover of stock. Slow-moving material may rob your business of capital needed for fast-moving items, the ones that support your shop. If space is limited, be sure to patronize a firm which makes frequent deliveries and has fairly complete stock.

Should you rely on one supplier or divide your needs among many? A dealer may try to convince you that he or she is able to fill all your needs, but shopping around may enable you to find bargains, such as ordering items directly from a mine or refinery. Ordering raw materials from too many suppliers, however, will prevent you from winning the strong allegiance of any of them. Your goal is to decrease costs; a supplier's goal is to increase sales. Cementing a mutual relationship can benefit both of you, for example, by earning you volume discounts made possible by the increased business given to the supplier. The supplier furnishing you the greatest share of your requirements will understand your business situation better and may well extend you privileges on your open account, such as payment extensions. However, if you are starting a new firm, you may be able to get more credit at first by spreading your purchases.

Be certain that the materials delivered by your suppliers are up to the standard of quality which your product requires. Prompt inspection should uncover any flaws or shortages. Check on the newly delivered parts by observing their use in production. If you have a complaint, make it promptly, giving supporting evidence.

Suppliers will also respect your word if you mark orders "rush" only when the need is critical. If you constantly use emergency terminology, your orders may only get routine treatment, whatever the need.

BUYING FOR
THE SMALL PLANT

How do you locate sources of essential raw materials and components? Obtain all available handbooks or data books issued by business papers and selling companies. They contain information on stocks carried by industrial millworks, supply houses, wholesale houses, manufacturers who sell direct, and retail stores. You may also advertise for bids.

Industrial-supply houses cater to factories and carry a complete line of materials. Since they sell in large volume, they buy their own stock at the most favorable prices and terms and can sell to factories at or near ordinary wholesale prices. The types of stock carried by industrial-supply houses are determined to a great extent by the principal class of customer served and so may differ from city to city or even within a single large industrial district. Conversations with the salespeople who call on you will soon inform you which of these houses can be of most service.

Many *wholesale houses* give special discounts to factory accounts. In certain areas, the wholesale hardware house and the industrial-supply house may compete with each other. When this is the case, the buyer for a shop can sometimes get discounts for which the shop would not otherwise qualify.

In some instances, the ordinary retail store may provide supplies for small plants. If the plant provides the dealer sufficient business, the dealer may allow credit while supply houses are demanding cash.

Direct purchasing from manufacturers may necessitate larger unit orders to avoid heavy express charges on small shipments. However, it generally does not pay to pad an order beyond probable needs merely to take advantage of a lower freight rate.

To circumvent the entire range of problems created by supplier dependency, you may decide to make your own components. There are instances when a company must produce its own parts to fit specifications which cannot be duplicated by another manufacturer. In that case, you will have to purchase the parts and assemble them or make the entire item from raw materials. This means a substantial outlay for machinery and equipment which might more profitably be used in expanding your product lines. The beginning factory usually fares best with purchased parts, if they are available.

INVENTORY CONTROL

Spot checks of inventory can also be used for theft prevention. Your front office records may show invoices and checks for goods that were never actually purchased. Keep the receiving end of your business separated from the personnel at the buying end to avoid collusion. Also, do not rely on inventory reports composed from tallying the purchases. Your purchasing system must check to verify that inventory is real. One trustworthy person on the receiving end can initial invoices. Front-office personnel can date and stamp incoming invoices. Check the invoices against your orders for accuracy of terms, prices, shipping quantities, and quality. Since actual bribery of a company's purchasing agent is not an uncommon practice, you should protect yourself against this type of fraud by irregular inventory spot checks and a continuous record of purchases that can be easily audited by your accountant.

Your perpetual inventory card should contain a description of the material as it will be entered on an order blank. Include data on the length of time it takes a shipment to arrive. Show the actual balance on hand, recording each receipt or withdrawal of material. If material has been allocated to a job scheduled for the near future, note the reserve on the card so the reorder point can be stepped up, if advisable.

Keep supplies of small items in stock even though they are obtainable quickly. Metal screws, wood screws, studs, bolts, and nuts will not tie up much money in stock, and it is a good practice to have them on hand. A glance at the floor sweepings will show whether they are being used carefully.

REDUCING EMPLOYEE ACCIDENTS

Statistics prove that the cost of accidents in small plants is high enough to demand a program for their reduction. In addition, no plant owner will want his or her laxity to be the cause of serious injuries or illnesses. Furthermore, the Occupational Safety and Health Administration (OSHA) of the U.S. Department of Labor requires that you maintain safe facilities and operational practices or be subject to penalties.

Many managers believe that insurance alone will tend to the total costs of accidents. However, as a rule there will be about 4 additional dollars of indirect costs for each dollar of compensation paid by your insurance policy. An accident will lead to lost time by injured employees, lost time of fellow workers who halt operations to help them and lost time of supervisors and managers who must select and train new employees while the injured workers are recuperating. Damage to machines is a frequent by-product of accidents, leading to lost production, destruction of materials, and other general lapses in output.

In recent years, many small plants, with the assistance of safety organizations, have developed successful safety programs without undue expense or additional personnel. Each of these programs is devised with the application of certain basic principles. Modern safety engineers have discovered that these principles must be adhered to in developing a successful program within any small plant. Here are the principles:

- Study the problem thoroughly yourself so that you can pinpoint the most vulnerable areas in the plant and the machines and tools that might become involved in accidents.
- Ask for assistance from the nearest office of your state department of labor, insurance company, or trade association. They can help you analyze your accident problem and assist you in planning a safety program that will reduce unnecessary costs, generally without charge. They can provide information and guidance on employee instruction, keeping accident records, methods of safety inspection, developing a safety committee, and controlling mechanical hazards.
- Learn how to recognize hazards of all kinds, especially those that are not self-evident, and learn how to remove them or safeguard employees against them. The following are some factors to consider:

- Machine safeguards.
- Plant construction, layout, and arrangement.
- Unsafe practices of employees, including those involved in house-keeping of plant and machines, maintenance, use of hand tools, lifting, carrying, and working on scaffolds, ladders, or other elevated places.
- Possibility of fire, explosion, or electrical shocks.
- Special occupational hazards.

- Sell the idea of safety to all employees. This is the most important and the most difficult phase of accident prevention. You cannot do it overnight. Encourage, demonstrate, and insist upon safety every day until each person has formed safe working habits. The following are some of the ways of selling safety to employees:
  - Recognize that, since safety is a management responsibility, it should be planned as a part of the plant operation.
  - Organize, guide and encourage safety committees, and delegate responsibility through them and through supervisors.
  - Publicize the problem, the program, and its results through group meetings, talks, posters, and bulletin boards.
  - Supply safety information and knowledge through committees, meetings, talks, posters, written instructions, sound-and-slide presentations, and movies.

New employees, inadequately trained or not yet comfortable with their machines, are safety hazards in themselves. On-the-job instruction can eliminate this danger. Try not to assign a new employee a job that tests the employee's capabilities if the employee's efforts to do the job may lead to unsafe conditions. Supervise new workers until they familiarize themselves with the mechanics of the operation. Keep records of accidents. These records will serve a number of purposes, such as the following:

- Providing information for a study of causes and frequencies
- Estimating total cost of accidents for consideration with profit-and-loss statement
- Identifying workers who have an unusual number of accidents
- Indicating progress and success of safety program

One of the best ways in which you can gain the worker's interest in safety is by eliminating those hazards over which you have direct control. The realization that you are doing your part in providing the workers with safe working conditions will make them more receptive to a safety program. A basis is thus provided for employee cooperation.

They will be more willing to do their part in maintaining safe working conditions and to support the entire safety program. Commence work in the following areas.

Inspection Accompanied by some key workers, make an *initial safety inspection* of the plant. Even though you may not have had safety training, you can recognize many situations as being dangerous if you study them closely.

Some hazards that may not be found by such inspections may be discovered by *safety engineers* or *inspectors* who can be brought in from state labor departments or insurance companies. They often are asked by safety-minded managers to analyze safety conditions in the plant, make detailed safety inspections, and recommend corrective action.

Once hazards are recognized, *corrective action* may be taken to eliminate them. It is sound business practice to do so since safety and efficiency always go together.

This process of inspection and elimination of hazards is a continuous one, since new hazards may be created by a change in operation or old hazards may reappear.

Plan Next, plan or replan your layout and arrangement intelligently. Proper planning of the original plant layout and adequate control of operations theoretically would eliminate all accidents. Many firms have come very close to that goal. At the time the plant is built, safe working conditions can be provided without additional difficulties or expense, since the most efficient operations are usually the safest.

Changes in layout or operations of existing plants are indicated for reasons of safety and efficiency when materials pile up at certain points, when the paths of materials in process cross each other, when employees do not have adequate working space, or when similar conditions become apparent. These changes, particularly if they are major rearrangements in plant layout or operations, cost so much that another change is not practical for some time. This emphasizes the importance of planning all changes carefully so that other dangerous conditions are not created by the change.

Poor lighting of buildings, rooms, and passageways is responsible, directly or indirectly, for many accidents. Where conditions do not permit constructive improvements, liberal use of white paint or frequent application of whitewash will be of much value. Light-reflecting wall surfaces do much to help the diffusion of available light, whether natural or artificial.

Plant housekeeping—cleanliness and orderliness—is a fundamental of good management. It prevents accidents by removing many causes. In a well-kept plant, there are no loose objects on stairs, floors, and platforms, no articles that can fall from overhead, no wet or greasy floors, no projecting objects in aisles, and no projecting nails or sharp pieces of metal to tear the workers' hands.

In plants where accident records are good, managers have paid very careful attention to maintenance of plant, equipment, and machinery in the following ways:

- Floors are kept in good condition, without holes or splinters that might cause slipping, tripping, falling or handling injuries.
- All portable equipment on which workers stand, such as ladders, steps, horses, or scaffold planks, are maintained in proper condition.
- Chisels, portable grinders, and drills are kept free of defects, or replaced. Machine guards are properly made, installed, and maintained, and workers are instructed in their proper use.
- Machines themselves, as well as pressure vessels, electric wiring, and other equipment, are kept in proper condition for both production and safety.
- Operations and methods are planned to eliminate hazardous situations and ensure adequate control at all times.
- Mechanical handling is substituted for manual handling. Often it is cheaper and faster as well as safer.
- Workers are carefully trained and adequately supervised to see that all supplies, products, and other materials are moved, carried, and stored in a safe manner as well as an efficient one.
- Workers are protected from electrical hazards.
- Protective clothing and equipment, such as safety shoes, goggles, and gloves, are worn by all workers on jobs where needed. Management usually supplies these items and insists on their use.
- A simple way to eliminate electrical hazards is to make sure that all circuits and lines are installed and maintained in conformance with safety standards.

Whether a worker wears suitable or unsuitable clothing is a matter largely within the control of the employer. Keep watch on this matter. A ragged sleeve, a flowing necktie, or a loose coat or jumper jacket can do incalculable harm if caught in any part of a moving machine. Workers should be required to confine their hair or wear adequate head protection when engaged in machine operations. For certain jobs, special clothing (hand and arm protectors, shoulder capes, hats, caps, welders' aprons, coats, overalls, leggings, shoes, etc.) is necessary for all operators. In the selection of such special clothing, four essentials should be considered:

● The garment should be reasonably comfortable when worn under the conditions for which it was designed.
● It should fit snugly and not interfere unduly with the movements of the wearer.
● It should offer adequate protection against the hazard for which it was designed.
● It should be durable under the conditions for which it is used.

Safeguarding of mechanical apparatus is of prime importance. You must convince workers that guards should be installed on machines and used at all times. Those who have become accustomed to working on machines without guards often resent their installation and will remove them whenever possible. They must be convinced that the guards are necessary for their protection.

Workers who have been trained on guarded machines prefer them. It has been proved that the correct kind of guards invariably increases production through enabling machines to be operated more steadily, or faster, or both.

You should emphatically maintain discipline in the interest of safety—particularly with workers who smoke when smoking is properly prohibited, who drink liquor at any time on company premises or report for work under the influence of liquor, or who tamper with safety protective devices. You need to be tough with those who disregard safety rules—particularly those operating without full use of safety equipment or without authority. Post notices conspicuously, describing the following:

● How to start, operate, and stop equipment
● What switches and controls must never be touched
● Where fire-fighting apparatus is accessible and how to use it
● How aisles are to be kept free for use in case of fire
● How waste is to be kept out of corners to avoid fire

Every shop should have a system for furnishing first aid to the injured. The effects of an accident may be intensified by lack of immediate and proper care of the injury; unskilled handling may do further harm, in addition to causing unnecessary pain. Where it is not possible to have a thoroughly equipped emergency room, there should be first-aid supplies available all over the plant. See that locations are known to all and that personnel are trained to render first aid, such as CPR (cardiac pulmonary resuscitation). Names, addresses, and telephone numbers of physicians and local hospitals should be conspicuously posted.

MAINTENANCE PROCEDURES

Small businesses are frequently guilty of poor housekeeping, and this disregard is reflected in their production records. Safety alone dictates the necessity for uncluttered aisles, quick disposal of waste materials that accumulate under machines, and regular cleaning of windows and walls.

To get the most out of your machines, follow an inspection procedure that adheres to a definite schedule. Delegate the responsibility for maintenance to competent hands. If you do not have enough work to employ a full-time worker, get regular inspection service from a local, qualified individual.

From your inspection reports and cost records, you should be able to detect any unwarranted maintenance expense and to adopt corrective measures. Sometimes the problem will be solved simply by the adjustment of a particular machine. Constant vigilance against machine malfunction and misuse will save you money.

You may find some of the following maintenance tips helpful:

- Keep all working parts free of harmful waste, shavings, and other extraneous materials.
- Immediately investigate all undue vibrations in machinery.
- Establish a lubrication routine that prevents rust and unnecessary wear.
- Inspect all valves, pumps, joints, fittings, and couplings according to a regular schedule.
- Inspect and test all emergency equipment at reasonable intervals.
- Mount safety or relief valves as closely as possible to the equipment.
- Be sure the pressure gauges with which valves are set are correct, usually at about 4 percent blowdown and not less than 3 percent.
- When a fuse is to be replaced, find the cause of its blowing first; it may be a stiff belt, tight bearings, unclean commutator, motor being brought to full speed too quickly, damaged motor, or worn bearings. Tending to these matters promptly may prevent accidents and save you money. Be sure you do not overfuse. See that the contact on the fuse block is good and that the right kind of fuse is being used for the circuit.

- If a motor or generator becomes wet, dry it out thoroughly with portable infrared lamps. Temperatures should not be raised above 194°F (90°C). The stator may be dried out in an oven.
- Be sure the frames of all arc welding equipment are grounded to avoid shock. When you are locating your welding equipment, remember that ventilation is important. Otherwise, overheating may result, shortening the life of the insulation.
- Have an expert go over your oil-burning system in detail.
- To keep firehoses in top operating condition, run water through them at least twice a year. If they should freeze, thaw them out before bending them.
- Get the manufacturers' data on setting saws, care of files, and proper usage. Stretch the life of your tools by using them properly.

14
DOING BUSINESS
WITH THE FEDERAL
GOVERNMENT

The United States government buys huge quantities of machinery, equipment, supplies, and services. For many companies, the government is their biggest potential customer. Many firms compete for government business. To succeed, they must do the following:

- Offer a good product at a highly competitive price.
- Be able to produce the goods or services in the time required.
- Know how to follow government purchasing-office procedures.
- Represent their firm and its products favorably to government purchasers.

This chapter will tell you how the government buys, how you find out which agencies buy your products, how you can compete for contracts, and how the Small Business Administration can help you sell to the government.

FILLING GOVERNMENT
CONTRACTS

Before making your bid, you should be certain that you can profitably manufacture the item which the government wants under the strict terms of the contract. If specifications are not precisely met, the government can reject your product. The government also has the right to terminate a contract at any time while production is under way. This has sometimes taken place because a business failed to live up to specific regulations, but cancellations also occur because of changes in the government's needs.

The specifications for government manufacture are very rigid. The quality, grade, size, and other characteristics of components are precisely detailed. This makes government items more expensive to produce than the typical civilian product. You will find the specifications listed in *The Index of Federal Specifications and Standards* available from the Superintendent of Documents, U.S. Government Printing Office, Washington, D.C. 20402, while the use and development of the standards and specifications are discussed in *The Guide to Federal Specifications and Standards of the Federal Government* available at General Services Administration (GSA) business service centers and field offices of the Department of Commerce and the Small Business Administration. Reproductions of federal specifications and standards are available from Specification Sales, GSA, Building 197, Washington Navy Yard, Washington D.C. 20407, as well as from GSA business service centers. Copies of military specifications and standards can be obtained only from the Naval Publications and Forms Center, 5801 Tabor Ave., Philadelphia, Pa. 19120.

If you wish to sell the government a new or improved product that exceeds existing specifications or eliminates the need for old products, you must go through channels to make the government aware that they might be interested in contracting with your company. File Form 1171, the Application for Presenting New or Improved Articles, with the GSA.

The government prefers to enter into contracts on a fixed-price basis. This means you must plan carefully both for the effects of inflationary cost increases over the life of the contract and for expensive difficulties that arise in performance. In some instances variations can be written into the contract providing for price redetermination and escalations.

BIDDING FOR CONTRACTS

Contracts calling for payment of the contractor's costs in addition to a fixed payment are used only when the nature of the work makes a fixed-payment contract impractical. Contracts calling for a payment of cost and a percentage of the cost are forbidden by law. When circumstances require the government to act quickly, it will sometimes allow work to begin with only a letter of intent from the contractor.

When you know which agencies buy the type of products you make or can make, apply to be put on their list of bidders by filing standard Form 129, the Bidder's Mailing List Application form. The local office of the Small Business Administration can help you find out which agencies normally buy your product. The Department of Commerce publishes the *Commerce Business Daily*, which lists most projects open to private contractors as soon as they are put out for bid. Also listed are sales of surplus property from various government agencies, foreign business opportunities, subcontracting possibilities, and the winning bidders on previously announced contracts. To subscribe to this important information source, write the Superintendent of Documents, U.S. Government Printing Office, Washington, D.C. 20402.

When awarding a contract, the government considers not only the size of the bid, but also the "responsibility" of the bidding company. The government wants assurances that your company is capable of performing within the terms of the contract. Thus, if your company has no experience in the field of the bid project, you are unlikely to be awarded the contract. An inexperienced company is more likely to have performance difficulties. Therefore, to assure a government agency that you can meet contract terms, send a complete résumé on your usual production, your plant capacity and equipment, number of workers, background of engineering and management personnel, and your firm's financial position. The agency may also send you a questionnaire to fill out so that it can gain a clearer picture of your suitability for government contracting.

Errors in the preparation of your bids can result in financial loss and also cast doubt on your ability to fulfill contracts. There is little benefit in cutting all your estimates to the minimum. You may win the contract but fail to make a profit, or may even suffer a loss in completing your product.

Businesses performing work under government contracts operate under restrictions which may raise the cost of doing business:

- The components of products you supply are required by the Buy American Act to be of American origin if possible.
- The Walsh-Healy Public Contracts Act requires employers on government contracts to pay overtime to employees working more than 8 hours a day or 40 hours a week.
- The Davis-Brown Act prevents a contractor working on a government project from paying workers less than the prevailing local wage and fringe benefits.
- Items produced for the Department of Defense that are on the qualified products list must be tested at the contractor's expense before they are delivered.

If you are sending in a bid on an item for the first time, ask for a copy of specifications and drawings. Instructions accompanying the invitation to bid will tell you whether you can bid on part of the total or on the total amount, your delivery date, and the deadline for withdrawal. It will also give particulars on packaging and shipping requirements.

After the bids are opened in public at the appointed time and read aloud, the lower bids are designated for further evaluation. As price is only one of the factors considered, the lowest bid is not always chosen. The government agency is sometimes influenced by its opinion of your financial stability and your ability to meet delivery and specifications.

At times, the government buys by negotiation rather than by advertising for bids. Using its list of bidders, a procurement office may ask several suppliers for proposals or quotations on the item to be purchased. Those making the best proposals are called in for further negotiation, during which government buyers try to get the best deal possible.

If you wish to bid on a Department of Defense contract, be sure to first familiarize yourself with the armed services procurement regulations which govern these contracts. The military procurement procedures are explained in the brochure *Selling to the Military*, available from the Superintendent of Documents, U.S. Government Printing Office, Washington, D.C. 20402. Each of the armed services, in turn, has its own set of regulations. When you deal with an agency, be sure you receive all your instructions from the contracting officer, who may be a civilian or in the military. The contracting officer, or his or her authorized representative, is the only person qualified to administer the contract and authorize changes.

Should you invent an item while under government contract, you will face the problem of patenting rights. Some agencies, such as the Department of Defense and the National Aeronautics and Space Administration, have flexible policies on patenting rights. Others, such as the Atomic Energy Commission and the Department of Agriculture, are required by law to take title to inventions and patents which are the product of a contract let by them.

SOURCES OF
PROCUREMENT INFORMATION

In addition to the *Commerce Business Daily*, government projects put out to bid by private industry appear in other sources. Construction projects soliciting bidders are noted in area newspapers, pertinent trade journals, and in industry technical publications.

The business service centers of the GSA are responsible for issuing the invitations for bids in their regions. Business service centers are located in Boston, New York, Washington, D.C., Philadelphia, Atlanta, Chicago, Kansas City, Fort Worth, Houston, Denver, San Francisco, Los Angeles, and Seattle. GSA business specialists work out of these centers to provide assistance to the business person in securing government contracts.

Defense Department contracts are sometimes issued separately through the Defense Logistics Agency. Interested businesses should send their Form 129, Bidder's Mailing List Application, to one of the Defense Logistic Agency supply centers, located in Columbus and Dayton, Ohio, Alexandria and Richmond, Virginia, and Philadelphia, Pennsylvania. Subcontractors should send their mailing list application to one of the regional offices of the Defense Contract Administration Services, located in Boston, Chicago, Cleveland, Dallas, Los Angeles, New York, Philadelphia, St. Louis, and Marietta, Georgia. However, your local office of the Small Business Administration, Department of Commerce, or General Services Administration should still be able to assist you in obtaining Department of Defense contracts.

DIFFICULTIES WITH
GOVERNMENT CONTRACTS

At times, economic conditions make it advisable for the government to cancel a contract. When this is necessary, the contractor usually recovers all allowable expenditures made up to the time of the termination. The contractor also will be awarded a reasonable profit on the investment of time and facilities, provided that records indicate a profit would have been made on the contract. If, instead, a loss is indicated, less than 100 percent of expenditures would be recovered. For this reason, it is essential to keep well-documented accounts on all transactions.

Most contracts contain a "dispute" clause which permits you to petition the Board of Contract Appeals on any disagreement you have with the contracting officer. Your appeal must be made within 30 days of the contractor's request or specification. While the board processes your appeal, you are obliged to continue filling the contract's requirements. If any disagreement occurs, be sure to contact your lawyer for aid in seeking redress.

SUBCONTRACTING OF
GOVERNMENT CONTRACTS

In competing for government contracts, the small enterprise is frequently hampered by the lack of facilities for mass production. At times, with the assistance of the Small Business Administration, groups of firms band together to bid on government contracts. Even more frequently, small businesses have received subcontracts from prime contractors who deal with the government. You can build up a good volume of subcontracting if you develop good relations with a number of prime contractors who can use your production facilities.

Before you approach a prime contractor, decide on the type of product you can make and the price you will charge. You will find end products and components bought by the military displayed at the SBA regional or branch offices. Get the specifications on items you think you can manufacture. Then, after a close examination of your costs, ask the SBA for the names of suitable prime manufacturers.

Initial contact with the prime contractor might be made by a letter including the same kind of information as is requested on the Bidder's Mailing List Application form (standard Form 129). Military security clearance for work on classified materials should be arranged through your prime contractor. Be sure to be specific about the services or products you are offering.

Subcontracting for government contracts has bolstered production levels for many firms during business declines. You may be able to rent idle government-owned machine tools if your prime contractor sponsors you. Subcontracting also qualifies you for financial assistance from the SBA.

If you should obtain a contract from a prime contractor, be sure to familiarize yourself with the government's terms. Many may not apply to you. Your requirements on patent and data rights, financing, disputes, and appeals will also be different from those of the prime contractor.

Subcontracting carries its disadvantages. If you allow defense work subcontracts to absorb the largest part of your volume of production and neglect sources of civilian work, you may find yourself idle when defense work slackens. You might also be left with specialized equipment which you do not need for your civilian work. Remember, too, that military production requires close tolerances and a precision on which you will have to pass inspection from the prime contractor as well as from the government. You are also open to termination of subcontracts during periods when the prime contractor's business slows down and it does the work which was formerly subcontracted.

GOVERNMENT BIDDING CONSIDERATIONS

Bidding for a government contract requires high standards of accuracy. Make sure your bid is in line with these considerations:

- Government packaging requirements may call for expensive materials, labor, and machinery not necessary for your civilian product.
- Make an allowance in your profit computations for delivery costs, increases in labor costs, and fluctuations in the prices of raw materials.
- Have a design which complies completely with the specifications and standards of the invitation to bid.
- Furnish the required information in your application. Government questionnaires and applications must be fully completed.
- Demonstrate your responsibility and ability to perform the contract at your bid price.

15
HIRING AND MANAGING PERSONNEL

Each company has a personal style of doing business which is reflected in the work and attitude of its employees. Your own daily experience should convince you of the value of efficient and courteous personnel. Almost every day you are in contact with employees of some company: a clerk in the local supermarket, a telephone operator, a receptionist, a bank teller, a manager, or a chief executive. The way he or she handles your business may encourage you to continue to do business with the firm or swear never to set foot on the premises again. What you expect from the personnel of other companies, people will also expect from the employees of your firm. In setting the tone for your personnel, your attitude is crucial—not only must you be able to hire competent people, you must also have the necessary style of leadership that encourages employees to give their best efforts and loyalty. It is not an easy task. Business pressures place strains on human relationships, and it often is difficult to find and keep the most desirable type of personnel. Compromises sometimes have to be made.

Moreover, as an employer you must be aware of and keep abreast of current labor law restrictions, their application to your industry, regulations on minimum wages, maximum hours, overtime pay, and child labor, and details of keeping the payroll records needed for government purposes. Maintaining an efficient staff is a major and continuous management problem of every business.

YOUR REQUIREMENTS

The very nature of your operations may fix the number of employees which you must hire. If you are planning to use 10 machines to produce a product which requires an operator and helper per machine, you of course need at least 20 employees for this part of your business. In other areas, determining the number of people you need is not that straightforward, and only after a period of experience will you be able to determine how many employees you need. Sometimes, the relative ability of the available employees may determine the number of employees required for a particular job. If you are fortunate, you may have an employee whose ability and efficiency makes him or her the equivalent of several employees.

In determining your requirements, prepare a description for every job in your company and the type of employee needed for that job, including education, skills, and experience. It is important, if you hire a person, that he or she have challenging and continuous work with which to be occupied. There is nothing as detrimental to an employee and a company as hiring employees for positions that do not demand their full time and energies.

RECRUITING HELP

You may utilize various sources and agencies to contact applicants. You can advertise in newspapers, or you can call agencies or offices operated by commercial firms, trade associations, schools, unions, and the state.

Whatever source you use, make sure that you adequately describe your job requirements. You do not want to waste time interviewing people who do not qualify for the position. Before accepting applicants for interviews, request their résumés of experience or similar records to determine whether their basic qualifications meet your objectives.

When you do interview a person, there are various steps to follow.

Have the applicant fill out an application form. This should elicit enough information to allow you to judge whether the applicant can do a particular job with minimum training and whether he or she will fit into your company.

Interview the applicant in private, and put the applicant at ease with a few general remarks on the business and the job. Plan the interview so that you have the résumé and application before you, and take some time to absorb some of the important information. Encourage the applicant to talk about points suggested to you by the application. Responses to routine questions often reveal a person's personality, and an alert interviewer can generally catch troublesome characteristics. Depending on the importance of the position, interviews should take between 15 minutes and an hour. Another interview, possibly by the supervisor of the department the applicant would enter, is advisable.

Provide some test of the applicant's job skill. For example, if you are hiring a typist, the applicant should be tested for proficiency and speed. If a technical skill is required, you may have to give some written test which can reveal the extent of the applicant's ability. After interviewing and testing applicants, check their references before making the final choice. Contact by telephone or mail is usually adequate, but for high-level supervisory positions, it may be best to meet with some of the references.

Verify whether the applicant has the skills the job requires or is capable of learning them in a short time. This is the only criterion necessary, unless the applicant has given you reason to suspect his or her trustworthiness or willingness to work (for example, consistent absenteeism with previous employers). It is illegal to discriminate against an applicant because of the person's race, religion, sex, or handicap. If a person can do the job, he or she must be seriously considered. In many positions, the disadvantaged will perform far more conscientiously and skillfully than the average worker. In most instances, you will have a choice of many applicants who can do the job. You will be able to concentrate on selecting the one most qualified.

HIRING AN EMPLOYEE

For certain classes of employees, you may wish to establish a *probationary period.* Inform the employee when hired that he or she is "on trial" for a specified time. During that period, the employee, too, will be able to judge the suitability of the job to his or her abilities.

Many companies give *physical examinations* before hiring a person. This is necessary if the work imposes any physical strain. It also helps you to comply with worker's compensation laws by giving you a record of an employee's health. Should any physical disability occur, you are protected by your written record of the worker's condition at the time of hiring.

TRAINING THE NEW EMPLOYEE

How you choose to train a new employee depends upon the job being taught, the personnel to be used for instructing, and how many new hirees are being instructed at one time. Unless your company is large enough to have specialized training personnel, the responsibility of instructing the new employee will fall on the person who will be his or her supervisor on the job. The employee must be able to work with the supervisor and meet the supervisor's standards.

Actual methods of instruction vary with the skills and procedures required by the job. More complicated functions may require seminar-type conferences and lectures for large groups of trainees, on-the-job training, and role playing. Lectures and conferences are effective ways to present a mass of background information that the trainee must study and commit to memory. However, an examination of the trainee's retention of background material is not a good indication of how the trainee will perform on the job. As most background information is usually available in reference materials, it is more important to know where to look things up than to trust one's memory for the information. Background information for a salesperson, for example, is not as important as the salesperson's ability to deal with people.

Role playing also allows the trainee to see things from the other side (that of the customer, for example), thus giving the trainee valuable insight into how to deal with a sales problem. Role playing also gives both the instructor and trainee an idea of how much the trainee must still master.

On-the-job training provides real experience, and mistakes can be corrected by the supervisor before they get out of hand. For many jobs, such as those requiring machine skills or cashiers, on-the-job training is the only effective method. Follow these four steps in on-the-job training when no other teaching method has been used:

1. *Teach.* Find what your employee knows. Take nothing for granted, even if the employee declared on the job application that he or she had similar experience. Then teach what is not known, keeping in mind that it is better to repeat some of what is already known than to have the employee waste time and material later.
2. *Demonstrate.* Following the job breakdown sheet, show the trainee how to do the job. Proceed slowly, asking questions which make the trainee think of why each step is taken in the demonstrated manner. Then demonstrate at normal speed.
3. *Let the trainee perform.* After the demonstration, let the employee perform the job alone. Your attitude at this point should be one of

encouragement. Avoid looking over shoulders. Demonstrate again, if a mistake is made.

4. *Inspect.* Either you or a supervisor should then check the trainee's work. Point out satisfactory progress, or explain what he or she is doing wrong and why.

For extremely specialized or intensive training, it may be worthwhile for your company to pay the employee to enroll at a local school of higher education. Your industry association may also sponsor educational gatherings such as conferences or symposia. Your employees can be given the incentive to advance their skills on their own if the company normally promotes people from within the company.

COMPENSATING PERSONNEL

From your experience and contacts, you can readily discover the going rate of pay. Depending on your needs and the pool of available prospects, you may be able to offer more or less than the going rate. Here again your actual experience will be your guide. In important positions, you may leave the exact amount open to bargaining within certain bounds.

The level of pay needed to attract talent will depend on your industry, the size of your company, your geographic location, and the responsibilities of the job. If your company shows promise of rapid growth, you may find a capable manager who is willing to start at a lower salary with expectations of a bonus for getting results. Straight-salary income may not be sufficient to attract personnel. You may have to provide added pay benefits: a profit-sharing plan, a possible part ownership of the business, educational benefits, and other fringe benefits. For example, women workers can be attracted by convenient day-care facilities or a subsidy paid by your company to a day-care facility.

Be aware that the Equal Pay Act of 1963 forbids wage discrimination on the basis of sex. As long as men and women are doing substantially equal work, they must be paid identically. Male and female telephone repairers were ruled to be doing substantially equal jobs, even though the males occasionally carried heavier equipment. Male and female bank tellers handling different kinds of accounts would also call for equal pay as the difference between their duties is minor. Even if an agreement between union and management calls for different wage rates, the pay must be the same if the differences between the jobs are insignificant.

PROVIDING FRINGE BENEFITS
TO EMPLOYEES

Fringe benefits is a term that describes pay benefits other than wage or salary income. There are benefits provided employees through group life-insurance protection, discounts on company products, education assistance, health and accident benefits, no-interest loans, and retirement benefits. Fringe benefits to some employees may be more important than a salary increase because a fringe benefit may be received partially or wholly tax-free.

Retirement Benefits   The federal government, through the tax law, encourages the creation of private pension plans by allowing (1) an employer to deduct contributions on behalf of an employee, (2) an employee to avoid current tax on the contributions made to his or her account, and (3) tax-free accumulation of income earned on funds invested in the plan. Tax is not incurred until the employee begins to collect benefits. If certain rules are met, this tax is generally lower than the tax otherwise due on similar amounts.

These tax benefits apply only to plans which meet technical rules that generally are aimed at preventing owners from discriminating in their own favor. When a plan is approved by the IRS, it is called a *qualified plan*. A qualified plan may not discriminate in favor of officers or other highly compensated personnel.

Qualified retirement plans may be based on *profit sharing* or *pension funding*. A profit-sharing plan adjusts itself to changes in your business. You may contribute according to a formula based on profits. In loss years you may contribute nothing, while in good years the contributions may be substantial. The employee is not promised a fixed or predetermined amount of benefits. However, the plan creates an incentive in the employee to help increase the company profits.

Thrift plans may be coordinated within a qualified plan, allowing the worker to contribute some of his or her own funds to the plan.

In a pension plan, contributions are not based on profits, and benefits are definitely determinable. A pension plan must be "actuarially sound"; that is, contributions must be substantial enough to fulfill the purpose of paying a fixed monthly sum when employees reach a predetermined retirement age, or when they can no longer work because of infirmity. If you choose a fixed-benefit plan, you must use a definite formula for determining an employee's benefits. Contributions are then determined actuarially to ensure adequate funds for benefits. If you decide on a money-purchase pension plan, you use a fixed rate of contributions, from which benefits are actuarially determined.

The kind of plan you choose will depend on the probable future of your business and the kind of benefits you want your employees to have. Consult with your accountant and insurance adviser before committing yourself. You want to know the cost commitment and how much flexibility you will have in annual contributions. Your consultants can give you cost estimates based on 20- or 30-year projections.

Life Insurance Plans A company may provide up to $50,000 face value of group-term life insurance without an employee being taxed on the value of premiums in income. The company may deduct the premiums. Group coverage is available at a considerably lower cost than could be obtained on an individual basis.

VACATIONS, HOLIDAYS, AND SICK PAY

Vacation pay practices vary with each company, but many companies give 2 weeks after a year's service and 3 weeks or more after an additional period of time.

Paid holidays are generally granted for the following 6 days: New Year's day, Memorial Day, Independence Day, Labor Day, Thanksgiving day, and Christmas. Additional holidays are often granted in some communities or industries. Other holidays which may or may not be observed in your type of business are Washington's Birthday, Lincoln's Birthday, Veterans' Day, Columbus Day, and Martin Luther King's Birthday. Federal legislation now ensures that 4 out of 11 holidays are celebrated on Mondays, giving many workers 3-day weekends.

Also inform new employees of company policy on paid religious holidays. Ensure that all your workers are treated equally in paid time off.

Sick leave practices vary. A certain number of days may be granted for the year. In some companies, a few days may be allowed under self-care, but above that a doctor's note is required. As for maternity leaves, employers may no longer refrain from putting qualified young women in vital positions because of the fear that pregnancy may interrupt their careers, without running the danger of being sued under Title VII of the Civil Rights Act, which forbids sexual discrimination in hiring, promotions, and all other conditions of employment. Employees who maintain health and disability plans are required by federal law to provide coverage for pregnancy and childbirth.

As more and more single parents join the work force, employers must face the problem of how to treat leave for caring for sick children.

Most companies require their employees to use their vacation time, rather than their sick leave, in order to remain home and care for their sick children. You may want to maintain a more liberal policy depending upon how valuable the contribution of these single parents is to your business.

AN EMPLOYEE'S HANDBOOK

A well-written employee's handbook can give the new employee an introduction to your company. It may tell the history of the organization, with possible attention to its financial status—past, present, and projected. It should list working hours, policy on use of the time clock or other sign-in procedure, rules on rest periods and coffee breaks, as well as the rules for absences from work, the length of the pay period, and the company's safety and accident-prevention programs. You might also economize and prevent future bitterness if you list restrictions on the use of telephones.

Your booklet can also elaborate on such company benefits as the following:

- Vacations and holidays
- Medical hospital and surgical benefits
- Pensions, profit-sharing plans, and bonuses
- Group insurance
- Training programs
- Parking rules
- Service awards
- Credit unions
- Company cafeteria location and fare
- Bowling and baseball teams and tournaments
- Monthly or weekly magazine or newssheet

You might also indicate company policy on jury duty and military leave, and state the employee's rights to unemployment compensation.

MAINTAINING GOOD RELATIONS
WITH YOUR EMPLOYEES

Communication with employees on company policies should be prompt and thorough. If you do not keep your workers posted on new developments, they will get their facts through other means, often garbled by rumors and misinformation.

Informal chats with employees help create a friendly atmosphere and give you a chance to uncover dissatisfaction, but even small companies need the regularity and definiteness of formal communications. Meet with your entire staff at regular intervals to impart general information and answer questions. Be sure that notices of holidays, schedule changes, and training and other educational opportunities are posted on bulletin boards. A house newspaper or magazine can serve to tell employees what is currently happening to their fellow workers and to the company. You might mail an annual letter to each employee, giving information about the company's status and expressing appreciation for past efforts.

Employees want to be treated fairly by management, not to be always assigned duties that could be shared by others, to be allowed to leave or arrive at other than normal working hours when personal emergencies interfere (doctor appointments, car problems), and to be rewarded fairly in salary negotiations for good work.

The employee wants to feel needed by the organization and to have the sense of being one of the team.

Encourage your workers to come forward with their complaints. They should feel assured that stating their grievances will not prejudice their positions with their immediate supervisor. You might have an employees' suggestion box. Choose an administrator to gather suggestions, and let the employees select a committee to consider new ideas and possibly make awards for ones that are adopted.

DISCHARGING EMPLOYEES

Sometimes a reduction in business or an employee's total unsuitability for a job makes it necessary for you to terminate the person's employment. This creates an unpleasant task for both of you. Try to schedule your talk for the end of the day when you can be free from interruptions. Give the employee your exact reasons for termination, mentioning the benefits available in both severance pay and unemployment compensation. Help the employee find a new job if he or she has some skills which you can honestly recommend. Do not forget that any lack of tact or feeling you might show when discharging an employee will cause resentment among other employees whom you need to retain.

USING A TEMPORARY
EMPLOYMENT AGENCY

If your need for office help is usually light or only periodically heavy, you may be able to use a temporary employment agency, as do 80 percent of American companies at one time or another. Although the rate you pay the agency that provides the temporaries may seem high, you are probably saving money because the agency, not you, provides the workers with insurance, pension plans, and other fringe benefits and takes care of the bookkeeping, payroll, and tax deductions, which may cost as much as 40 percent on top of wages.

Proper use of temporaries can keep an employer's unemployment tax from rising. The rate of unemployment tax you pay to the state and federal governments depends upon how often you hire and fire your employees. Because temporaries are the employees of the agency from which you hired them, moving them in and out of your work force will have no adverse effect on your unemployment tax rate. Moreover, temporaries may be well-suited for certain types of jobs that do not require the background of your regular work force.

However, if the position requires extensive training and you cannot keep the same temporary for a sufficient time, your work output suffers. Many established firms prefer to hire a full-time "floater" who goes from one temporary assignment to another as workloads develop within the office.

16

DEALING WITH FRAUD AND THEFT

White-collar crime has shown a steep rise in recent years. The profits of small business are substantially cut each year by internal theft. In the plant, workers may express dissatisfaction with their jobs by making off with tools, parts, or the finished product. In the office, forgery, embezzlement, and manipulations by trusted employees and executives siphon off hundreds of thousands of dollars, driving even long-established firms into bankruptcy. It is not uncommon for retailers to have 30 percent of their losses come from theft by their own employees. In addition to the fear of burglary, robbery, and swindle faced by small businesses around the country, the retailer must also deal with the hazard of shoplifting. Although some measure of theft loss is inevitable, the individual business owner can take precautionary measures.

PREVENTING EMPLOYEE THEFT AND PILFERAGE

Care in screening job applicants is the first step in preventing inside theft. Like the large organization, the small business should provide a form for the job applicant to complete. All previous employment should be listed so that dates can be checked and lapses between jobs can be accounted for. The employer should follow up on personal and business references with telephone calls. Previous employers and personnel managers tend to open up more on the phone than in letters.

Some employers ask applicants for handwriting samples to be professionally analyzed for personality traits. Lie detectors are another screening method used by some firms to test the stability of employees, but note that it is illegal not to hire someone solely because the individual is unwilling to take a polygraph test.

Incentives that the employer provides can help to reduce motivations for dishonesty. The employer who rewards performance as consistently as he or she enforces rules is respected. Nor should the employer overlook the need for honesty in his or her own dealings with the public and with suppliers. A high standard and a good example can deter dishonesty among employees.

HOW EMPLOYEES STEAL

The following are the most common forms of employee theft for which employers should be on the watch:

- Stealing petty cash and covering theft by false vouchers
- Stealing cash payments by mail
- Stealing cash payments by customers for sales in store, office, or on the road
- "Lapping" cash by using today's receipts to cover yesterday's embezzlements
- Purloining stamps, large quantities of which may be sold on the black market
- Manipulating payroll, including salaries for fictional, discharged, or deceased employees
- Forging a company check to one's own order and destroying check on return by bank
- Cashing company checks made out for fictitious bills from nonexistent vendors
- Altering legitimate bills to get an additional payment that is cashed by the thief
- Lowering amount of customer's bill in book entry and keeping difference when customer pays full amount
- Adjusting or writing off customers' accounts, sometimes in collusion with customers
- Sending goods to nonexistent customer that are then sold for personal profit
- Directly stealing company supplies or stock
- Selling company property (by-products, fixtures, machinery, automobiles, investments) and withholding proceeds

- Taking kickbacks, splitting commissions, or making other deals with suppliers or customers
- Using correctable typewriters to change the figures on checks

Total protection against the ingenuity of the determined internal thief may be beyond reach. You can, however, make the way hazardous and curtail losses that arise from a lack of system, from carelessness with cash and checks, and from opportunities for impulse thievery.

SAFEGUARDS IN OFFICE PROCEDURES

In general, the possibility of fraud in the office can be cut by instituting such methods as the following:

- Have one employee record a sale, but another charge the customer's account.
- Have one employee receive the collection, but another record the credit to the customer.
- Have one employee handle the cash, but another keep the cash-ledger account.
- Have one employee accept an order, but another receive the goods.
- Have one employee approve the invoice for payment, but another issue the check.
- Have one employee make up the payroll, but another issue paychecks and take receipts.

Of course, two or more employees acting in concert can circumvent these safeguards. Good friends can be tempted to act together to commit a crime if their job duties combine to give them the opportunity, for example, if one employee is the bookkeeper and his or her spouse works in shipping and receiving.

Business owners with few employees should themselves supervise their employees as much as possible and spring spot checks so that the employees are aware of the owner's watchfulness. However, one should avoid making such supervision appear to be anything but a businesslike care for proper fulfillment of procedures. To stir up the antagonism of honest employees by obvious suspicion is an invitation to trouble. The potential thief will get the message, even when it is subtle.

Petty-cash theft is the most common form of employee larceny, made easy by some employers who allow vouchers to be made out in pencil, so that the amount can be altered. Unmarked vouchers can be reused by the petty-cash manipulator. Take these four simple precautionary steps, which auditors consider essential:

1. Requests for payment from petty cash must be made out in ink to prevent forgery. As a further precaution, all slips over $5 must have the amount written in both longhand and figures.
2. In every possible case, the request should be supported by invoices or receipts and approved by a designated official.
3. After each petty-cash voucher has been paid and date of payment entered, it must be stamped or punched to prevent reuse.
4. The vouchers must not remain under the control of the cashier.

SAFEGUARDING MAIL RECEIPTS

If your mail customarily contains checks, cash, or stamps, you need a strong protective system. Find out whether a registering machine, which creates a cash record and registers the customer's remittance documents, would be an economic safeguard in your business. Install these office routines:

- Mail is opened under competent supervision away from other staff.
- Mail openers sort orders or payments immediately. All papers and mailing documents are fastened together with cash or check.
- Coins or stamps are put into envelopes for attachment to other papers.
- Amount of money received is marked on the papers.
- Checks and money orders are endorsed "for deposit only." Company endorsement stamp is used.
- Other employees take over. Paid orders are channeled one way; payments another. A clerk who opens mail should not be the person making book entries of the receipts.
- Staff is rotated so that no one person can easily set up a system of pilferage or book falsification.
- Customer complaints of unfilled orders or bills rendered again after payment should be investigated immediately. Have such complaints directed away from mail openers or bookkeepers who might have reason to suppress them. If complaints make you suspect mail pilferage, you might want to plant a couple of pieces of mail containing cash in the incoming mail.
- Tighten security and let employees know you are watchful.

CASH-HANDLING PROTECTION

Take the strongest measures possible to safeguard cash:

- Bond all cash-handling employees from cashier to outside salespeople.
- Install a modern cash register. Use of a till or cash box invites larceny.
- Demand a regular check of petty-cash funds.
- See that the cashier does not make disbursements from receipts; an imprest fund is usually more advisable.
- Make sure that the cashiers are required to give a full receipt for all funds taken in.
- Educate the payer of funds to get a receipt for proper credit of payment.
- See that the cashier registers funds immediately upon receipt.
- If the registry is by a duplicate receipt, number it serially so as to control it fully.
- Make certain that lapping, the holding back of funds despite entry in the receipt records, is not possible.
- Compare your receipts with budgets, standards, and ratios in daily or periodical reports. Investigate all unusual divergences from forecasts or normal trends.
- Make certain that it is impossible for cash to be taken by a clerk's not reporting sales.
- Be sure that unauthorized or improper allowances cannot be entered.
- Make certain that it is not possible for cashbooks to be juggled or forced, particularly in the discount columns.
- Be certain that it is not possible for a charge to be made to an expense account to cover stolen cash.
- Have independent office personnel or accountants balance the cashier's funds and salespeople's registers.
- See that the person receiving money on charge accounts does not have access to the ledgers.
- Segregate the person handling cash and cash operations from the rest of the office.
- Provide an adequate safe room; make certain that the safes are modern, burglarproof, and fireproof; permit only authorized persons to know the combinations; and change the combinations periodically.
- Make use of the protection given by mechanical equipment—cash registers, analysis machines, autographic registers, check registers, automatic cashiers, paying machines, and change-making machines.

- Avoid any "payouts" from receipts which should be deposited in the bank intact.
- Preferably avoid cash collections by outside salespeople. Bond any collecting salesperson. Have sales force's receipt books serially controlled in duplicate. Have orders and cash balanced by someone outside the sales department. Investigate quickly if customers complain that cash payments were not credited to their accounts or if they fail to pay for a salesperson's order. If salespersons must use customer cash payments for their expenses, ironclad control and recording are needed. Spot-check from time to time to prevent salespersons from overcharging customers and pocketing the difference.
- Banking should be done by a bonded person other than the cashier. Have that person accompanied to the bank, and make sure the money is carried unobtrusively. Bank nearby and insure against crime loss.
- Make deposit slips in duplicate to receive bank proof and prevent forgery.
- Check daily deposits through bank records. If possible, have this done by someone other than the person receiving the cash.
- Reconcile all bank statements regularly. If possible, have the reconciliation made by a person other than the cashier.
- Reconcile the bank balances occasionally at periods other than the close of the month.
- Review all bank accounts yourself or have an accountant do so to guard against borrowing from one account to cover a shortage in another. Question all transfers between banks, particularly those at the end of the month.

SAFEGUARDING THE USE OF CHECKS

Permissive use of checks leaves the door wide open to the forger. Install positive routines and a sound verification system in the writing of checks. Remember that in too many cases the trusted, long-time employee has proved to be an embezzler. These protective measures guard management from loss and the employee from unjustified suspicion:

- Require more than one signature on a check. Have at least one of the authorized signers thoroughly audit the vouchers. This prevents the use of false, previously paid, or raised invoices. The latter are sometimes rendered by vendors who conspire with employees to defraud a company.

● Have checks numbered serially and prepared with a checkwriter; retain all voided checks; and route checks returned by the bank to a person other than the issuing employee. Have the bank reconciliation made by a disinterested person.

● Permit no checks to be made out to "cash" or "bearer," no presigning of blank checks, and no signing of checks without seeing the bills to which they correspond.

● Blank checks must be locked up safely.

SUPERVISING YOUR ACCOUNTS

Constant supervision of your accounting system is necessary. The new business owner needs a qualified accountant for guidance in setting up a system; the established company needs the auditor's eye. Sloppy bookkeeping and indifferent checking up enable the embezzler to cover tracks for years. Note these pointers:

● Review all reductions of accounts carefully. Bad debts, allowances, discounts, and all kinds of write-offs should be properly authorized and subsequently audited.

● Make sure that reductions can be charged nowhere but to the account provided.

● Check all deductions from remittances, such as cash discounts and commissions. Make certain that a cashier or salesperson cannot misappropriate any payments received on accounts that have been charged off.

● Be sure that items cannot be lost. Points to watch include goods sold without an entry in your books; interest received from customers on their notes and accounts and not entered; proceeds from sales of by-products, waste, etc., that have not been properly protected; and interest or dividends due on investments that have not been received.

The computer has opened up new areas in employee fraud. Computerized embezzling is more difficult to detect than earlier varieties of embezzlement, particularly because some auditors are not fully attuned to unraveling that type of fraud. Control and audit techniques have to be built into the system from the start. When one person or one group follows a transaction from beginning to end, the possibility of manipulation exists.

Computer manufacturers are at work to incorporate security checks into their systems. In the meantime, experts have some advice for business owners who use computers:

- The programmer and the operator of the computer should not be the same person. Both should be carefully screened when first employed, the programmer in particular.
- The officers who authorize checks should be in a department apart from computerized check-writing operations so that a dishonest company officer cannot easily convert falsified data into checks.
- Change job responsibility frequently. When programmers and operators do not work on the same job for long, they have less opportunity to set up a system of fraud.
- Require that programmers and operators take their annual vacation time; most computer theft schemes fall apart without constant monitoring.

If computers are used in your accounting system, you need auditors who have been trained as programmers and are experts in checking through all phases of a computerized operation to detect fraud.

Workers, not inherently dishonest, may be tempted to steal if your methods of loss prevention are slack. People who begin by taking a few nails for a job at home may eventually cost you thousands of dollars in inventory or equipment.

Let your employees see that you mean business regarding security, whether that means a ban on lunch boxes at the job area or sophisticated methods of inventory control. *See that rules apply to all.* If the system requires that everyone sign for stockroom items, then you, and members of your family also in the business, should comply too.

Here is a checklist of essential security measures:

- Control keys effectively; install time locks and alarms. Use locks that need a key on both sides if permitted by local regulations. Employ a central-station alarm system, motion detector, or electric eye. You need every protection against the employee-thief who hides until the plant is closed and then leaves freely without evidence of forced entry.
- Guard against collusion between employees and outsiders. Rotation of security guards should be established. Make spot checks of truck loading to see that no stolen goods are on the truck. Consider closed-circuit television to guard the loading area. Supervisors should have a clear view of operations from their desks.
- Employees must not park cars in the receiving area.

- Trash cartons should be flattened; trash bins should be checked at unexpected times. Have trash collections supervised in case employees and collectors have a theft deal going.
- Make sure the receiving door is shut and locked when not in use. An alarm should ring when it is opened, and only managerial employees should have a key to turn the alarm off.

Top security areas should be guarded by a card entry system to prevent access by other than needed personnel. The latest entry systems employ fingerprint scanners and even voice-activated controls. Card systems, run in conjunction with a computer system, are cheaper and usually sufficient for most security needs.

Prosecution of employee-thieves is advised; to settle for less would encourage others to steal. Many companies now sue the thieves to recover what monies they can. Formerly, companies would hesitate to press for recovery; some even dropped criminal charges because of the fear of adverse publicity. However, because insurance companies rarely pay the full amount of the loss, more companies now try to recover the theft by any means possible.

GUARDING AGAINST BURGLARY AND ROBBERY

Crime prevention begins with elementary measures that are too often overlooked. Business premises should be thoroughly inspected when acquired for ease of access to thieves. Locks may easily be picked, doors pried from hinges, and windows and skylights broken. If you do not know who might now hold the keys to your premises, have the locks changed. Changing the locks from time to time is one method of preventing use of old keys by former employees or other persons.

Sheer carelessness can invite burglary. Doors, windows, and even safes are sometimes left open after closing hours. A regular routine of double-checking the premises should be established. When the owner or supervisor will be absent, other responsible persons should be designated for this duty.

Be sure that no unauthorized person is concealed on the premises at closing time; that certain lights inside and outside are left on, particularly those illuminating the safe, which should be visible to a patrolling security guard or police officer from outside; and that any adjacent alleys are also adequately lighted.

In high-crime areas, retail storefronts are now protected by various types of folding metal gates. Similar gates can be installed at particularly vulnerable windows of offices and plants. Where the glass of doors or windows can easily be broken and access gained to a lock, such protective measures should be taken.

Check with your police department whether it links up with alarm systems of local businesses. In your area there may be a commercial center which provides response to alarms. For both police and commercial alarm centers, false signals provide a real problem. If you have an alarm system installed at your business premises, make thorough arrangements for its use. Designate who will activate the system and turn it off; cover absence of the responsible person; and guard against accidental triggering of the alarm. Sometimes nothing more than the wind rattling poorly fitting doors and windows activates the alarm. Tests at set intervals will be necessary to check on a system and on its power sources.

Maintenance of an alarm system may seem costly, but it can reduce your insurance premiums. The more you do to stop crime, the less risk the insurance company will be taking, and they may be able to reflect this in your rates. An alarm system is a kind of insurance, one that may save you grief and money in the long run. In areas where crime insurance is unavailable, the preventive measures you take yourself are your only protection. These may include dogs, alarms, and private security guards.

Among your antiburglary measures, list these precautions: Leave cash registers empty and open so they are not damaged by hopeful thieves. Bank frequently so that little cash remains in a safe overnight. Keep the safe combination out of unauthorized hands, and change that combination when employees who know it are shifted or leave the company.

Armed robbery is an ever-present danger at many retail stores and at other places of business where cash or high-price merchandise is available. Large cash payrolls have proved to be a temptation to armed bandits; when possible, payment by check is preferable.

Prevention of a holdup may not be possible, but you can take reasonable precautions and instruct your staff on their conduct in the face of robbery. In general, individuals should not resist or do anything that would provoke a robber's use of arms. But if possible, a silent alarm should be triggered or, through prearranged signals, other employees alerted to the situation. Whatever happens, observation of the robber's appearance and methods of robbery and getaway can provide police with necessary clues.

HAZARDS OF CASHING CHECKS

If you intend to accept checks in your business, you should establish a specific procedure that will help to weed out fraud:

- *Know your state law* regarding fraudulent checks.
- *Decide if checks made out for more than the cost of goods or service will be accepted.* Establish the limit.
- *Examine all checks carefully* and refuse those which show signs of alteration or an illegible name, have more than one endorsement, differ in figure and written amount, are stamped or typed with a company name, are not properly imprinted with the bank name and location, are not dated or are postdated, or are more than 30 days old.
- *Require identification* from the check passer, preferably a driver's license or government or military identification. Compare the signature on the identification with that on the check; record the identification number on the check. The person passing the check should record his or her address and telephone number on the back.
- *Preferably know the check passer.* Refusing to cash a stranger's check may lose some business, but the loss on a bad check may be greater. Government checks are sometimes stolen, so use particular care before cashing. Even certified checks have been altered by forgery. Check with the issuer when in doubt.
- *Acceptance of invalid credit cards can also result in losses.* The issuing company should provide a phone verification service so you can quickly find out the maximum that can be charged on that card, or whether the card has been stolen.

PROTECTION THROUGH INSURANCE

Preferably all employees, not only those directly involved with financial transactions, should be covered by fidelity bond. There are many ways in which a dishonest employee can operate, quite apart from "dipping fingers in the till." Nor should long-time, trusted employees be excluded from coverage. Change of circumstance and unusual pressures have driven many a formerly honest person to crime.

Loss through forgery may be covered in separate categories. You may protect your checks, bank drafts, etc., and forget that you have other negotiable instruments, such as bills of lading and warehouse receipts, that are also vulnerable. Where a hazard exists, you may decide to expand your coverage.

Know the terms of your insurance. You may think you have the situation covered, but after your employees are held up on the way to the bank, you may discover that all the conditions laid down by the insurers have not been fulfilled. See that your employees know special precautions demanded of them and that they do not become slack in carrying out their assignments.

STOPPING OVER-THE-COUNTER SALES THEFTS

The owner of the retail store must protect over-the-counter sales from the light-fingered salesclerk as well as from customer theft.

Employee theft at the retail level may take the form of ringing up items for friends and relatives at less than the ticketed price. The salesclerk who is too popular with customers or who has many friends visit the store may be doing favors that are costly to the store owner.

If clerks are permitted to buy store-damaged or returned items at a discount, see that they do not go home with substituted first-class merchandise. At no time should a clerk be allowed to ring up his or her own purchases on the cash register.

These steps may also help reduce employee theft:

- Use modern equipment for counter sales, particularly cash registers, autographic registers, and charge registers. Balance the sales that are registered against cashier's funds daily. Such balancing should preferably be done by persons not in the sales or cashier's group.
- Do not permit counter salespeople to disburse any funds received.
- See that customers know they are entitled to a receipt. Advise them that subsequent adjustment depends on showing their receipts.
- Salespeople taking cash should give a receipt that is serially controlled in duplicate.
- Maintain a perpetual inventory of stock in stores where counter sales are made.

THE MENACE OF SHOPLIFTING

Shoplifting costs retail merchants some $8 billion annually. Merchants can expect losses to run between 2 and 15 percent. Some security people claim that one out of every three small business bankruptcies can be attributed to shoplifting losses. Some city jewelry firms now only let one customer at a time into the store. Other firms are trying to derive more of their income from mail orders.

The shoplifter is 20 percent more likely to be female than male. One survey of teenagers revealed that 70 percent had some shoplifting experience. As many as one customer in every ten may be leaving your store with merchandise for which he or she has not paid. While professional shoplifters can clear whole racks at a time, amateurs, by their sheer numbers, will account for most of your losses.

The small retailer is more vulnerable than the large corporation. The merchant may be unable to afford the more sophisticated protection devices. Moreover, a local merchant who catches a member of the community shoplifting, or possibly the son or daughter of an important customer, will think twice about a theft charge. Large department stores have become less hesitant, believing that a reputation for prosecution lowers shoplifting losses. Even though convictions occur at about a 95 percent rate, time-consuming court proceedings may represent a financial loss to the small merchant. If you are actively going to combat, arrest, and prosecute shoplifters (as opposed to figuring your losses into the cost of doing business), make sure your confrontations take place according to local law. Also, have your business insurance cover you for damages relating to suits for false arrest. Settlements of several hundred thousand dollars have been won by people falsely arrested.

ALERTING EMPLOYEES
TO SHOPLIFTING TECHNIQUES

All salespeople and cashiers should be aware of typical shoplifting methods. Let them know that the failure to report acquaintances who steal will result in the loss of their own jobs. Your employees may know which of their friends shoplift and give them the message.

The most common shoplifting method is to conceal the merchandise in an innocent-appearing object, such as a handbag, shopping bag, box, briefcase, or closed umbrella. Ambitious shoplifters sometimes prepare boxes with ingenious fake tops or bottoms. They slip stolen items into the boxes by raising the false tops or bottoms which are pulled back into place by strong rubber bands attached to the inside of the package.

The second most common method is to conceal the merchandise

in clothing. A raincoat over one arm is a useful screen. Pockets are, of course, invaluable to the youngster stealing at the local variety store and to the professional, who may wear specially prepared clothing with concealed pockets. A slit in one pocket of a coat may enable the shoplifter to transfer merchandise to a larger one inside.

Another technique is the switching of price tags. This can be foiled by the merchant who is also the cashier and remembers the price of each item in the store, which is only possible if the price is not changed frequently. Computerized price markings used by supermarkets help to combat this ploy. There is one price stamped for the customer's eye and another for the optical scanner used by the computer-assisted checkout system.

Baby carriages or strollers are often banned in stores, not only because they block the aisles, but also because they are used as a cache by the shoplifter. Collapsible shopping carts are also sometimes used for store theft.

Stout thieves need no special equipment. Their clothing often contains sufficient space to hold merchandise they intend to remove from the store. The change in their gait is hard to discern, though short steps may be a clue.

In apparel stores, fitting rooms are, of course, invaluable to the clothing thief who walks out wearing more clothes than on entering.

Jewelry shoplifting has some specialized techniques. One involves the accomplice who distracts the salesperson while the theft is made by sleight-of-hand substitution of a cheap but accurate imitation of a valuable piece. In another method, a shoplifter conceals in one hand a clamp attached to strong rubber bands which run up the sleeve and are fastened securely. While examining a ring or some other piece of jewelry, the thief fastens the clamp to it and so whisks the prize up his or her sleeve.

Pairs and groups of shoplifters will often work together to divert attention. Young people particularly, not necessarily professional shoplifters, may enter a store en masse. A disturbance is a favorite cover for theft.

Devices other than "lifting" an article may be employed by the store thief. Returning an item for refund that was in fact taken from the shelves is one method. The clerk accepting the returned merchandise should see that it comes in a bag and has the sales check with it and that the customer has not been roving the store before coming to the checkout counter. Insistence on the return of sales checks helps retailers to protect themselves from giving refunds on merchandise stolen from other stores, as well as from their own.

Retailers need the cooperation of employees in antishoplifting tactics. Employees should be trained to recognize likely theft devices and to be alert for new ploys. Watchful employees patrolling the aisles, particularly when the store is busy, can help to safeguard stock against the amateur or impulse shoplifter. The determined thief is full of tricks. Salesclerks should try to keep the customer in view when filling a request and reckon with the fact that people who appear to be strangers to one another may in fact be accomplices.

ANTISHOPLIFTING DEVICES AND METHODS

The interior arrangement of the retail store should provide maximum visibility. Racks, counters, and tables should be as low as possible and not offer cover to the shoplifter. Convex wall mirrors that enable store personnel to watch the aisles are necessary in many types of businesses.

Locked display cabinets should be used for expensive merchandise. The checkout counter where cashiers are in attendance is frequently used for the display of items that are easily stolen.

Signs warning against shoplifting may usefully be posted in some types of business. Letting the potential thief know you are alert and employing protective devices may serve as a deterrent.

A customer going to a fitting room should be handed a tag corresponding in number to the number of garments taken in. When the customer leaves the fitting room, a clerk checks that the number on the tag and the number of garments are the same. Shoplifters may try to take more garments than are permitted into the fitting room. Salesclerks should be alert to this possibility.

Doors not in regular use should be locked unless such locking would violate fire ordinances. Check with your local authorities.

Fast service is recommended as a deterrent to shoplifting. Sales checks should be given to the customer to confirm payment and should not be discarded by the cashier. Shoplifters watch for sales checks scattered around. They use them to protect themselves or to return a stolen item for "refund."

When shoplifters are suspected in a store, the staff should be able to alert one another by the use of a prearranged signal or code.

The arrangement of merchandise and its tidiness are important. Do not stack goods so that they obscure the view or make it easy for a thief to sweep items into a bag or pocket.

Lifting from the cash register, a type of theft known as "till tapping," can be discouraged by placing registers away from customer access and keeping the amount of cash at a low level. Drill employees in a register routine which calls for closing the drawer immediately after giving change. Employees should avoid being distracted by a customer while the drawer is open, thus making it easy for an accomplice to rifle the till. A register not in use must be locked.

The marking of merchandise with sensitized tags has proved a useful deterrent to retail-store theft. The tags cannot be removed by a would-be shoplifter without damage to the merchandise. The thief trying to sneak out of the door with stolen items that are still tagged will set off an alarm system.

At larger stores, walkie-talkies and computers are used in the antishoplifting war. The use of television to keep its ever-present eye on cashiers, clerks, and customers alike is increasing. The cost of such surveillance is worthwhile in a large operation where losses have been extensive.

Apprehending Shoplifters   Many retailers shrink from confronting shoplifters. Consult with the police to determine what local law permits in such confrontations. Less than half the states have criminal legislation specifically covering shoplifting. You may have to make a citizen's arrest, or you may be able simply to detain the suspect until the police arrive; find out for sure before you open your doors. A storekeeper should fear accusations of false arrest or defamation of character.

In some cases in which the store owner is certain of the theft, he or she or a representative may follow the shoplifter outside and say, "I believe you forgot to pay for something." To wait until the thief leaves the store makes sure there is no intention to pay and no opportunity to get rid of stolen goods. Many states allow arrests inside the store if the retailer can prove intent. Intent may be shown if the customer has taken the item past the cash register for that department or has secreted the item inside his or her clothing. Check with authorities to see how local law views arrests when the customer has merely put an item in his or her pocket. After all, the customer may be legitimately absentminded.

Some shoplifting laws allow retailers to detain someone for a reasonable time in a reasonable manner. Some laws allow a retailer to deny a suspect telephone calls.

17
OFFICE MANAGEMENT AND EFFICIENCY

The office is the nerve center of almost every business. Here, all the activities of the business are generally coordinated. Orders are received and records are kept and stored. The office is where you and other executives plan and execute management decisions.

Physically the office may be one room, a suite of rooms, or extend over several floors. Size obviously depends on the nature and size of your business, but common to all offices are the basic office furniture and equipment—desks and filing cabinets, typewriters, telephones, calculators—and the need for efficiency in coping with the volume of paperwork, telephone messages, and daily mail produced by business communications.

Offices are very much like the people that run them. As there are people who make an immediate impression by their style of dress, there are offices which by their layout and design also give an immediate impression of the business's style. Yet, as often as you enter an attractive office, you will also step into an office which strikes you as a sloppy afterthought of its owner. No reason or planning has entered into its layout. There is a blindness not only to efficiency but also to the fact that the office is a place where people have their first contact with the business and receive their initial impressions. Sometimes with just moderate attention to detail, an office can be made efficient and also can present a positive public image.

DESIGNING THE OFFICE SPACE

The layout of your office should be designed with an eye toward efficiency. Consider which tasks could be performed better and more easily if personnel performing related duties were located next to each other or next to a frequently utilized machine. Frequent reviews and, more often, your experience through trial and error will reveal the most efficient office routine.

When you employ a large office staff, you generally have to decide between having (1) separate rooms for each worker or group of workers or (2) an open office space in which the staff works and which may be divided by partitions to separate space according to an overall organizational plan. Many manufacturers offer freestanding screens and panels, modular and L-shaped work units, and furniture with built-in shelving and filing space, all of which can be easily combined into any pattern the business finds convenient. The open office is popular because it permits less expensive changes and because the partitions can be easily shifted. Only one thermostat control or air-conditioning system is needed for the comfort of many workers. Electrical wiring and telephone lines are less costly to pull up and rearrange.

However, some workers require a separate office, especially those who are often on the telephone as part of their job and who may disturb other workers unless situated in separate quarters. Individual offices also help insulate those who need quiet to concentrate or need privacy because of the nature of their work. Managers and executives also prefer separate office space, if only to reinforce their image and status.

When planning your firm's office space, make adequate provision for reception room, conference room, storage, and vaults. The reception room should have 10 square feet per person for the maximum number of people who may come at one time and a minimum size of 50 square feet.

Your office should contain adequate personal comfort facilities: restrooms, coatrooms, locker space, drinking fountains, and coffee machines. The average office needs at least one toilet and one sink for every 15 persons; more sinks may be necessary depending upon the type of work being done. Offices sometimes provide shower facilities as a consideration and encouragement for employees who jog or bicycle to work.

FILLING LIGHTING REQUIREMENTS

Be sure you have adequate lighting in the office. Poor lighting means eyestrain and tired and grumbling employees. Fatigue can be reduced by better lighting. Compare your existing light with accepted standards by use of a light meter. The electric company in your vicinity will aid you willingly in your study. Finer detailed work requires more light. For instance, drafting workers need 6 times as much light as mail room workers. Artificial lighting should be of good quality to avoid glare and shadows and to increase efficiency of workers.

Study equipment to obtain fixtures that will properly direct the light. Glass-top or highly polished desks cause glare. Avoid too great a contrast of light in different parts of the same room. Consider use of indirect lighting and translucent bowls or fluorescent lighting to increase diffusion of light.

Efficiency of lighting may depend largely on getting maximum reflection from ceiling and walls. Flat white is the most satisfactory color for the ceiling, but flat white paint on the walls reflects up to 90 percent of the light, causing glare. Buff, light blue, or green will reflect about 60 percent, creating a more restful condition for the eyes.

EQUIPPING THE OFFICE

To determine standards for buying office equipment, ask yourself the following questions: Does the item speed up office work by making records easier to find, fill out, or understand? Does it promote greater accuracy or provide greater protection in the handling of cash, securities, mail, and other office valuables?

If you are considering equipment which will change routine operations, first seek an office demonstration of the equipment, especially with the employees who will use it. Listen to their comments; do not buy equipment with which they will not feel comfortable and which they may resist using, unless you believe they will accommodate themselves to the equipment in a short time.

Before buying new office machinery, find out if there is used equipment available that will meet your needs at less cost. There are dealers who specialize in renting or selling used equipment, in addition to the nationwide brokers who handle used office machinery. Less expensive still are sources of used machinery available from bankruptcy auctions and General Service Administration (GSA) auctions of used government equipment. Here, however, the machinery comes "as is," so that repair costs may cancel out your savings.

In acquiring office equipment, do not buy equipment that does not use the same standard supplies as other equipment in the office. Do not buy equipment for which use, though advantageous, is confined to short periods. Machinery is often acquired in the mistaken hope that it can be used more extensively.

The desks and chairs of your office workers, secretaries, typists, and clerks should conform to certain standards of comfort to eliminate backache and general fatigue. Desks of about 29 inches, a natural working height, should have adequate drawer space and compartments, racks for cards, stationery, and accessories, letter and filing trays, and partitions for particular jobs to be done.

Make a card for each piece of equipment, recording the manufacturer, serial number, model, cost, date of purchase, type of work performed, location, etc. Keep a record also of maintenance costs, perhaps on the reverse side of the equipment card, showing the dates of repairs.

If you enter into a maintenance contract with the manufacturer who made your equipment, see that repair people come regularly to clean and oil machines and that they respond to emergency calls as well.

Maintenance can drain finances. If repair of a purchased machine is running more than 15 percent of its cost, consider replacing it.

The rental of office equipment may save costs. Some machines are, in fact, usually rented rather than sold to small businesses, for example, a photocopying machine or specialized electric typewriter with a magnetic card system. Check into rentals for your office needs before committing yourself to purchase.

USING COMPUTERS

A favorite cliché of computer experts is that any computer you buy will be obsolete by the time you finish paying for it. Although this statement is meant to illustrate the rapid technological progress being made in the computer field, it is also a warning to businesses that any computer purchase should be evaluated carefully.

Current computers do have vast potential when used correctly, but the benefits of having one are more easily demonstrable for large companies. An individual business may use a computer system for linking its offices; management support and information; processing and filing statistics, documents, and correspondence; electronic mailing; coordinating and implementing schedules and calendars; and specialized accounting, scientific, or analytical purposes, depending upon the capacity of the system and the requirements of management.

Computers with compatible transmission sources can be linked to each other, so that networks of users can communicate directly from computer to computer. The computer system will also file and store the transmissions for later review.

Many commercial computer services are also available for compatible systems and give access to research materials, stock market reports, news services, or other information that may be of use to your business.

It is even possible to transmit microfilm by using high-speed computerized electronics. This combines the storage capabilities of microfilm with the processing speed of semiconductors.

Do not purchase a computer system that does not benefit you financially just for the sake of being modern. Computer consultants encourage business persons to own computers, but they are in business to sell them. In the face of such pressures, it is advisable to be skeptical until true utility, time savings, and financial benefit to your business are demonstrated. Take pains to determine that the computer will perform the duties expected of it. Your expectations of time and trouble saved may be impossible to realize. Buy a computer because you have specific problems to which the computer has a definite application.

In buying a computer, pay special attention to its *software*. Software is the technical term for the computer program that tells the computer what to do. The computer itself is just a machine, known as *hardware*, that the program operates. If your business needs require that a computer program be specially tailored to fit your situation, the cost of the software may make a computer system impractical for you.

When considering a computer system, keep in mind the future needs of your business as well as present requirements. If you foresee your business expanding, look for a system that is easily modified to increased tasks and capabilities. Expansion is not as simple as just adding another computer because the software for one computer will rarely work in a computer of a different make. Now is the time to anticipate whether the computer system you buy today will be flexible enough to meet the demands of your business tomorrow.

What will it cost you to learn how to use the system? A computer designed for small businesses should be nearly self-explanatory. For comparative purposes, figure the cost of the time you must spend operating the computer. Measure this cost against your regular method of doing the same tasks. You may well find that programs written for accounts receivable are more trouble than they are worth and that a program for general ledger is superfluous for your small business.

Some computer experts recommend buying machines that have proved themselves in service (but this means these units will be outmoded sooner). Try to talk to a satisfied user. Some broken-down computers must remain inactive while parts are ordered. It may pay the user to have a few spare parts on hand (which adds to the computer's cost) to prevent such a delay.

It is best to have an uninterrupted power supply for your machine. Phone-line power sources, for example, are expensive and subject to interruption as often as normal telephone service. If a power failure should cause the computer to shut down, data vital to your business may be destroyed. For safety's sake, a duplicate set of data must often be stored elsewhere. If such data are noncomputerized and must be kept anyway, there may be no point to having a computer. How much do the computer's speedy operations actually mean to your company?

The worst computer stories concern security breaches. Unscrupulous computer programmers have set up dummy payrolls and bogus disbursements and have stolen company secrets stored on computer tapes. Since most computer crimes go undetected (although discrepancies should be obvious in a small company), the nationwide scope of these abuses probably is much larger than actually reported. The business person should check noncomputerized records often against the computer figures, both to stop theft and to spot errors. The misplaced decimal point is a common mistake between the computer, programmers, and transcribers.

When you do decide to adopt a computer system, do not be afraid to admit that you find it difficult to understand. Computer jargon may seem impenetrable. Make sure that everything is fully explained to you before you buy. Then you will not expect performance for which a particular machine is not designed.

EFFICIENT WORK HABITS

Although the capital investment for office equipment and overhead can be sizable, the cost of labor contributes the largest part of the expense of running an office. Work efficiency can lower costs.

Check for wasted motions and duplicated efforts:

- Is there a specific and understood purpose for each office operation?
- Does work move directly from one person to another without unnecessary repetition, duplication, or delays?
- Do certain details or records require more time than the results are worth?
- Are personnel supplied with the necessary materials to perform the step or operation without unnecessary delays to get material?
- How does your staff work? Can you eliminate unnecessary interruptions, arguments and gossiping, absences from desks, delays in answering questions, procrastination, or unnecessary questions?

If your salespeople or executives dictate their letters, instruct them to organize their thoughts and make meaningful notes before dictating. They should try to adhere to a definite dictating schedule, preferably at the same time each day. They should make a practice of spelling out all technical terms and proper names. An office dictionary is a necessity.

When possible, standard form letters and paragraphs should be used. Keep these on file. Specialized typewriters combined with computers provide storage and easy access to standard form responses. Sometimes time may be wasted in preparing individualized business letters when phone calls may be quick and cheaper. But if you want your instructions or discussion on record, written correspondence is more effective.

A style manual will help your stenographers to prepare neat, well-organized letters. The stenographic station should also contain a file of names, addresses, and telephone numbers of all clients and suppliers and a list of difficult spellings and terms that commonly appear in your business.

Insist on written messages; concise interoffice memos save time, minimize misunderstandings, and serve as reminders. A three-tiered basket on each desk can receive all incoming, outgoing, and file papers.

Be sure your senior office personnel impart to their juniors the tricks of the trade. For example, experienced typists know that envelopes can be fed into a typewriter, one on top of another. Then, as one envelope is finished, a turn of the cylinder rapidly brings a new one into position. Experienced clerks who send mail to the same branch offices every day know to address a supply of envelopes to the branch offices in their slack time. Rubber stamps are also advisable for commonly used addresses.

Economical Habits   Teach your staff to use office supplies as sparingly as if they were personally paying for them. Recognize that waste in supplies can be due to mere lack of control. Avoid serious waste in deterioration or obsolescence of supplies, and issue supplies in limited quantities to each desk to reduce spoilage and waste. With sufficient tact, you can discourage wasteful habits on the part of your staff. Of course, you do not want your company to become known for a petty attitude over minor concerns. A contented staff will be willing to observe little economies out of habit. Encourage your workers to turn off lights and electrically driven machines when leaving their desks, at noon, at rest periods, and at closing time. Nothing that can be reused for another purpose should be thrown away. Discarded photocopies and obsolete forms can be used for scratch paper.

Select the most economical grade and size of paper for each purpose, except in situations in which quality paper is necessary to create an impression.

Copy machines may be used to reduce costs. Copy machines can be used to produce form letters, business forms, or even artwork. Many copy machines today do not require special paper, which thus reduces costs.

Review Office Expenses Periodically review office expenses by examining payroll records, purchase records, and service-charge records to determine payments for office rental, light and heat, machines, supplies, postage, clerical help, and telephone use. Translate each expense into a percentage of the total. Supplies will run 10 to 20 percent, while maintenance should be 15 to 20 percent.

The use of outside services for particular jobs such as addressing and mailing may be more economical than using skilled employees. Some savings may be made by using part-time help, such as students working after school, who can be paid the minimum wage for unskilled work and short-term, routine jobs.

The Office Manager The larger your office, the more you need someone to serve as an office manager. There should be someone to help facilitate office procedures by assigning and overseeing the work, to see that supplies are distributed and accounted for, to make sure that all relevant memos are circulated, to make sure that the proper reference publications are subscribed to, and to act as a troubleshooter in making temporary adjustments to office equipment. In many small offices, these matters are too trivial for the chief executive's attention, so the responsibilities of maintaining office functions should be delegated to the head clerk or secretary.

FILING PROCEDURES

- Devise an overall filing plan and adhere to it. Train your personnel to sort papers before filing, through the use of sorter trays, etc.
- File promptly, preferably daily, so that work does not pile up. When folders are full, use expansion folders or divide folders; this will conserve supplies.
- Insist that folders taken from the files be returned as soon as possible.

If you have difficulties with this, consider making a rule that all outstanding records be returned to the files at the close of each working day.

- Keep track of records through the use of a tickler system, so that you will know when records are outstanding for more than the usual length of time.
- Examine the contents of file drawers occasionally to see if all papers are worth saving. Material with a limited usefulness should be preserved for a limited time.
- Do not fill drawers so full that papers cannot be removed easily or without pulling out unwanted material.

Establish and adhere to a time schedule for the retention of records in the files. Clean out the files regularly. Organize the transfer system carefully. Appoint someone to work out the procedures and be responsible for the follow-up. Work this way:

- Classify what is to be destroyed and what is to be transferred. Decide how long various types of papers and records are to be kept.
- Recognize that filing affects a good many departments and people with differing views and requirements.
- Survey what is being filed. Eliminate from permanent files unnecessary duplicates that may come back to the filing department from several departments. Decide which copy to keep—preferably one of distinctive color.
- Set up a routine for automatically disposing of unneeded carbons or photocopies after some established interval has passed.
- Mark on the copy, at the time written, the date for its disposal. Have the filing department remove outdated material from the files as they file new material.

Consider these three methods of sorting outdated material for the needs of your business and choose the most economical:

- Regularly switch the entire contents from current files to transfer boxes.
- Regularly transfer out of current files only the material over a given age (say 1 year old) to transfer boxes.
- Maintain two sets of filing cabinets; use the upper row of drawers for current files and the lower for transferred documents. This expedites reference to recent files and material not recently transferred. At fixed periods transfer the old files to storage. Always maintain a cross index of materials in transfer files.

Make sure your transferring is at fixed periods.

Consider the use of microfilm. Many firms save on storage costs by having their records microfilmed. A roomful of records can be condensed to small rolls of film occupying a mere cabinet of space. These rolls can also be safely stored in bank vaults. Film has the advantage of binding records in a definite, unchangeable order, making loss of one record in a group impossible. Fraudulent alteration of records becomes impossible, and the transportation and transfer of records are accomplished more economically.

Microfilming can be handled by outside services, but if use justifies the cost, obtain a microfilmer for your offices through lease or purchase.

DESIGNING FORMS
FOR YOUR BUSINESS

The stationery, documents, and other forms you choose for your business should simplify your company's activities. Clarity is an objective of good form design. The instructions, printed across the top, should leave no question as to procedure and purpose. Columns should be aligned under their proper titles, with an occasional horizontal line to break up the page and keep the divisions separated.

Assorted forms, labels, folders, letters, and memos are sold in stationery supply stores or are available more cheaply from mail-order firms. Businesses can choose unadorned letterheads or designer forms. Carbon duplicates offer a savings over the more popular, less messy, carbonless paper products. Money can be saved by ordering the correct size paper products to suit your business. For example, an invoice may have 8 lines or 20. If your typical customer purchases only one or two items, the smaller pads offer a savings. Consider the average size of your memos for the most efficient memo pads. The same forethought can save you money when ordering stationery, folders, ledgers, etc. No forms should be ordered without consulting the workers who do your paperwork every day. They are in the best position to know your needs and requirements.

Review your paper requirements periodically. Some forms and documents may no longer be essential and can be eliminated or adapted to other paper documents. Self-copying documents may become unnecessary as photocopying or multiple-entry bookkeeping practices become routine. Also, rubber-stamping certain information may be cheaper than printing certain special, seldom-used letterheads. Paperwork is the biggest problem for many entrepreneurs. The forms you must file for others are troublesome enough. Do not create more of your own paperwork than is really necessary.

DUPLICATING AND PRINTING SERVICES

Your needs for duplicated or printed material may be small. A photocopying machine or mimeograph is sufficient for many offices; others with greater needs find it cheaper to install more complex equipment, even to set up a small offset print shop or phototypesetter on their premises. You should consider leasing rather than purchasing certain types of equipment, especially if your needs arise only at particular times of the year.

Outside services are available for all types of copying and duplicating, as well as printing. Check the yellow pages of your telephone directory under letter shop services. copying and duplicating services, duplicating machines and supplies, photocopying, data processing services, and typesetting (which includes computerized typesetting). Request brochures and watch for new developments which take place constantly in the equipment and services offered in this area.

Every year improved technology expands the capabilities of electronic paper copiers. Each year new purchasers looking for a copier to suit their needs generally find more choices and better bargains. Machines now can copy on both sides of the page, change the size of the material being copied, copy materials of many different sizes, and make three-dimensional copies and transparencies. Copiers can also sort and collate the documents being reproduced.

In determining the cost of a copier, do not overlook the cost of making a copy. The paper, electricity, and developing chemicals may run anywhere from 1 to 10 cents a page. The more copies you make, the better it is for you to purchase a machine with a low cost per copy. A business making infrequent copies might get a copier with a high cost per copy but a low initial purchase price, making the overall copier costs inexpensive. A copier can cost anywhere from $100 to $10,000, so an infrequent user may indeed find savings in an inexpensive machine with higher operating costs.

Dealing with Your Printer   Your printing needs will be best served if you can locate a printer who can fill all your requirements quickly and to your specifications.

Invite bids from printers who are properly equipped to do your type of work. Ordinarily they will be able to turn out the work at the best price. When seeking estimates, give complete specifications. Get bids from at least two sources. If one bid is unreasonably higher than the other, you can assume that the printer does not have the necessary equipment to do your work economically. Among reputable printing establishments, higher costs do not necessarily indicate better quality.

Consult with your printer before planning a job in detail. You can get valuable tips on effective type size, style, paper, folding, and mailing. Weigh the advantages against the cost whenever you consider the use of extra color, tricky layouts, oversized pages, or excessive corrections.

To control your composition costs, give the printer clean, typewritten copy. Edit it to avoid later corrections which may be expensive. It does not pay to send copy to the printer long in advance of publication. Changes may occur which make it necessary to alter the material. After copy has been set in type, these changes can be very costly.

Be aware that an unspoken custom in the printing trade permits the printer to 10 percent deviation from the number of copies ordered by the customer. On small orders, a 10 percent deviation is common; on large orders, it is usually smaller. For example, it is not uncommon for an order of 3000 pamphlets to produce as few as 2700 or as many as 3300 copies. You are charged for the actual number of copies produced. Take such possible deviations into account when planning your orders.

TELEPHONE SERVICE

Telephone expenses can seriously inflate a company's overhead. Every desk in the company does not need a fancy push-button intercom unit available from the phone company. Better and less costly telephone systems may be available at electronics stores. Also, in an open-office setup, where several people work in the same area, several workers may be able to share the same telephone, provided none of their jobs requires heavy telephone use. Many offices are adequately served by three incoming and outgoing lines. Note that it is not necessary to list all the business lines in the yellow pages. Just list enough lines to handle incoming calls; use the nonlisted lines for placing calls.

Check your monthly telephone bills. They may contain errors which you can trace and rectify, or your billing statements may reveal that your lines are being abused for personal calls.

The telephone company no longer has a monopoly on long distance phone service. Competition comes from private companies offering cheaper rates for communications between major cities. They charge less because they do not provide local service while they make use of the most modern equipment, such as communications satellites, to relay long-distance calls.

REDUCING MAILING COSTS

Watch these details to cut your mailing costs:

- If you want an envelope to hold no more than 1 ounce, you need not necessarily confine the contents to one sheet. With some lightweight paper, especially useful for airmail, nine sheets weigh only ½ ounce.
- Large first-class envelopes should be clearly marked or stamped "first class"; otherwise, they may be mistaken for slower mail and delayed in transit.
- In place of stamped, self-addressed envelopes for reply, business-reply cards and envelopes permit you to pay only on those actually returned.
- Demurrage charges on c.o.d. mail can be avoided by using address labels recommended by the U.S. Postal Service, giving specific instructions if undelivered.
- Check with the post office for the least expensive mailing arrangements when mailing books or catalogs.
- Your covering invoice, if it applies strictly to the package contents, can be enclosed in the package. That saves postage and the time of preparation that would be required if the invoice were mailed first class later.
- Special delivery should not be confused with special handling: special handling gets extra speed in handling only to the post office in the addressed area; special delivery mail is also speeded to the addressee's post office, but it is also delivered directly to that address by other than the usual letter carrier. Check what actually happens with special delivery mail to the areas that you service. In some areas, special delivery means later delivery. You and your mail contacts may find time and money saved by using regular mail delivery.

Investigate mechanical aids that might save money and time in handling:

- Hand stamp affixers
- Envelope openers

- Sorting racks and tables to facilitate sorting and dispatching mail to various departments
- Folding and inserting machines
- Addressing machines
- Postage scales
- Parcel post machines
- Scaling machines
- Combined sealing and stamping machines
- Metering permit machines
- Nonmetering permit machines
- Tying and bundling machines

Avoid the use of clips or other weighty material in your mail. Charge postage to the department sending out the mail. If you request periodic reports on the postage ordered, your department heads will be more careful about usage. Finally, investigate the services of private carriers. For certain deliveries, you may find that they offer faster and more economical service than regular mail, with greater reliability and better insurance on the delivery.

Electronic Mail Electronic typewriters at different locations can be linked to a central computer brain that allows a message typed out in one office to appear on a screen hundreds of miles away. When computers and word processors are made compatible with telephone lines, telecommunication will be possible between almost any electronic sender and receiver. Use of computer communication networks between distant offices of the same company is practical. A computerized word processor is also capable of remembering all communications transmitted, exchanging background information, and allowing workers to skim through and recall any of the data base in its memory.

18
SELLING THE PRODUCT

In less-developed areas, you can still see simple and straightforward methods of selling. A seller sits by a road and sets up his or her wares: baskets, weaving, or produce. The few products are clearly seen. Marketing problems are quite simple, even when the sellers offer the goods in the town's public marketplace. The products are clearly displayed to the potential buyer. The seller can on the spot tout the wares, set and change prices, and after the day count profit or loss. The modern world, with its thousands and thousands of products and markets, is much more complicated. To sell your wares, you must determine your market, which may be in thousands of locations. You must rely on the services of others, you must bring the product to the attention of potential buyers, you must transport the product, you must meet the standards of complex laws, you must offer discounts and credit, you must meet intensive competition, you must tailor your product lines, and you must be prepared to change your style. These problems make selling the most demanding challenge of modern business.

DEVELOPING AN EFFICIENT SALES FORCE

Even the "born salesperson" finds stiff competition from carefully trained and coached competitors who are imbued with a respect for the company and product they sell.

Select applicants whose attitudes and honesty you respect. They do not necessarily have to be fast talkers. The most successful sales-people are usually the ones who are convinced of the value of what they are selling and who have a thorough grasp of all the factors which distinguish their product from others in the same line.

Be sure your sales force has a detailed understanding of the man-ufacturing processes used in producing your merchandise. Purchasers often wish to know these details, and salespeople should be able to supply information without fear of misstatement. Through regularly scheduled sales meetings, keep your sales force informed on any short-ages, delayed deliveries, changes in packaging, and discontinued items, so that they can effectively handle criticisms and complaints. In turn, you should listen carefully to any data your salespeople obtain from their customers to help make your own production and marketing effort more profitable.

Develop files on customers and prospects that go beyond a mere record of their prior orders. Certain fundamental information con-cerning your customers may be of use to you in both sales and mar-keting strategies. Keep a record of all the business endeavors of a customer, the operations of its subsidiaries, the locations of its branches, and for each the floor space, sales volume, and number of employees. Also keep a record of the customer's customers, if you know them, of other suppliers from which the customer buys, and, of course, of the dealings the customer has with your competitors.

The time spent in contact with prospects is the productive part of the salesperson's day. Plan routing carefully, assigning each person a territory which can be efficiently and economically covered. There is a real risk in allowing a salesperson to drop in too often on good accounts to the neglect of places which need greater cultivation. Plan just how often you want a salesperson to call back on a customer or prospect.

CONTROLLING SALES EXPENSES

A sound business establishes a fixed policy on sales-expense arrange-ments. Definite rules should state how each allowable expense should be reported by the sales force on a permanent reference form.

Before establishing the system, consider providing for these ex-penses in the salary or commission paid each salesperson. That frees you from further responsibility. Or you might set a per diem or other flat-rate system.

If, instead, you decide to use the reimbursed-expense system, com-pose an instruction sheet covering your policy on hotel bills, meals, tips, use of trains, airplanes, and taxis, automobile costs (mileage rate, insurance, depreciation, parking, etc.), entertainment, club initiation fees and dues, and other receipted bills pertaining to sales effort.

Audit of all traveling-expense accounts is essential if you wish to keep claims on a reasonable, honest basis. A liberal interpretation of a travel voucher will cost your business money.

Many businesses are trying to reduce their automobile costs for traveling sales personnel in this era of higher gasoline costs. More emphasis is put on trade shows, where many clients and customers can be contacted at once. Better-planned travel routes, more frequent phone contacts, and even the mailing of samples to old, familiar customers can help to reduce automobile expenses.

USING INDEPENDENT
SALES AGENTS

For many small businesses, independent agents or representatives are the most effective means of distribution per dollar of cost. Your independent agent is not your own employee. The agents run their own businesses, and your product will be only one of the manufacturers' products they sell. However, none of the other items should be competitive with yours. Generally, an agent sells to specific areas and industry groups.

Your agreement with an independent agent usually provides the agent a commission on sales and the exclusive rights to your products in the territory. The agent gets orders for you, but you ship directly and bill the purchaser. You control sales conditions such as prices, terms, and credit, but the agent may have useful suggestions in dealing with certain customers with whom he or she has had sales and collection experience.

The use of independent agents enables you to avoid the expense of training, recruiting, and supervising a sales force. Your fixed selling expenses are greatly reduced. When sales drop, your selling cost declines automatically since the agent is paid a percentage of sales.

Your own sales force would not find it remunerative to call often on small customers located across the nation. However, an agent carrying the lines of a number of manufacturers can sell a larger total amount to one of the regular stops in the agent's limited territory. For the new firm, the independent agent gives the advantage of immediate service without the time- and money-consuming training program entailed in creating one's own sales force.

On the other hand, when the volume of sales becomes high, the independent agent may claim too large a percentage, seriously draining your profit. With your own sales force, you automatically reduce commission rates as the volume rises. A further disadvantage is your lack of control over agents' selling methods. They give you only a part-time selling effort. Should you ever break relations, the agent would probably be able to switch a large part of your business to a competing client.

Your decision to use independent agents will be influenced by your need to gain quick product acceptance and your ability to train qualified personnel if the selling requires high technical skills and knowledge. You might also wish to use an agent if your volume will not be sufficient to support your own salesperson or if the market is too thin and too widespread, causing excessive travel costs. If your market is seasonal and yet you need year-round contact, or if your product sales volume varies greatly with the economic cycle, you might benefit from the services of an independent agent. You will probably get fullest satisfaction from an agent who handles products that are closely related (but not competitive) to yours in type, price, and quality.

WORKING WITH YOUR WHOLESALERS

A cooperative relationship with your wholesalers will enable you to operate more efficiently. Wholesalers can buy goods at the time they are produced and store them until they are needed by local retailers or industrial consumers. This greatly reduces the amount of warehouse space needed by large manufacturers and lessens the amount of capital they need.

The quick cash provided by wholesalers often gives a manufacturer the money with which to continue operations until the season is ended.

A manufacturer can get national distribution more quickly and more thoroughly through wholesalers than by any other means. Retailers buy more readily from the wholesaler because through past dealings they know the wholesaler is reliable and will not burden them with goods that are known to be unsuitable to their trade.

Your wholesaler can be the agent through which you distribute advertising to retailers. The wholesaler will make your material up into kits, which are given to the sales force to deliver to each of their retail customers. The only cost to the manufacturer is shipping the bulk material to the wholesaler. The cost involved is minute in comparison with the expense of your making up individual kits and mailing them to thousands of retailers.

PROMOTING SALES
THROUGH RETAIL OUTLETS

To establish closer ties with retail customers, you might institute a regular mailing program to keep information on your product up to date.

Some manufacturers offer product exhibits, store demonstrations with factory representatives on the job, dealer contests for window display or newspaper advertising, prize contests for clerks, and many other promotional devices that may create interest in your products.

OPERATING FOR MAXIMUM
PROFIT BY REVIEWING
COSTS OF SALES

You must always be alert to the possibility that a large proportion of customers, orders, or commodities may bring in only a minor proportion of sales. If this is so, your current marketing efforts are costly. Too frequently, expenses increase in proportion to the number of customers, orders, and commodities, rather than in proportion to the number of actual dollar sales. Thus, a large part of marketing expenditures may secure a small part of total sales and gross profit.

You must decide whether there is any advantage to you in continuing unproductive accounts which entail expensive sales calls, delivery costs, and the cost of processing payments.

A survey of physical distribution and storage may uncover some products whose handling expenses nullify any profit you realize on their sales. You may benefit by their elimination. However, if you need to maintain these items as a convenience or attraction to your customers, investigate other methods of storage to conserve space.

What is the ratio of sales to the marketing costs involved in any part of your business? Are you using the most economical channel of distribution? Have you chosen the best territory for the product? Is your price viable? If your competitors are claiming a larger share of the market than you are, your research should show you why.

Elimination of unprofitable sales is not the only method—or the most desirable method—for dealing with unprofitable business. Here are some of the ways a good cost-analysis system helps you convert relatively unprofitable commodities into sources of profit.

Simplify the line. Reduce the number of sizes, styles, qualities, and price lines. Simplification may result not only in reducing distribution costs, but also in increasing sales by permitting concentration of advertising, selling, styling, and design on fewer items. One knitting mill, for example, sharply reduced its storage costs and inventory losses by restricting the variety of articles offered for sale, and attributed a rapid increase in sales to that policy. A simplified line will also help you fill reorders faster. You can also reduce production costs while increasing production.

Repackage the product. A change in the package may reduce the direct costs of packing, and the new container may make possible reductions in transportation, storage, and handling costs. A new package may also influence the volume of sales.

Increase—or decrease—the amount of advertising and promotion work. Whether it would be profitable to increase or decrease advertising depends on such factors as the effect of advertising on volume of sales and the effect of the volume of sales on unit production and distribution costs.

Decrease the price. Sometimes it may actually pay to reduce the price of unprofitable commodities. When consumer demand is so elastic that a small reduction in price leads to a substantial increase in sales, the greater volume decreases your distribution costs allocable to the item, allowing profit.

Increase the price. Where an increase in price may lead to only a small reduction in sales, it may be possible to raise the price in order to recover the loss on unprofitable products. The increase in dollar gross on margin would have to exceed the increase in per-unit cost of production and distribution that might result from the lower volume or the smaller unit orders.

You might minimize losses suffered through small and relatively unprofitable orders by doing the following:

- Reduce services offered, such as special storage, free acceptance of returns, and repair services.
- Make a special-handling charge for all orders below a minimum size.
- Devise special routines that reduce clerical costs on small orders.
- Establish a minimum-size order that will be handled.
- Turn small orders over to jobbers, brokers, or agents.
- Substitute mail-order solicitation for personal calls on a number of customers of certain classes.

You must be constantly alert to innovation and substitutions in packaging, production, and materials. Listen to the information your salespeople pick up on product improvement and criticism. Give someone in your organization specific responsibility for keeping alert for suitable additions to your line.

When you get an order from an unusual source, find out why your product was purchased. The information may disclose a market for your commodity or an application of it that has not occurred to you. If your competitors publish lists of users of their products, study them closely for suggestions of classes of prospects or uses for your merchandise which you have overlooked in your sales work.

Either you or someone you appoint should read the publications of your trade or industry for items regarding new businesses in any of your markets, personnel changes in firms on your prospect list, and news about your competitors.

Your trade association may be another valuable source of information in your profit-improvement program. Many trade groups collect statistics on the industry for use by members and by the government. They print and distribute specialized data on sales promotion, creating markets for the industry's products. They also maintain credit-reporting services that can guide you, and they prepare economic studies on wages, sales, and prices. They act as clearinghouses for technical advice that may be especially helpful to smaller businesses which cannot afford their own technical staffs.

Your trade association will aid you in promoting efficient methods by keeping you informed of government legislation, public events, and technical or trade changes that affect the industry. Detailed manuals on record keeping have been printed for some industries. These are the result of years of familiarity with the problems of the industry and knowledge of the ways adequate records can help solve such problems.

ADVERTISING

Your advertising should convey your message to an area where sales will most likely result. Available media are newspapers, magazines, radio, television, direct mail, billboards, transportation signs, and business papers and magazines. You may find it effective to concentrate on several of these, experimenting occasionally with less adaptable forms.

If you are in a suburban area, you will probably find advertising in a large city newspaper too expensive and its coverage too wide. If you have a local radio station, you may get quick results through spot radio advertising. Make the wording bright and catchy enough to alert the listener within the first 5 or 10 seconds. Trade and business papers are an essential medium for reaching other businesses or dealers. Try leafing through trade journals for ideas that can be adjusted to your product.

Experiment in Your Advertising   If you use several newspapers or magazines as outlets, try scheduling advertisements in different publications in consecutive weeks and check your increase in sales for the corresponding periods. Coupons, games, lotteries (depending upon local law), and discounts are also ways of stimulating and measuring consumer response. A good way to reach business customers is to advertise in business magazines, such as trade publications and industry journals. A product useful in many factories could be advertised in magazines geared to executives.

You will want to make use of two different kinds of advertisements: *commodity* and *institutional*. The commodity advertisement sells one or more definite items. The primary approach creates interest in an unestablished item. Selective advertisements direct the customer to a specific brand of goods, whereas mass advertising appeals to a cross section of the population. Or you may consider advertising by class, directing your message toward a special group for which your product may have greatest appeal or use.

Institutional advertising conveys a message that may have nothing to do with a particular product. It may concern a change in policy on credit, the enlargement of a department, or the acquisition of a new line of goods. Institutional advertising, judiciously placed, can often enhance a business's stature in the community. Some firms identify with a drive for charitable contributions or some other local cause of importance.

Just as a product is sold, services or atmosphere can be sold. In fact, there may be no difference between the shoes sold by your shoe store and the shoes sold by the store down the street. To attract customers you must establish some apparent differences by your advertising campaign. The success of your store will be determined by your marketing skills. For example, have your advertising feature the attentiveness or experience of your sales personnel, your refund policy or layaway plan, or a sale on one or two styles that the competition may be unwilling to match.

Another way of selling something else besides the shoes in your store is to create an image for your store through advertising and then sell the image. Be careful to select an image that will attract consumers, for instance, "Dancin' Shoes," a shoe store decorated in an electric motif with disco background music and a modest colored-light system.

You must use your judgment to weigh the extra decoration and advertising expenses against the increase in sales brought about by the campaign.

What is a suitable amount for a firm to spend on its advertising program? Your deciding factor is: How much can you afford? Some industries devote 1 to 2 percent of their profits to advertising. Among retail establishments, furniture stores run highest with 3 to 4 percent, apparel stores average 2.5 percent, and drugstores 1.5 percent.

An industry might choose to assign an expense figure on advertising for each individual product. In advancing your product through advertising, be sure to keep the message clear. Run the advertisement long enough to be certain that the average shopper will have absorbed its contents.

Manufacturers, wholesalers, and newspapers may help you plan more attractive advertisements. They often provide excellent cuts, mats, and suggested copy slants. This expertly planned material generally will be furnished without charge. Make full use of it, for it will help to keep your advertisements up to date, appealing, and effective.

Many manufacturers have promotional campaigns in which they contribute financially to retail-store advertisements calling customer attention to specials on, for example, hosiery, cosmetics, and items of apparel. Many customers rely heavily on these annual name-brand sales.

Strategic placement is essential to capture the casual reader's interest in a *newspaper advertisement*. The reader will be affected by the position of the advertisement on the pages, its size in relation to surrounding ads, the interest of adjacent editorial matter and advertisements, and the effectiveness of your layout and display.

Direct mail, on the other hand, gives you almost unlimited freedom in illustrations and their size and treatment, within limits of the format selected and the reproduction process used. Unlike a newspaper, direct mail focuses the recipient's entire attention on your message, no matter how briefly. If the item appeals, your advertising has found a customer. (Direct mail is discussed in Chapter 12.)

A good advertising program promotes items that are timely because of seasons, holidays, local events, or national advertising of manufacturers and producers. Use tempting pictures or descriptive phrases which highlight the characteristics of your merchandise that make it superior to the offerings of other merchants or manufacturers. The use of humor requires a deft touch. Do not attempt it unless the results seem spontaneous and light.

Be certain that you make no misleading statements in your advertising. The Federal Trade Commission has set up trade practice rules which prohibit false advertising, misbranding, and deception.

USE OF AN ADVERTISING AGENCY

If you turn your advertising program over to an agency, be sure you choose a firm that is experienced in handling your line of work. It is not necessarily true that a small agency will give smaller accounts more attention. A large agency, offering more specialized facilities, may be interested in your business because of your growth potential.

You will find advertising agencies from all over the country listed, together with their accounts, in the *Standard Advertising Register*. You can also use your classified telephone directory to locate local firms, but remember that not all firms listed as advertising agencies are fully equipped to give all types of service. Choose one that is recognized by the various media associations and is free from control of any one advertiser or media owner. It should have a staff of sufficient size, ability, and experience to meet your needs. Examine its former work on your type of merchandise carefully to see if its presentation is suitable.

EFFECTIVE PACKAGING

Packaging should supply adequate protection against rough handling in transit and delivery to users. It should be able to withstand climate and temperature changes, provide interior reinforcement and cushioning, and be of minimum weight for proper protection.

Your package should allow you the greatest possible shipping economy. Occasional breakage and replacement may be more economical than penalizing every shipment by the cost and weight of damage-proof containers. Your shipping department should observe standard practices which eliminate extravagant use of crates, nails, padding, wrappings, etc. If your container can be used by the purchaser for display or some other purpose, be sure to explain this in prominent lettering on the exterior of the package.

When designing for retail display, make sure the package will be distinct and visible on shelves and counters and in windows. It should "look its price"—that is, give the impression of being worth what is asked for it. If it contains one of a line of similar items, it should probably bear a "family resemblance" to the packages of the other items. If the appearance of the contents is a sales asset, consider transparent wrappings, or a box with a clear plastic window, or a bulk display of packages with one sample exposed to view. Make sure that the labeling on your package is informative as well as distinctive and that it includes all the information required by law. Experimentation may show you whether you might enlarge your sales market with cartons of a different size or containing a different quantity.

Your packaging prices should be modest in comparison with the value of the contents. If you package your product for ultimate retail purchase, try to keep the tone consistent with the style of the merchandise. Producers of cosmetics, for example, would probably benefit from very careful consideration of bottle and package designs before settling on the one they will use.

MARKETING A NEW PRODUCT

Before introducing a new product, you should answer the following questions:

- What consumers will use the product? What are their ages, locations, and occupations? How many are likely to ignore the product because it is too expensive or not expensive enough for them? How many are likely to be out of the market because they already have similar items giving satisfactory service? Customers often resist changes in their buying patterns.
- Will its price compare favorably with that of existing products of its kind? Can your product compete favorably with similar products already on the market with regard to price, quality, style, and service? Are other manufacturers likely to enter the field with products similar to yours? What is the present consumption of items of this type? Is consumption likely to expand in the next 2, 5, or 10 years? How often will consumers buy it; is it durable or does it need frequent replacement? At what season does it reach peak sales?
- Through what channels are customers accustomed to buy products of this kind? You will want to discover the basis on which your competitors usually sell similar products to retailers. What selling techniques and agencies do you intend to employ? You might choose to sell through established wholesalers or jobbers, through exclusive distributors, or through your own sales force. Some manufacturers use a combination of these.

Market Survey Introducing a new product is risky and costly. To reduce the amount of loss that might follow a failure, manufacturers test-market new products in selected cities. Of course, a test courts the danger that your competitors will be tipped off. They can audit one of your test areas, and if they are impressed, enter the market at the same time you do. This deprives you of the benefit of being first and getting the largest part of the market.

As manufacturers test in several cities, they are able to note the results of different advertising slogans, techniques, and packaging. They also have an opportunity to test the consumer's reaction to several colors and smells, to unit assembling, and to price. To test advertising techniques for the product in various cities, for example, you might try different combinations of light, average, and heavy advertising (TV, radio or newspaper), alone or combined with redeemable coupons, door-to-door selling, or free samples.

Makers of high-priced products not for mass distribution generally do not find such testing techniques suitable and must rely on other market information and experience.

If you plan to use a professional firm to survey your market, tell them clearly what you want surveyed. They will then submit a written proposal defining the assignment as they understand it, the names of the people who will handle the operation, and an estimate of the time involved and their charges. Charges are often calculated on a daily or hourly basis, but some consultants and research organizations work on a retainer, or fixed fees, or on a cost-and-percentage basis. In addition, the consultants expect to be reimbursed for certain expenses. These should be specifically defined.

Setting a Price The price you establish for a new product may be the pivot on which the success of your marketing efforts will turn. Prices must be in line with competition for the same quality, service, or style. You may find it necessary to set up a schedule of discounts and allowances to wholesalers, retailers, and others as an inducement for them to add your line.

Your price policy should embrace everything that goes into the establishment of a true price, including especially such items as credit and collection policies, whether goods are sold f.o.b. factory or on a delivered basis, consignment policies, and policies on returned goods, cancellation of orders, and credit for damaged or unsatisfactory goods.

Legal Advice Legal counsel can examine your product, labeling, and advertising, as well as your sales agreements and price policies, to see if you have abided by any applicable regulations set up by the Food and Drug Administration for industries engaged in interstate commerce. Be aware of any statutes in your area governing the use of premiums and contests to promote your merchandise. State laws vary widely in their restrictions on advertising and display material on alcoholic beverages and various other products. In many states, particular items, such as drugs, may be sold only in specified types of retail outlets. A substantial number of cities throughout the country have adopted ordinances circumscribing the activities of house-to-house canvassers and frequently requiring a license. In other states, restrictive laws have been passed which tend to cut down or eliminate sales of out-of-state products competing with dominant local industries.

Health laws, building codes, and sanitary codes are in operation in most, if not all, cities. In many instances, these laws prohibit the use of certain types of products in the construction of homes, offices, and factories.

AVOIDING SALES TERMS
THAT DISCRIMINATE

The law forbids price discrimination that injures competition. Special sales terms that amount to price reductions, or price increases, should be quoted to all purchasers on an equitable and consistent basis. Special terms may be granted in good faith where necessary to meet competition, but shaded prices or discounts should normally be applied uniformly to all competing customers who purchase the same product in the same period of time.

Rebates in a Market Decline The law permits a seller to give a buyer a guarantee against a price decline. However, the seller must give the same terms to all customers who place orders on a single date and have rebates computed as of a single future date. Any shift in the initial date, or the rebate date, justifies a change in terms—provided changes in the seller's cost or in future market conditions have occurred.

Future Delivery Contracts A price quoted for future delivery need not be the same as a price quoted for immediate delivery. This is so because the law does not prevent changes in price based on changes in market conditions. A seller may, for example, take an order from a customer for delivery 1 or 2 months ahead, at either more or less than the price prevailing on the day when the order is placed. On the other hand, if the seller quotes different prices to different purchasers who place orders for the same amount of the same product for delivery on the same advance date, the seller runs the risk of violating the law.

Options for Future Purchases A seller may give a buyer an option to purchase a given amount of an item at any time up to a given future date at the price prevailing on an earlier date. It is true, in this case, that a buyer who does not have such an option may be paying a different price when purchasing on the same date as the buyer who has the option. This fact will, however, not result in violation of the law if all similar buyers have had the same rights and opportunities to enter into a like option.

Return Privileges A seller is, in general, free to permit buyers to return merchandise under any conditions he or she may care to establish. All buyers must be given the same rights to return damaged or imperfect items, goods that are delivered after their due date, and goods which cannot be sold after a specified length of time.

Special Discounts for Large Orders Quantity discounts are legal if they do not injure competition or if they are based on specific cost, market, or competitive conditions. Quantity discounts are permissible when a seller's costs actually do vary with the size of the order the customer places. Difficulties may be encountered, however, if a seller's exaggerated discounts for large orders bear no reasonable relationship to discounts on smaller orders.

Credit terms and special delivery services must also be extended to all customers without discrimination.

CONDUCTING BUSINESS OVERSEAS

If you are interested in selling your product overseas, contact the Bureau of International Commerce of the U.S. Department of Commerce. The department maintains up-to-date lists of foreign buyers, distributors, and agents for a full range of products in many countries. Their representatives will help you make contact with foreign businesses and sales agents.

A thorough perusal of Department of Commerce literature will help you decide on your best potential foreign market. Their *Trade List* supplies names and addresses of foreign companies dealing with specific products in 100 countries. The *World Trade Directory Reports* provide exhaustive information about overseas firms—their products, territories, owners, and officers.

To initiate your export program, you might register with the Department of Commerce for inclusion on the *American International Traders Index*. This index contains the names of more than 20,000 American manufacturers who wish to sell in foreign markets, along with the data about their products.

To give your product effective foreign exposure, you can arrange with the Department of Commerce to have an exhibitor display your commodity at one of the U.S. trade centers overseas. Centers are located in Milan, Stockholm, Tokyo, London, Frankfurt, and Bangkok. Consult the *Overseas Trade Promotion Calendar* for further details.

Before choosing a country as a market for your product, evaluate its trade restrictions, including tariffs, quotas, import licenses, and exchange permit requirements. The *tariff*, a tax imposed by foreign governments on imports, may be based on value or quantity, or both. A schedule of tariffs, published by the International Customs Tariffs Bureau in Brussels, Belgium, is on file at your nearest field office of the Department of Commerce. Some groups of countries, such as the European Common Market, publish their own common external tariff schedule. This document may be obtained from the European Economic Community headquarters in Brussels. Be certain that the tariff schedule you obtain is up-to-date. Changes are frequently made. If your product is difficult to classify, you may have to send a sample to the appropriate authorities to gain a decision on its tariff rates.

The quota system limits the number of a specific item which a country can import within a certain length of time, usually a year. Sometimes the limitations are directed toward specific countries, or they may encompass the entire world. In some cases, where the quota is exceeded, a product is not banned but a tariff is imposed on any additional items imported into the country.

Import licenses are often used by countries to keep track of their imports or to regulate the amount of importing done. Some countries, when they have balance-of-payment difficulties or shortages of hard currency, may require exchange permits. This form of import licensing enables the government to ration the supply of hard currencies available for imports. Preference is always given to essential items.

Consult with your field office of the Department of Commerce for full information on your requirements.

19
EXTENDING CREDIT
TO YOUR
CUSTOMERS

Credit makes the American economy go. While "buy now, pay later" is the national slogan, your perspective must be somewhat more conservative when you have the responsibility of extending credit. Obviously, not all people granted credit will honor their debts. Yet, to do business, you may have to give credit. Your objective then is to reduce your risk while benefiting from the buying power of the credit society. You must know what it costs you to extend credit. Giving credit increases your sales. However, if the sales are only on paper, you will be forced to borrow to replenish your stock. In extending credit, your working capital must be sufficient to carry the accounts receivable, to buy stock, and to pay for operating expenses. As a retailer, you may need a monthly cash flow of at least 3 times the outstanding credit balance. As a manufacturer, you may need sufficient funds to operate during the time lag between billings and payment. You also must anticipate as best as possible economic recessions that may extend the average length of time that accounts receivable will be outstanding. When the nation hits a slump, slow-paying customers may force your business to seek credit and, if your are overextended, they may even jeopardize your business. Businesses have gone bankrupt because of the domino effect through the failures of their customers.

Often, you will be guided by the credit policies usual in your specific line of business. Competition must be met and surpassed. You may offer specified discounts on bills paid within a certain period, or, if it is usual in your trade, you may allow your customer to defer payments under the *extended datings* system. For example, a manufacturer may sell seasonal merchandise by taking payment from a dealer in stated installments spread over 4 months. This allows the dealer to resell and to raise the money to pay the manufacturer. Cash discount policies may also relieve credit problems. Customers may find it advantageous to take out a bank loan to meet the discount terms, rather than ask for credit.

CHECKING THE CREDIT STANDING OF A BUSINESS

Your business should extend credit to other companies solely on the basis of present ability to pay. However, credit policies should be kept flexible. In a recovery phase of the business cycle, expand credit. Reduce it when recession is imminent.

In determining the amount of credit to extend, evaluate the character, reputation, and business abilities of those who conduct the business. Collateral circumstances should also be studied. Check a prospective credit customer's business location and see if the customer's insurance coverage against fire is adequate. Are there outside mortgages, liens, or control on the management by other creditors or interested parties? Is the business subject to unusual price cutting and excessive risks? Have others ever had to institute legal action for collection?

There are many sources of information concerning a customer's business. Among them are the mercantile credit agencies dealing with your particular trade, suppliers that deal with your customers, credit bureaus operated by trade associations, data collected from banks, and financial services such as those of Standard & Poor's, Moody's, and Dun & Bradstreet.

Instruct your sales force to obtain all possible information on prospective credit customers. They should study the financial condition of the firm and analyze its character and trade practices. However, you should weigh your sales department's reports carefully. Too often their compensation depends on the volume of sales produced, and they may extend credit too freely.

Local attorneys may often supply a report on the credit status of a firm you are investigating. They may know of liens, claims, judgments, or actions pending against the debtor.

You may find that personal interviews with proposed customers yield first-rate credit information. Use the meeting to encourage complete expression by the customer about prospects, finances, and policies. Get a financial statement of your customer, if that is possible. If the customer makes a false financial statement, knowing that you intend to rely on it for credit purposes, the customer may be subject to prosecution. Know, too, the federal mail statutes that make it a crime to send a false statement through the mails.

Periodically, you can request financial statements, certified by reputable independent accountants, from your customers. These statements can alert you to an account's approach to its credit limitations. Be sure that the statement reflects recent conditions. Have it sent by mail as a means of taking full advantage of the penal laws should the statement prove false. Insist upon a detailed report, with supporting schedules on an analysis of receivables, investments, inventories, and creditors. Be sure the information offers comparisons with preceding periods and helps to discover trends.

Many essential facts do not customarily appear on financial statements. It will be up to you to find out what contractual commitments the customer has at higher-than-market prices and whether the customer has unfulfilled contracts for sales at too low prices. See if the cash position is adequate for anticipated business requirements. How much of the available cash is needed for imminent payment of wages, dividends, bonuses, loans, and purchase commitments or expansion programs? Is the ratio of sales to accounts receivable increasing or decreasing? An increasing ratio may reflect a favorable business trend.

A study of notes receivable and trade acceptances should inform you as to what portion is fully negotiable, what portion is restricted, and what notes are worthless and should be written off. Your estimation of inventory should disclose any liability included in accounts payable. Estimate the liquidity of inventories in the event of seasonal changes, priorities, freezing orders, or other factors.

Intelligent analysis of the company's assets, investments, and debts should give you a good notion of its probable risk as a credit customer.

Composite balance sheets and income statements of successful firms of approximately the same size as that of the prospective customer may help. Many such figures are now available. Good management often checks the significant ratios on composite statements. Then it compares the ratios of the prospective customer and seeks an explanation of unfavorable variations.

An especially sensitive indicator is the ratio of current assets to current liabilities. When this ratio falls continuously, it is a sign of deterioration. Another important ratio is that of net worth to total debt. If this ratio continues to fall, it may indicate disaster.

CREDIT BUREAUS

The credit bureau acts as a clearinghouse for credit information in the community. It provides a dependable source of information on the credit of local customers. The records reveal the actual trade or credit experiences of individuals with banks, retail stores, automobile dealers, finance companies, physicians, dentists, and hospitals. Credit bureau files include such highly important public records as judgments and deeds, mortgages, chattels, and conditional sales.

Where the bureau also operates a collection department, it provides much information of value to the bureau files.

A reputable merchant or business can pay a local credit bureau for its verification services. Of the almost 2000 credit bureaus in the United States, 95 percent are affiliated with the Associated Credit Bureaus of America, Inc. Through this affiliation, your local bureau exchanges information nationwide, helping to prevent a bad risk somewhere else from taking advantage of businesses in a new locality.

Computerized credit reports will be returned to you, scored on the basis of the answers on the credit application filled out by the customer. Reliance on the computer's weighted score helps prevent the merchant or the credit bureau from being accused of discrimination. The computer is free from prejudice of race or sex, although age is a factor in determining credit risk.

An applicant turned down on the basis of a credit report may, under the law, ask you to find out the source of the negative report. Be aware of the potential for error in the credit report. Customers should be turned down diplomatically and invited to resubmit their application at a later time when their credit is better established.

If there is no credit bureau in the community or when the information developed in the credit investigation does not clearly suggest a decision, certain other factors might be considered before you open or decline the account. You may be able to obtain information from other stores and businesses. Some merchants will base a favorable decision on the good record of the applicant's parents, on a stable employment record, or on the maintenance of a checking or savings account.

RETAIL CREDIT POLICIES

Occupations and income of customers will influence you, as a retailer, in your choice of a cash or a credit policy. In a community made up largely of farmers or ranchers, you may have to give credit until your customers have sold their crops or stock. Lower-income, but steadily employed, families often find it necessary to charge purchases from payday to payday. Buying on credit has long been the preferred method among many higher-income families also. They like to charge purchases, then pay for all of them at the end of the month. Today, they are joined by the middle-income customer who is in the habit of using various types of credit cards to postpone cash payment.

When you sell for credit, you gain a number of advantages. First, you are able to build a clientele of regular customers. Cash customers are anybody's customers. Charge customers are customers of record. The following are some other important points:

- Charge customers usually are not as concerned with the prices of goods as are those who pay cash. They tend to buy a higher quality of merchandise, and they frequently buy more of it.
- Credit is an accommodation to customers. Because of this, charge customers generally have a feeling of goodwill toward the store.
- Goods can be sent on approval to customers.
- Charge customers provide an excellent mailing and promotion list.
- Adjustments can be made more easily.
- A more intimate relationship can be built up between the customers and the store.

Along with these advantages come disadvantages, which you must also consider:

- Capital is tied up in merchandise charged by customers.
- Credit adds to the interest charges on money borrowed.
- Losses are bound to occur. Credit customers may purchase beyond their ability to pay.
- Credit customers have a greater tendency to return goods than do cash customers.
- Credit adds to the cost of operations since accounts must be maintained and monthly statements prepared and mailed.

Depending on your business, you might run ordinary, *open-end monthly charge accounts* only, or you might also have such variations as *budget accounts*, under which the customer makes a down payment and incurs a service charge for paying for goods on an installment system. In *revolving accounts*, you and the customer agree on a credit ceiling; the customer pays a preset amount each month, plus a service charge. *Option accounts* combine open-end and revolving accounts; if the customer pays in full at the end of the month, there is no service charge, but otherwise a finance charge is assessed, the amount of which depends on the size of the monthly payment. (Some stores call this a revolving account. Credit account nomenclature varies.) You may also offer *long-term installment contracts*, as is usual in the selling of heavy appliances, furniture, and automobiles.

To change the terms of a credit account, you must give 30 days' notice, as required by the federal consumer credit restraint program, and you must explain the changes in the credit program. The consumer may pay off the existing balance under the original terms of the credit account. However, use of the charge account by the consumer after the 30-day period is considered acceptance of the new terms.

MAJOR CREDIT CARD PLANS

Whether you are a retailer or in a service business, you will have to consider participation in one or more of the various credit card plans. Shall you accept cards issued by clubs, banks, and oil companies and be relieved of billing and collection responsibilities? In a credit card transaction, you will probably receive your payment for the sale or service long before the customer pays the issuer of the credit card. On the debit side, you will have to consider the cost of participation: fees, percentage of sales, charges for imprinting machines, and possibly a point-of-sale checking system.

The trend is toward a cashless society, and you stand to gain more customers through participation in credit card plans. You offer the same convenience in charging that the department store gives, and customers are tempted to spend more when they do not immediately have to lay down cold cash. Business, too, is picked up from travelers and transients who do not wish to carry large sums of money with them.

Losses of $1 billion a year stem from the theft of credit cards. As schemes for counterfeiting credit cards grow more sophisticated, this total can only increase. Various protection devices exist, ranging from signatures and photographs on the cards to computerized systems of authorization. The future will see more credit card processors linked to central computers.

Merchants accepting credit cards should know that the Fair Billing Act of 1975 allows customers to stop payment on items with which they are dissatisfied. The bank issuing the credit card will automatically deduct the disputed amount from the account of the business. The credit card customer has the legal right not to pay for an item he or she has tried to return or for a defective item that the buyer has tried to get the merchant to correct. This return feature can negate the effects of your sales skills if customers should later decide they do not really want an aquarium or encyclopedia.

On the other hand, most credit card plans do not require you to refund the money directly to customers returning credit purchases. You give the customer a copy of the slip which you send in with the customer's credit card billing, so the customer is credited from the credit card company. The credit card company then adjusts the merchant's account. This gives the merchant the benefit of a free float between the time the item is returned and the time the account is adjusted. Another advantage to credit cards is that the issuers of credit cards will credit payments to you directly to your bank account.

DISCOUNTS FOR CASH

With the granting of credit, whether through your own billing system or through credit card plans, you will be increasing your cost of doing business. You have the overhead cost of raising the extra cash flow necessary to grant credit, plus you may be paying a percentage of the credit card sales to the banks handling the credit cards. Although credit transactions are increasing your sales volume, obviously there is an advantage to doing as much of your business as possible in cash. However, dealing in cash has its drawbacks. You must be careful and consistent.

Credit card companies will try to discourage you from a cash discount policy. Obviously this is contrary to their interests. Their pressures will be subtle, via billing rates or services. Formerly, credit card issuers prohibited the merchants in their programs from giving cash discounts, but Congress prohibited this form of control by law.

Unless a cash discount policy is posted in your store, or you otherwise notify all your customers as to cash discount practices, you are in violation of the Truth in Lending Law. Also illegal is giving different size discounts to different customers. In effect, a cash discount policy is assessing a finance charge on credit customers; that is why the Truth in Lending Law is applicable.

A way of increasing your cash business without running afoul of these restrictions is to have a minimum purchase amount for charges. If credit cards are only allowable on purchases of over $20, for example, a merchant's cash flow will increase. Be careful to set a limit that will not have an adverse effect on sales volume, a cash amount that most of your customers will have in their pockets.

SELLING ON
THE INSTALLMENT PLAN

Installment selling facilitates the sale of machinery and durable or "hard" goods, such as refrigerators, ranges, and furniture for the home, which have a long life and a relatively high value. They can be repossessed and resold if the customer fails to make payment.

Any form of credit business entails a larger capital investment than sales offered strictly for cash. Installment-plan selling requires an even larger investment than credit sales of charge account type. Money tied up in installment sales is frozen for a long time unless arrangements are made to transfer the contracts to a sales finance company.

In arranging an installment sale, the down payment should be large enough to make the buyer feel like the owner, not merely the renter, of the merchandise. The actual percentage asked depends on the type of merchandise. It might run from 20 to 33⅓ percent or more of the total price. Some dealers will sell with no down payment and try to reduce their risk in other ways. Retailers tend to ask a higher down payment on soft goods since they rapidly decrease in value through use, wear, or changes in fashion.

If the article is repossessable, the unpaid balance on it always should be sufficiently below resale value to protect the retailer from loss if repossession becomes necessary.

The monthly payments should be large enough to increase the customer's claim to the article faster than the item will depreciate from time and average use.

Repossessing Property Check the laws in your city and state on repossession, and also federal law which may supersede local law. The debtor is generally entitled to have a say before the property is seized. A Supreme Court decision prevents state laws from allowing creditors to repossess goods summarily for installment defaults. Repossession can occur only after the debtor has received a fair hearing.

TRUTH IN LENDING LAW

Credit provided consumers through open-end credit or installment plans is subject to the federal Truth in Lending Law. The law does not, however, apply to trade or business credit.

Complying with Credit Regulations Say you are a home-improvement contractor. Your customer wants credit. You must explain the details of the installment contract and also tell the customer that, even after signing, he or she may back out of the contract, provided the cancellation is made within 3 days. Such a grace period—exact periods may vary in different states—is generally effective in door-to-door selling and is sometimes limited to sales above $10, or above $50; again, state regulations vary. If home-solicitation sales are your business, see that your salespeople understand and observe state and federal regulations.

When you offer an installment contract, inform the customer of various points of the credit transaction and include the same information on the instrument presented for signature. Details will vary according to the type of business.

Disclosure Under the federal Truth in Lending Law, the following information must be included in credit agreements: the cash price of the goods or service, the down payment (include any trade-in), and the difference between the cash price and down payment; all other charges, itemized but not part of the finance charge; the unpaid balance; amounts deducted as prepaid finance charges (or required deposit balances); the amount financed; the total of the cash price, finance charges, and all other charges (which amounts to the deferred payment price); the total dollar amount of the finance charge; the date when the finance charge begins to apply if it is different from the sales date; annual finance charge, expressed as a percentage; the number, amounts, and due dates of payments; total payments; the amount you will charge for delinquency or default, or the method used for calculating the amount; a description of any security; a description of any penalty for prepayment of principal; and an explanation of how the unearned part of the finance charge is calculated in case of prepayment (charges deducted from any rebate must be stated).

If you offer open-end accounts which customers may pay in full or in installments, you again must tell the customer in writing or on a form the terms of the credit offered: the conditions under which a finance charge may be made; the period, such as 30 days, during which no interest is due if payment is made; the method of determining the balance on which a finance charge may be incurred; an explanation of how the actual finance charge due is calculated; the finance charge rates (for example, 1½ percent on the first $500, and 1 percent on amounts over $500); the conditions under which the cost of new purchases is added to the account, and details of how the finance charge is then calculated; a description of any lien that may be made on a customer's property, as, for example, the right to repossess a refrigerator; and the minimum periodic payment you require.

Finally, credit terms on any sale on which the price may be paid in more than four installments must be disclosed. The disclosure is obligatory even if no finance or carrying charge is involved.

Billing Your Credit Customers   You must send out periodic statements (usually once a month) for accounts on which finance charges may be applied or on which there is an unpaid balance of more than $1. You must show the unpaid balance at the beginning of the billing period; the amount and date of each new purchase and a brief description thereof; customer payments and credits; the finance charge (in dollars and cents) and the rates used in calculating it; the annual percentage rate; the unpaid balance on which the finance charge was calculated; the closing date of the billing cycle; and the unpaid balance.

Federal regulations require you to show some of these items on the front of your statement; others may go on the back or on a separate attachment.

The question of what constitutes the balance on which revolving charge account finance charges are computed has been fought in the courts. Retailers like to bill on the *previous balance*, not taking a customer's payments into consideration; customers prefer the *adjusted balance*, under which their payments and credits are deducted before the charge is computed; a compromise, in some cases, is the *average daily balance*, whereby the customer is credited for payments but charged interest in proportion to the time he still has not paid. Ascertain state and federal law on this point if you are just setting up charge accounts. Some states have outlawed the previous-balance system, but at this writing federal law covering the practice has yet to be passed.

When mailing a statement to customers, allow plenty of time for them to pay before finance charges become applicable. In many states, the minimum time before such interest can be charged is 30 days. However, a reverse strategy, a discount policy for bills paid promptly, can make your collections easier. For example, offer 2 percent off on bills paid within 10 days and 1 percent off on bills paid within 20 days, with the normal finance charge being assessed after 30 days. Many businesses find this form of positive incentive to be a more effective means of collection than the typical penalty approach.

In response to customer complaints that their open-end credit account bills arrived too late for timely payments to be made, states may also regulate the mailing dates. For example, one state requires that statements be mailed at least 9 days before the end of the next succeeding billing cycle or payment-due date, whichever is earlier. Another state demands 15 days. Be sure to comply with current law in this regard, too.

COLLECTING OVERDUE ACCOUNTS

A sale beyond the customer's ability to pay can be the unhappy birth of a bad collection problem. If such a problem develops and the customer shows cooperation and honesty in facing it, have him or her start with a token payment to get collection under way. If the buyer is sluggish, prod gently at first, in order to retain the customer's goodwill for future business, and then become increasingly firm. Make the plan of debt payment definite. Exact promises, and press the customer to fulfill them. Get collateral security, notes, dated checks, sureties, or other feasible assurances of payment. Perhaps return of merchandise or extra time allowance would be acceptable. If your customer's business is in serious danger, see if you can give sympathetic help that might help him or her to save face. This often spurs the customer's efforts to repay you.

In some businesses, notices of delinquent accounts are sent out, say, 5 to 9 days after the due date. But in many other businesses, the business person just adds a reminder about the overdue balance to the next month's bill, and initiates collection actions if the overdue balance grows to a sizable amount. The first approach to the collection of delinquent accounts should be low-keyed; the customer may have been ill or dealing with urgent family or business matters. If a written approach fails, the retailer may try to reach the customer by telephone. Care must be taken not to harass debtors with continual or untimely phone calls and not to employ bad language. The law has become more stringent on debt-collection practices, frowning on threats of repossession when, in fact, an item could not be repossessed; on threats to damage the customer's credit status with a credit-reporting agency when such action would not be taken; and on threats to have the debtor's wages attached without a court order permitting the action.

Some creditors have fallen afoul of the law by sending out official-looking letters that look as if they came from a government department. Intimidated debtors have imagined that they are about to be jailed for nonpayment.

If you are a retailer, you will probably turn delinquent accounts over to a collection agency 4 to 6 months after the purchase. However, if a customer comes to you with a reasonable explanation and a plan to make regular payments, you may be able to make an arrangement. Be ready to meet the willing debtor halfway; the source of the financial embarrassment may only be temporary—perhaps occasioned by heavy medical bills or a business loss. In future, the debtor may be a good customer.

LAWS AFFECTING
COLLECTION METHODS

Certain laws, which your lawyer can explain to you in full, affect collection efforts. For example, the acceptance of a promissory note from a debtor, particularly if it is endorsed by a third party, will usually prevent you from taking action until maturity of the note. Extensions induced by fraud will not be binding. An extension by you may release endorsers, sureties, and guarantors.

If you are using trade acceptances, see that the face of the documents contains a statement that the debt arises from the purchase and sale of merchandise. These documents should include definite orders to pay without any qualifying conditions. If you are having difficulties with a dishonest customer, you may make use of false-statement laws and federal mail statutes if written statements misrepresent material facts. These might deal with the amount and the nature of assets and liabilities, the amount and the terms of sales, the percentage of profit, the amount of goods produced, and the nonexistence of liens and assignments.

In dealing with partnerships, the firm signature is generally equivalent to the signature of all partners. As a rule, it is not necessary to exhaust the firm's assets before proceeding against the individual partners, and you can proceed against a retired partner if you have not received proper notice of retirement and if you had been doing business with the firm prior to the date of his or her retirement. If you are dealing with a limited partnership, not all the partners are personally responsible for the firm's debts.

If you have a judgment against an individual partner, you may levy against the partner's interest in a partnership but not against the firm's assets. The partnership's creditors will get priority over you with respect to the firm's assets, but generally with respect to the partner's private property, the reverse is true: you will get priority over them.

In transactions with social clubs, hospitals, cooperatives, and other unincorporated associations, make sure that the party with whom you deal is authorized to act. Also see that the obligation incurred is within the scope of the organization's purposes.

When dealing with corporations, make sure that the person with whom you deal can bind the corporation. It may become helpful to know that stockholders who have not fully paid for their stock are directly liable to the corporation for any unpaid balance and, therefore, indirectly liable to you, the creditor.

In trying to collect past-due accounts, be sure to keep your statements to debtors private. Avoid repeating statements you have heard that might be slanderous or libelous. Do not imply that the debtor is bankrupt, dishonest, or without credit, especially within the hearing of someone else, including your own employees.

Do not drop the matter when a problem has been turned over to an attorney for collection. Your knowledge of the particular facts will frequently be of great assistance. Inquire about third-party proceedings under which money or property that is due your debtor can be applied to your claim as long as the debtor has an established right to the money or property, or about proceedings when a third party has been given possession of your debtor's money or property through a fraudulent transfer in order to avoid satisfying your claim.

Avoid proceedings in bankruptcy if you can find other and better remedies. See if another plan might not yield a better financial return. You then will keep an honest debtor in business, and you may make up any losses through subsequent dealings. If you want to give your customer a chance to save his or her business, you might make a private agreement with the customer, either with or without the assistance and protection of the courts.

COMPREHENSIVE
INSURANCE
PLANNING

It is impractical to purchase insurance coverage against every conceivable contingency. Some small risks can be covered by loss-prevention programs. However, in the case of a major catastrophe, most firms can hope to stage a recovery only if their loss is covered by commercial insurance.

Major risks confronting a business are losses due to fire, storms, floods, or other natural disasters and losses arising from legal claims for death or injury caused by negligence. Loss may also be incurred through the dishonesty of employees; fidelity bonds guard against this eventuality. Where applicable, worker's compensation insurance pays benefits to injured employees.

CHOOSING YOUR INSURANCE
COMPANY

Four types of insurers vie for the protection policies available to businesses:

- *Stock companies* are owned by investors who look for profits.
- *Reciprocal exchanges* are unincorporated associations in which each member is an insurer of, and is insured by, every other member. Insurance is offered at cost.
- *Mutual companies* are similar to reciprocal exchanges in that they are cooperatively owned by their policyholders; however, the policyholders receive dividends, and as a result coverage is often as expensive as that offered by stock companies.

- Lloyd's groups, such as Lloyd's of London, are composed of individual underwriters who provide coverage on types of risks that other insurance companies refuse to cover. A firm with a record of heavy loss may, at a price, obtain coverage from a Lloyd's group. Many Lloyd's groups deal exclusively with one kind of risk. The Factory Insurance Association, the United States Aircraft Insurance group, Associated Aviation Underwriters, the American Hull Insurance Syndicate, the Oil Insurance Association, and the Food Industries Federation each cover a single industry. Ask your insurance agent if your company should be covered by such a specialized underwriting group.

Since different companies use different formulas for setting rates, it is difficult to appraise their overall economy without a knowledge of their entire spectrum of premiums. You might save in one area to the detriment of another. Be wary of low-premium insurers if they have a very strict claim-settlement policy attached. You may never be able to collect.

Limit the number of agents who handle your insurance needs. Having more than one policy can complicate a claim. Regardless of coverage, you will not be able to collect more than the price of the damage. When several companies are involved, disputes often arise over which insurer bears the responsibility for settling the claim. Payment is delayed, causing the insured additional inconvenience.

GUIDELINES IN BUYING INSURANCE

You can check with the state insurance commissioner or your lawyer to determine the financial stability of the companies that want to insure you. Their ratings can be found in books such as *Best's Insurance Reports* (Fire and Marine edition), published by A. M. Best Co., Morristown, New Jersey. *Best's* gives data on the current year, based on the companies' balance sheets, income statements, and underwriting results. A large public library where there is a technical or an economics division will have this reference volume available. Before contacting an agent or broker, formulate your insurance program with the aid of an insurance consultant. The consultant should be an impartial adviser with a full knowledge of your business needs.

It may be advisable for a small business to buy insurance in as large a unit as possible, with a *package policy* that covers everything. The insurance company has less administrative costs in overseeing one large policy instead of several small ones, and its savings can be passed along to you. Some package policies may be specifically designed for specific types of businesses, to give the best coverage possible. Blanket policies for commercial or industrial property will give all-risk protection on stocks of goods against freezing, flood, earthquake, seepage, landslide, war, radioactivity, dishonesty, etc. Exclusions from blanket coverage will be specifically stated.

The one problem with package policies is that they have one premium. Package buyers may have difficulty evaluating costs against other policies when they seek competitive quotes. When you look into such blanket coverage, try and find out how the premium is computed. Get the price broken down into each type of coverage.

Miscellaneous perils to your business that are not covered by other policies can be covered in one lump in a *difference-of-conditions* policy. This can protect you against anything not covered by fire, boiler, and crime policies and excludes only the specifics you designate. The exclusions keep your rates lower than if you had your policy cover every possible event (falling spacecraft, for example).

Deductibles A deductible is normally a stated dollar amount, although it can be a percentage or even a time period. For instance, in a business interruption policy, the first 24 hours might be deductible; the insurance company would not reimburse you for a loss of business during that time. They would start reimbursing you for your loss of income on the second day. The deductible feature of a policy causes you to shoulder a part of your loss, but it does reduce the premiums you pay. The higher your deductible, the less your insurance cost. You can keep your insurance costs to a minimum by using the deductible to insure just the amount of loss that you cannot afford to bear.

For example, the premium might be $100 for a policy with a $50 deductible as opposed to $70 for a policy with $100 deductible. For that extra $50 of coverage (the lower deductible) you are paying $30. Unless you make a claim 3 years out of every 5, you are losing money.

There are three different values for each object that can be insured. Make sure your policy covers the amount of value you wish to protect. A policy that covers the *cost* of an object will not provide enough money to replace the item if the cost has risen in the meantime. A policy covering the *tax value* of an object is providing even less protection. The tax value is the figure remaining after depreciation has been subtracted from the cost, so even if the object has increased in value, your insurance would pay you less than you originally paid for the asset. The most extensive policy covers *replacement cost*. This policy provides you with enough money to buy the asset at today's prices so that you can get back in operation right away without the need to raise additional funds. Note that a replacement-value policy may produce gain subject to income tax if the insurance company pays more than the asset's value as carried on your books. However, tax elections may defer tax on the gains.

Coinsurance   This term is used in more than one sense in insurance terminology. It generally implies that the loss is shared by the insured. In health insurance, for example, coinsurance means that the insured is required to bear a percentage of the medical cost. In fire insurance and related lines of insurance, coinsurance means that the insured is required to carry a specified percentage of insurance, based on the property's value; carrying a lower percentage results in the insured bearing the additional loss. For example, if instead of carrying insurance on 80 percent of the value of the property as required, you carry only 60 percent, on loss sustained the insurer would only pay six-eighths, leaving you with two-eighths loss to bear yourself. Coinsurance penalties may be avoided if property is appraised often enough and sufficient insurance maintained.

It is usually possible to obtain a substantial rate reduction under coinsurance.

BUYING FIRE INSURANCE

Your fire insurance policy should include protection against fire, lightning, hail, wind, explosion, smoke damage, riot, vandalism, malicious mischief, sprinkler leakage, and aircraft and vehicle damage. These and other extra hazards may be covered by a "difference-of-conditions" policy or by added endorsements to the basic fire policy.

To obtain the most effective coverage, base the amount of protection on the actual replacement value of your property at the time of the fire. Fire insurance policies are customarily written to supply a recovery based on the actual cash value of the damaged property at the time of the loss. This provision, which considers the physical depreciation of the property, will not allow you a sufficient return to purchase new equipment. Obtain coverage which can be reviewed at regular intervals to determine whether repayment will be adequate to make the replacements necessitated by fire.

The rates charged will depend on the fire experience and safety conditions in your locality. All cities of 25,000 or more are rated periodically and ranked 1 to 10 according to water supply, efficacy of fire-fighting equipment, and other circumstances. Companies will also consider the kind of business being operated, the construction of the building, and the nature of adjacent buildings and their occupancy.

You may find it advantageous to insure your inventory separately. In that way, its rates can be adjusted periodically to coincide with its shifting values. While it is not wise to underinsure, there is no advantage in paying excessive premiums on property that has decreased in value. Review coverage regularly.

A good insurance program will not only provide coverage in the event of a disaster but will also serve you by implementing loss-prevention programs. You may be able to obtain lower rates if you install sprinkler systems, keep your property free of trash, have wiring properly installed, maintain fire extinguishers and shelters, and use approved containers for inflammable liquids. You should insist upon strict adherence to "no smoking" rules in prohibited zones.

Your broker may suggest that you fireproof your buildings or install fire escapes, automatic sprinklers, fire extinguishers, or smoke detectors. Your plant might maintain guards and private fire brigades. A good water supply, first-aid rooms in your building, and emergency rooms in nearby hospitals reduce your risk and may also result in lowered rates.

Be sure you understand all the qualifications and exceptions in your coverage. Most fire insurance policies will suspend coverage if an insured building is left vacant for more than 60 days at a time, unless a special endorsement to the policy states otherwise. The comprehensive approach, which automatically covers any newly installed equipment, is strongly recommended. Otherwise, your coverage might be terminated or invalidated on the grounds that your new equipment has created an additional fire hazard on your premises.

WHEN DISASTER INTERRUPTS YOUR BUSINESS

Should your firm suffer the losses of a fire, flood, or other unforeseen calamity, you will need money to pay taxes, interest, utilities, and salaries to key employees while the facilities are being rebuilt. *Business interruption insurance* will cover these expenses. How long would it take to rebuild your business? Your interruption insurance should give you enough to maintain necessary upkeep during the reconstruction period. Most factory owners arrange for payroll coverage for a 90-day period, but your policy can be written for a longer or shorter time. There is an *extra-expenses insurance* available for industries which must maintain production following a fire, a toxic chemical spill, or other mishap. This kind of insurance is commonly needed by businesses such as newspapers, laundries, and dairies, whose customers depend on them for uninterrupted service.

Make sure you design your interruption insurance to cover a long enough period of time that it will cover a typical interruption for your business. Some companies have run tests of mock computer breakdowns to determine their repairer's response time. Many businesses come to a halt for the length of the computer "downtime," often several days to a week.

Whereas business interruption insurance covers problems that stop your business from operating, *contingent-business insurance* covers your losses when other businesses stop operating. A fire at your supplier can interrupt your operations, a vital material can be held up by a railroad strike or a bank failure can play havoc with cash flows and start a chain of bankruptcies. Contingent-business interruption insurance costs about half as much as regular business interruption insurance for protection against circumstances beyond your control. Make sure you understand which kinds of situations the two policies cover.

Also, note that business interruption policies may not reimburse you for trying to minimize the time your business is inoperable. While the policy may reimburse you for an expense that gets the business going again, they do not usually reimburse your expenses for efforts that fail to start the business again.

WATER DAMAGE INSURANCE

Water damage is almost always written as a separate policy and covers a number of accidents that are likely to beset the small business or plant. Such protection reimburses the insured for damage from overflow of water or steam from plumbing, heating, refrigerating, and air-conditioning systems, standpipes for fire hoses, and rain or snow admitted through defective roofs, leaders and spouting, windows, or doors.

FLOOD INSURANCE

Floods annually cause millions of dollars in property damage in the United States. Yet most private insurance companies do not offer flood insurance because the same localities are threatened year after year, causing the insurer to lose money on underwriting coverage. The federal government has stepped in to provide protection through the National Flood Insurance Program (P.O. Box 34294, Bethesda, Md. 20034). Also, the National Flood Insurers Association serves businesses in communities designated by the Federal Insurance Administration.

The Small Business Administration will aid damaged businesses in flood-struck towns. The SBA helps victims of all kinds of natural disasters, ranging from earthquakes to tornadoes. As a requirement for receiving SBA aid, the business may have to purchase National Flood Insurance.

POWER PLANT COVERAGE

If you own your building, plant, or equipment, power plant insurance is essential to cover boilers and machinery. Explosions have resulted in deaths, injuries, property destruction, and litigation, which have ruined many businesses. Insurance companies further protect plant owners by making periodic inspections to detect cracks, deterioration, and vibrations that could cause explosions.

Insurance companies are increasingly combining boiler insurance with fire coverage in one policy. This eliminates the controversy that can ensue from a loss that was originated by a boiler explosion which resulted in fire.

LIABILITY INSURANCE

You may be liable for any mishap which occurs through your business operation, the maintenance and use of your premises, your employees' activities, or the use of your product. Liability can also result from accidents that emanate from the ownership or operation of vehicles used by your business.

Many proprietors tend to limit their liability coverage to the value of the business. This is faulty reasoning. There is no guarantee that an attachment to the assets of the company will not follow after insurance maximums are reached. A recommended method for determining the amount of liability insurance you need involves setting a limit of liability for each person who might be injured on your premises, a limit for a number of people injured at one time, and a limit for property damaged. An alternate method fixes a single limit for all claims that might be brought against you as the result of an accident. An insurance consultant can advise you on the specific amount you will need.

A comprehensive general liability policy protects you against nearly all hazards. (There will always be exceptions. Be sure you note them.) With a schedule system, each hazard is insured under a different policy. You will want the comprehensive policy for all liability risks except the ones that can only be carried separately.

Automobile coverage, protecting vehicles used by your company, must be purchased separately. However, to avoid confusion in the event of a liability, it is advisable to use the same insurance company for your comprehensive liability and automobile policies. If an accident should occur, for instance, in the loading of your vehicle, there would be no wrangling between companies over which should bear the responsibility for payment.

You may insure each vehicle separately, on a schedule basis, or obtain comprehensive liability coverage which will insure any vehicle operated in the business, even leased ones when not covered by the lessor.

MALPRACTICE INSURANCE

Doctors are not the only ones sued for malpractice; many other professionals are liable as well. Lawyers, real estate agents, accountants, insurance agents, engineers, therapists, social workers, architects, and corporate directors have all been held by courts to be responsible for their advice or actions. One out of every three malpractice insurance policies is taken out by a nonphysician.

High rates are usually reserved for doctors because more claims are made against them. Whereas a doctor might pay $15,000 for $1 million in coverage, the same coverage might cost an architect $1000 or a lawyer $500.

Many professionals refuse to believe they need such coverage because of the confidence they have in their own ability. However, how much confidence do you have in the ability of your employees? A document misfiled or a deadline missed can lead to a malpractice suit. Forty percent of the claims against professionals are due not to incompetence, but rather to administrative foul-ups.

WORKER'S COMPENSATION INSURANCE

State laws obligate the employer to provide personnel with a safe place to work. Employers must limit hazards by hiring competent employees, providing safe tools, and warning employees of existing dangers.

Worker's compensation programs operated by states protect the worker in the event that an injury is sustained while on the job. In some states, laws exempt employers who have only a few workers. Agricultural, domestic, and casual labor are often excluded. Some states do not insist that employers provide worker's compensation for their employees. However, since the expense of settlements in court can be high, most employers choose to carry worker's compensation.

Premiums are determined by payroll, based on an audit. Rates are as low as 0.1 percent for "safe" jobs and as high as 25 percent for dangerous ones.

CRIME INSURANCE

Available statistics indicate that crime equals or exceeds fire as the chief culprit in property loss. Many firms, unprotected by insurance, have had to liquidate their remaining assets after suffering drastic losses through burglaries or robberies. Your insurance should cover the contents of safes and inventoried merchandise. You might investigate the storekeeper's burglary and robbery policy designed specifically for small businesses. This covers specific sums for loss from outside robbery, inside robbery, stock and safe burglary, kidnapping of owners, etc. Although larger amounts of coverage are available, this policy does not adapt itself to the medium-size or larger business.

Maintenance of an alarm system may seem costly, but it can reduce your insurance premiums. The more you do to stop crime, the less risk the insurance company is taking, and they may be able to reflect this in your rates. An alarm system is a kind of insurance, one that may save you grief and money in the long run. In areas where crime insurance is hard to get, the preventive measures you take yourself may be the best protection—dogs, alarms, private security guards, etc.

If you are in a high-crime area and cannot get insurance through normal channels, you may be able to obtain government insurance through the Fair Access to Insurance Requirements Plan. Rates will vary according to your geographic location, the crime statistics in your area, and your gross receipts. You will be classified as a not very, moderately, or highly hazard-prone business in paying premiums.

Businesses that are not very hazard-prone include barber and beauty shops and children's clothing shops; moderately hazard-prone businesses include grocery stores, drugstores, restaurants, and auto sales and service agencies; and highly hazard-prone businesses include dry cleaners, gas stations, and liquor and jewelry stores.

Federal crime insurance is available in 25 states. This insurance policy cannot be canceled no matter how many claims are made, assuming none of the claims is fraudulent. Businesses in high-crime areas, where insurance coverage is often unavailable, can thus get up to $15,000 in coverage from the Federal Insurance Administration, a division of the Department of Housing and Urban Development. Your local insurance agent can provide you with the application forms, or you can contact the agency directly.

FIDELITY BONDS

Although burglary, robbery, and theft account for substantial business losses each year, the largest crime losses arise from employee dishonesty. Small amounts are sometimes drained from the company over a period of years until losses reach thousands of dollars. Fidelity bonds which protect you against employee dishonesty are a wise investment.

The bond concerns three parties: the employee, the firm, and the bonding corporation. You may get *individual* bonds to cover each employee separately, *schedule* bonds which list all names or positions to be covered, and *blanket* bonds which cover the entire labor force. Some companies make the mistake of bonding only the workers who directly handle money. However, it has been no rare occurrence for a supervisor, for instance, to make out orders to fictitious names and collect on them.

The bonding company further aids the business owner by conducting a check on employees for any record of dishonesty. The bonded employee tends to adhere to more scrupulous practices.

Bonds are continuous until canceled by either party.

SPECIAL PURPOSE COVERAGES

Sometimes a standard insurance policy does not cover a particular risk in a business. Insurers will often design special contracts to meet such needs. For example, you may need *credit life insurance*. Such a policy can be tailored to meet your specific need.

Credit life insurance may be required if you are a retailer selling goods on credit, particularly on installment terms. Should a customer die, his or her debt is covered by this plan; you, the retailer, receive payment, and the debtor's estate is also free of obligation. Small loan companies also use this type of insurance.

Commercial credit insurance covers you if you extend open account credit to buyers of merchandise for commercial purposes. It does not apply to retailers, but might be beneficial if you sell extensively to relatively few customers.

Profits and commissions insurance will cover a manufacturer or selling agent who might lose substantially in expected profits or commissions should a large stock of goods be destroyed. Fire insurance might cover the cost of replacement, but not the profit that will not be realized. This type of insurance is applicable in businesses in which goods could not be speedily replaced.

Accounts receivable insurance reimburses you for customer billings that prove uncollectible. Such an insurance reimbursement is more valuable to you than the tax deduction for bad debts.

Valuable papers insurance will protect your business against damages caused by the destruction of important documents.

Consult with your insurance adviser for special coverage that might be necessary in your type of business.

REDUCING THE NEED FOR INSURANCE

Take advantage of any loss-prevention program or other device which reduces your need for heavy insurance premiums. One method of avoiding insurance involves a transfer of risk to another party. For example, you might lease vehicles under an agreement whereby the lessor maintains the insurance. Use services that perform your operation whenever possible, rather than hire personnel. In this way you fix the supplier of the service with the responsibility for loss or liability. The cost of insuring inventory can be shifted to manufacturers or wholesalers by "hand-to-mouth buying," through which you avoid the storage of merchandise.

USE OF LIFE INSURANCE IN BUSINESS

Business life insurance meets the hazards of loss by a business from the death of someone associated with it. This insurance is a basic life policy, but requires a special application to meet the problems peculiar to the business. The many legal, financial, tax, and technical complications require careful study by experts.

Key-employee insurance.   Almost every business has one or more men or women upon whom it depends heavily for its success. Frequently, it is the proprietor or manager. It might be the financial expert, the sales manager, or in the case of the retail shop the leading salesperson, or it might be a chemist, an engineer, or a scientist whose technical efforts produce the firm's lifeblood of ideas. If key-employee insurance is taken out because it is required by a bank or other lender in order to protect a business loan, the cost of the insurance would not be a tax-deductible business expense.

Partnership insurance.   A partnership automatically dissolves at, or shortly after, the death of any one of its partners.There is a vital need for life insurance protection to safeguard the business against forced liquidation. An adequate partnership insurance program will enable surviving partners to reorganize at once and continue the business. It will liquidate the interest of the deceased partner without loss, enabling the beneficiaries to secure full, fair value for the partner's interest in the firm. It lends support to the credit standing of the firm as well.

Corporation insurance.   The death of a shareholder may not have dire consequences for a business, but there are distinct hazards. Sometimes with the transfer of the deceased's shares, new shareholders who are unfamiliar to management may gain control. A shareholder's death can deal a severe blow to a firm's credit. A corporation insurance program helps reduce the shocks of these changeovers. It gives the deceased shareholder's heirs the full value of their inherited interest at once.

Proprietorship insurance.   This provides for maintenance of a business upon the death of a sole proprietor. Heirs are given sound valuation of the business, which enables them to effect its continuity. Provisions should be written into the policy to meet the conditions of a will or trust agreement concerning the sale or liquidation of the business.

One plan may call for the sale of the business to stated employees, with the purchase money provided by the insurance. Another may provide that the business will be run by the executor of the heirs. Or a trust company may be named as beneficiary, and management control may be established. However, the plan must be specific. Many a small business flounders upon the death of the sole owner because the proprietor did not provide the business with insurance to maintain it.

Proprietorship insurance can also aid the firm's credit status by covering the new owner or key person during the period of a loan or during the duration of a mortgage on property held.

Other Considerations in Purchasing Business Life Insurance Most business life insurance plans utilize life insurance that has cash values. These provide the firm with a valuable reserve for emergencies in the event of any sharp dislocation in business conditions. When necessary, the policy's cash values can be used as the basis for loans.

Before determining your business life insurance plan, consult at least three experts to make certain that every angle of the firm's interests is being safeguarded: your accountant, your attorney, and your life insurance agent. The first two provide the essential information on which the plan is based, and they double-check it when it is completed. Your agent will give you technical advice on the arrangement of the policies.

Tax factors, both income and estate, are involved in almost all business life insurance arrangements. Avoid plans which will necessitate additional taxes. On the other hand, tax laws often change, and the plan set up today on the basis of a certain tax advantage may prove to be disadvantageous next year. Periodically the business life insurance plan should receive a checkup by experts. Valuations of the interests of the owners are never constant. Revaluations should be written in whenever necessary on partnership and corporation policies.

INDEX